AF251046

whatever works to get the day done!

THE FANTASY ART TECHNIQUES OF
Tim Hildebrandt

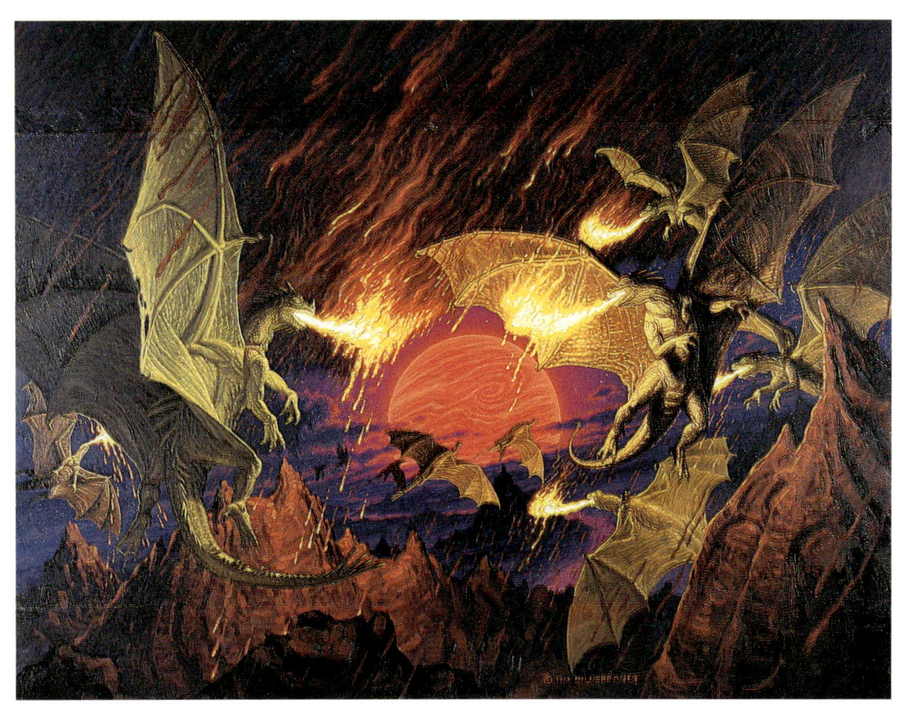

JACK E. NORTON

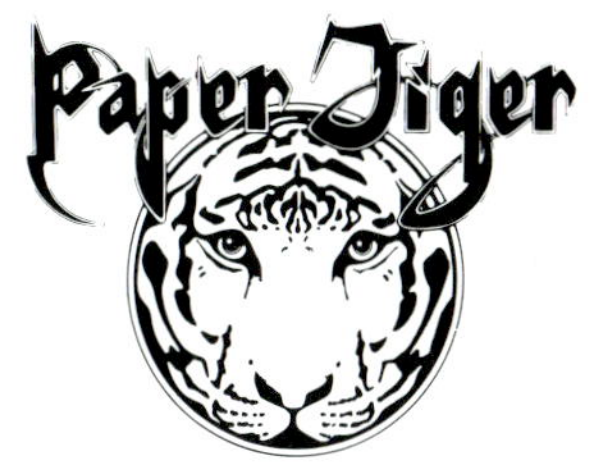

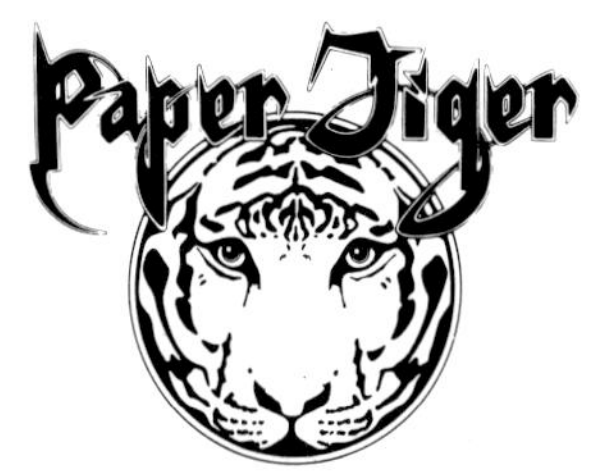

Paper Tiger
An imprint of Dragon's World Ltd
Limpsfield
Surrey RH8 0DY
Great Britain

First printed in 1991
Reprinted in 1992

The catalogue record for this book is available from the British Library.

ISBN 1 85028 161 0 (limpback)
ISBN 1 85028 162 9 (hardback)

Editor Michael Downey
Designer Ken Wilson
Art Director Dave Allen
Editorial Director Pippa Rubinstein

Typeset by Bookworm Typesetting, Manchester, England
Quality printing and binding by
Kyodo Printing Company Ltd, Singapore

Contents

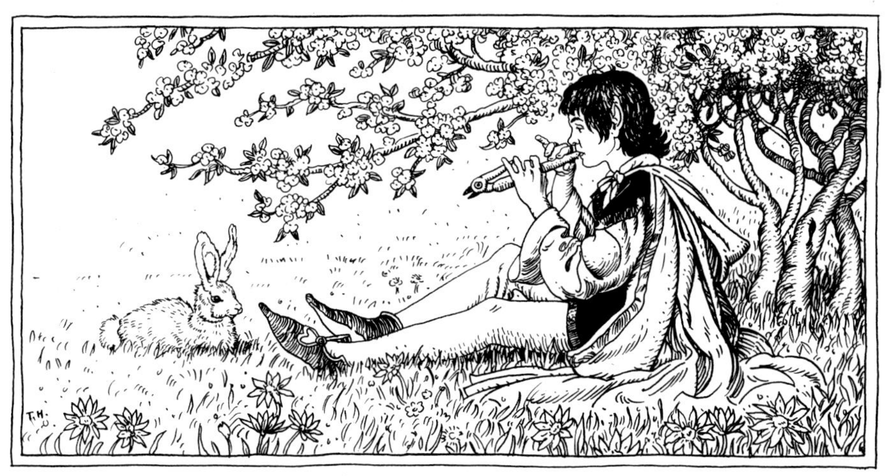

9 Foreword · *Boris Vallejo*

10 Introduction

Section One 28 Influences & Resources

Section Two 42 Concept & Composition

Section Three 76 Black & White

Section Four 106 Painting & Colour

Section Five 146 Presentation

154 Conclusion

156 Afterword · *Alan Dean Foster*

158 Index

Foreword

Illustration has been thought of by the so-called 'experts' as a minor art; illustrators, consequently, as 'minor' artists. Within the field of illustration, fantasy and science fiction art was considered of even less value. This, in my opinion, was due largely to the fact that, with very rare exceptions, the illustrators that specialized in fantasy and science fiction were shamelessly underpaid. Only those of limited talent ventured into that area. Even worse, if a talented artist would feel attracted towards the genre, the low payment he or she would receive would not justify the amount of time and effort necessary to produce a painting of any exceptional value.

During the decades of the sixties and seventies a select group of artists (with a capital A) began to change the concept of fantasy art by displaying a previously unseen combination of out-of-this-world imagination, sensitivity, strength, and, in some instances, a prodigious technique as well. These artists opened the doors for an art form that now has millions of faithfully following fans all over the world. As a consequence of their efforts, a new generation of gifted fantasy illustrators has sprouted whose skill and talent rivals that of any other in the field of the visual arts.

Among this élite of revolutionaries I was particularly impressed with a group of paintings published as book covers by Ballantine Books. They were signed simply: Hildebrandt. I was later to find out that 'Hildebrandt' was not one single artist, but two very unusual twin brothers who worked together on the same paintings. Their names were destined to become legend in their chosen field.

In 1977 I started doing covers for Ballantine Books. It was then that I first met Tim Hildebrandt and his brother Greg. That year marked the beginning of what has been a long and close friendship.

The stories that surrounded the Hildebrandt brothers were nearly as fantastic and bizarre as the extraordinary illustrations they produced. Among other things, I was told they would not only work on the same painting but would also work on it at the same time. Each of the brothers would start at opposite ends of the huge masonite boards they painted on and work their way towards the centre, where they would meet at exactly the right point with unfailing precision. Alas, as with most legends, this one turned out not to be true. At the time I met them, both of them sported a beard and were about the same height and build, making it difficult to tell them apart at first glance. I used to wish, especially when under the pressure of tight deadlines, that I also had a twin brother that could do at least half of my workload.

The search for our own identities as human beings and, in our case, as artists, take us through hard roads. It is difficult enough to establish who we are and what we are as individuals. This quest, as Tim and Greg found out, was twice as hard for them as two halves of one team. In their search for wholeness, the two halves of 'Hildebrandt' became two whole human beings as well as two whole artists, each one with his distinctive style and personality. As a friend and fellow illustrator, I watched the emergence of Tim Hildebrandt as a fully mature artist.

My love and respect for Tim as a friend and a human being is only matched by my admiration for him as an artist. I have spent many an evening at Tim and Rita's place. A wonderful Victorian house full of treasures: their not-to-be-found-anywhere-else old Walt Disney movies (I remember the marathon cartoon shows that would run all night and well into the next morning for their close friends), the antiques they have collected for years, and, most important, all those magical paintings all over the house.

After several hours of tearing pages and some of my hair I realized I should not attempt to describe Tim Hildebrandt's art. Not being a writer, I lack the eloquence to do his work justice. Instead, cast your eyes on this collection of treasures. They will tell you what I cannot put into words.

Boris Vallejo
Allentown, Philadelphia
Summer, 1991

Introduction

In the world of professional illustration, it is often difficult to determine where illustration leaves off and fine art begins. Nowhere is this more true than in the field of fantasy art. Much of Leonardo da Vinci's work from the late 1400s was considered at the time to be nothing more than pure fantasy, and Michelangelo's frescoes on the ceiling of the Sistine Chapel were commercial illustrations commissioned by the Church. Yet today, few people would argue that these artists had produced anything less than 'fine art'.

Fantasy in art can be traced back to prehistoric times in the earliest of cave paintings, yet it didn't become widely accepted as an art form until the middle of our century. The tremendous advances of technology and medicine made it possible, perhaps for the first time, to question openly previously held dogmas concerning humanity's place within our universe. At the same time, fantasy in literature and art provided an escape for many who were disillusioned by the realities of war and civil conflict. It was this environment that gave birth to the new masters of fantasy art, and allowed such names as Frazetta, FitzPatrick, Vallejo and Hildebrandt to become household words.

The art of Tim Hildebrandt first became widely known in 1976, when he and his brother Greg collaborated on the first of three calendars for J.R.R. Tolkein's *Lord of The Rings* trilogy. During this period, Tim and Greg were known as the Brothers Hildebrandt, a label given to them as a marketing tool by Ballantine Books. It's doubtful that the brothers needed the hype to promote their work; their paintings for the 1978 Tolkein calendar sold more than one million copies, the most that any single calendar had sold before or has sold since.

The year 1978 was also the year that *Star Wars* was released, and again, the Brothers Hildebrandt were in the spotlight. The poster advertising the movie earned them instant celebrity status, and is perhaps as well known as the movie itself. Interestingly enough, Tim and Greg Hildebrandt were not the first illustrators chosen to paint the movie poster. It happened that, shortly before *Star*

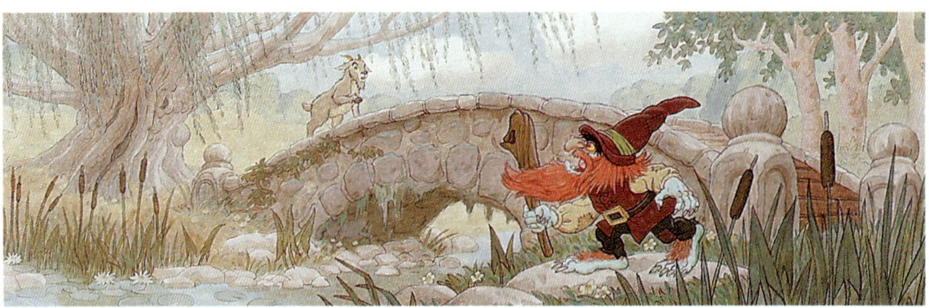

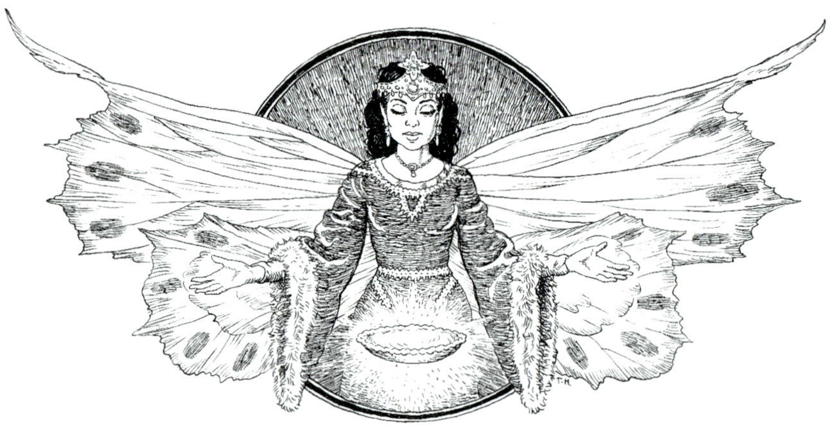

TOP **Billy Goat's Gruff**
A scene from a children's book, 1986. Tim here chose to use as media some magic markers, watercolours and coloured pencils. The magic markers allow him to work very fast. 'It's instant colour,' he says.

ABOVE From Tim and Rita Hildebrandt's *The Fantasy Cookbook*, Bobbs-Merrill, 1983, pen and ink. All the figures in this book are drawn with the aid of models.

RIGHT From *The Fantasy Cookbook*, 1983, watercolour on illustration board. Tim: 'I think the influence of Disney's *Pinocchio* is visible here in the building designs.'

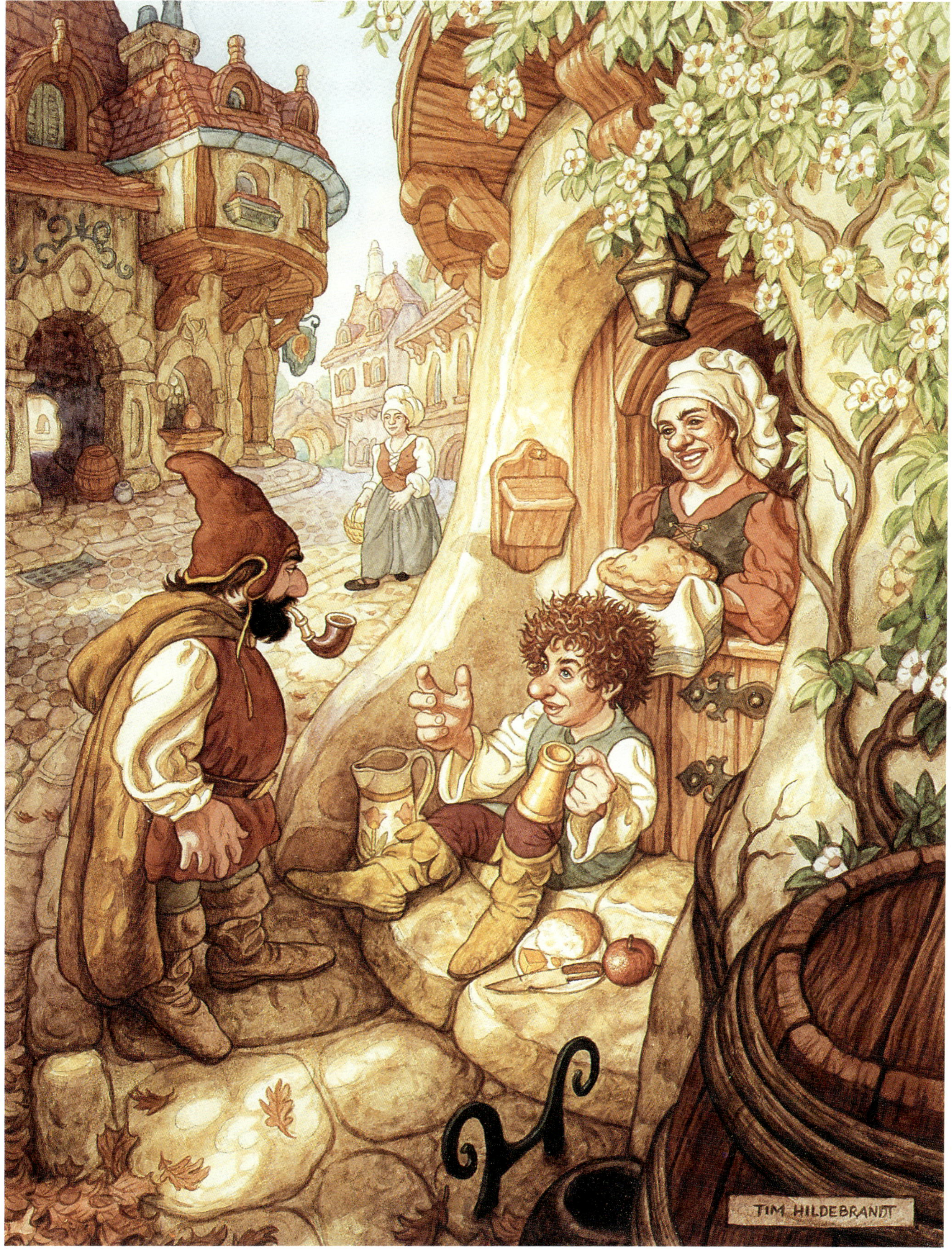
TIM HILDEBRANDT

12

Wars was to be released, the producers decided that the
original artist had not captured in his painting the element of fantasy that was inherent in the movie. The
brothers were called in to produce a second version,
mainly due to their reputation of producing quality
illustrations at great speed.

In the beginning, however, neither Tim nor Greg had
intended to become illustrators. In 1944, when Tim was
five years old, his mother took the brothers to see Walt
Disney's *Pinocchio*. The movie had a profound effect on
Tim. At that time, he was old enough to realize that the
pictures on the screen weren't real, yet he wasn't quite
sure what they were. He decided, at that very moment,
that it didn't matter. Whatever it was, that was what he
wanted to do. This early exposure to the art of the animator began an obsession with the films and characters of
Walt Disney that continues to this day.

It was the realism in Disney's animation that intrigued
Tim, and he would spend countless hours copying the
figures of Snow White, the Prince, and many other
Disney characters. He was determined to learn the secrets
of fluidity of motion, and though he copied the figures he
would provide them with movements of his own. By the
time he would discover what rotoscoping was, or even
obtained the use of this first camera, he had already mastered the human form.

The brothers were eleven when they actually began
animating their drawings. Together, they built a simple
light box, in order to view their drawings in relation to
each other. Without the benefit of animation school they
painstakingly taught themselves the 'in-between' method
of animation. In this procedure, the artist draws two
extreme poses of a figure, then makes a series of 'in-
between' drawings to fill in the motion. The characters
they used were mainly Disney's, but the brothers would
breathe into them a life of their own. They also used characters from *Prince Valient*, a Sunday comic originally written and drawn by Hal Foster. Here again, the characters
belonged to someone else, but the action belonged completely to the brothers.

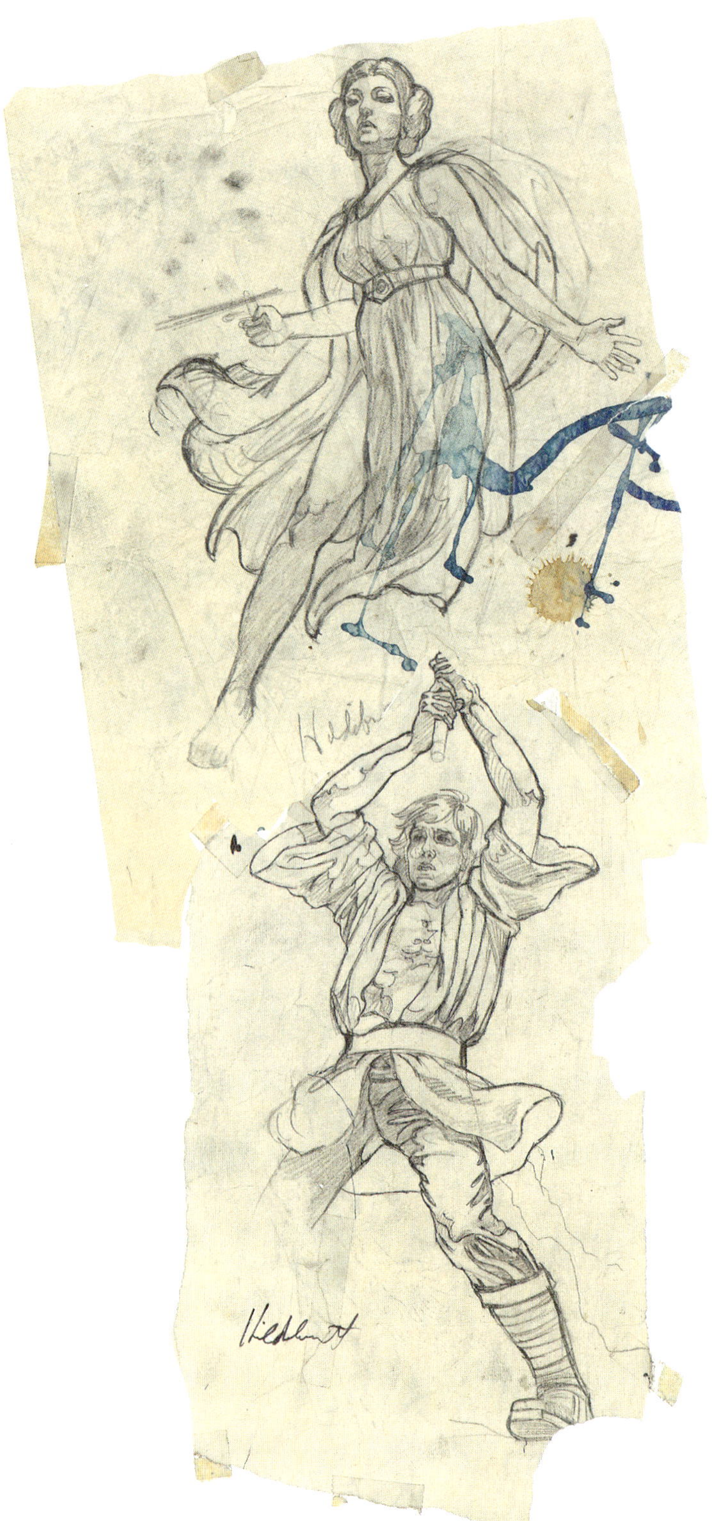

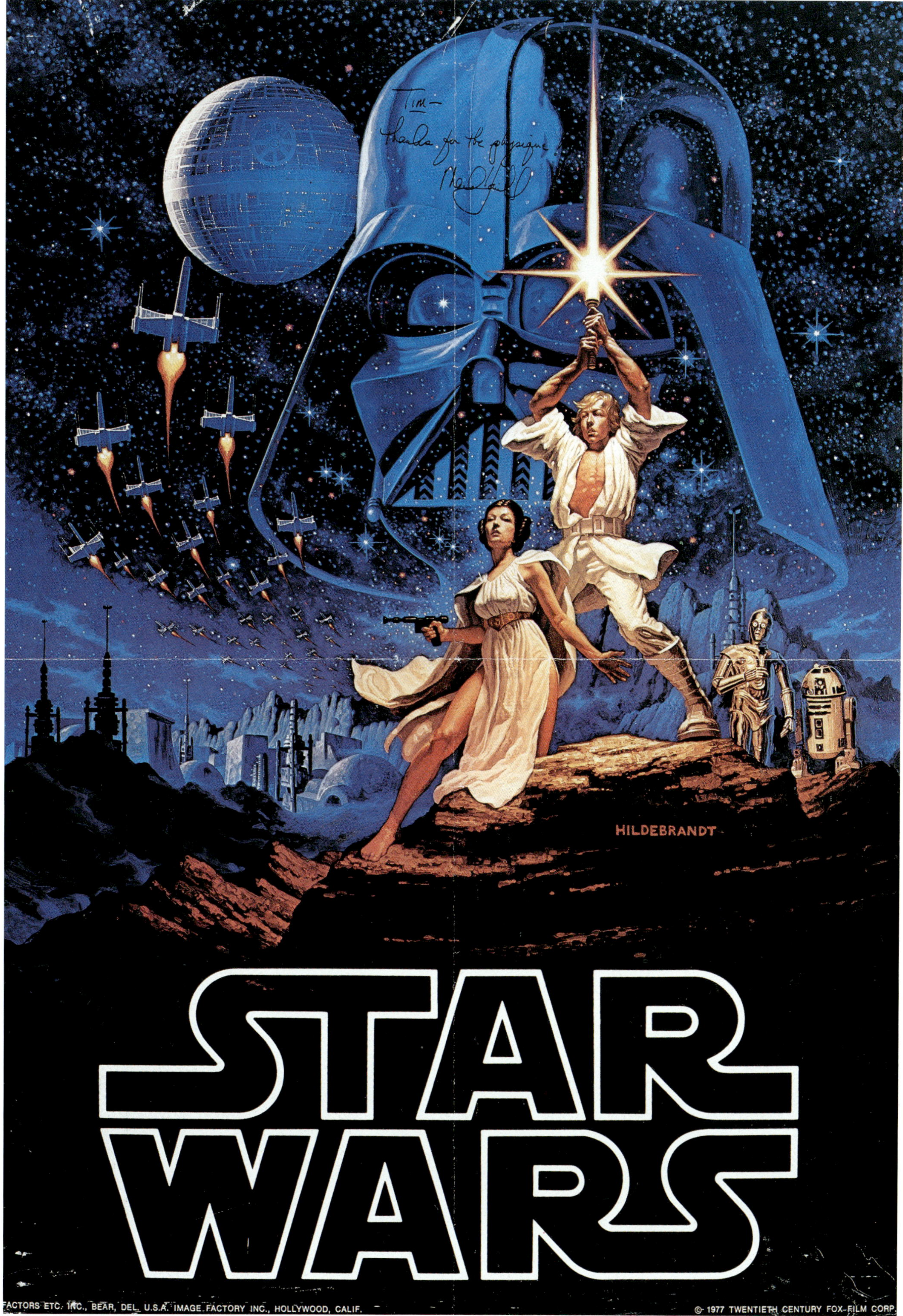
HILDEBRANDT
STAR WARS
FACTORS ETC. INC., BEAR, DEL, U.S.A. IMAGE FACTORY INC., HOLLYWOOD, CALIF.
© 1977 TWENTIETH CENTURY FOX-FILM CORP.

14

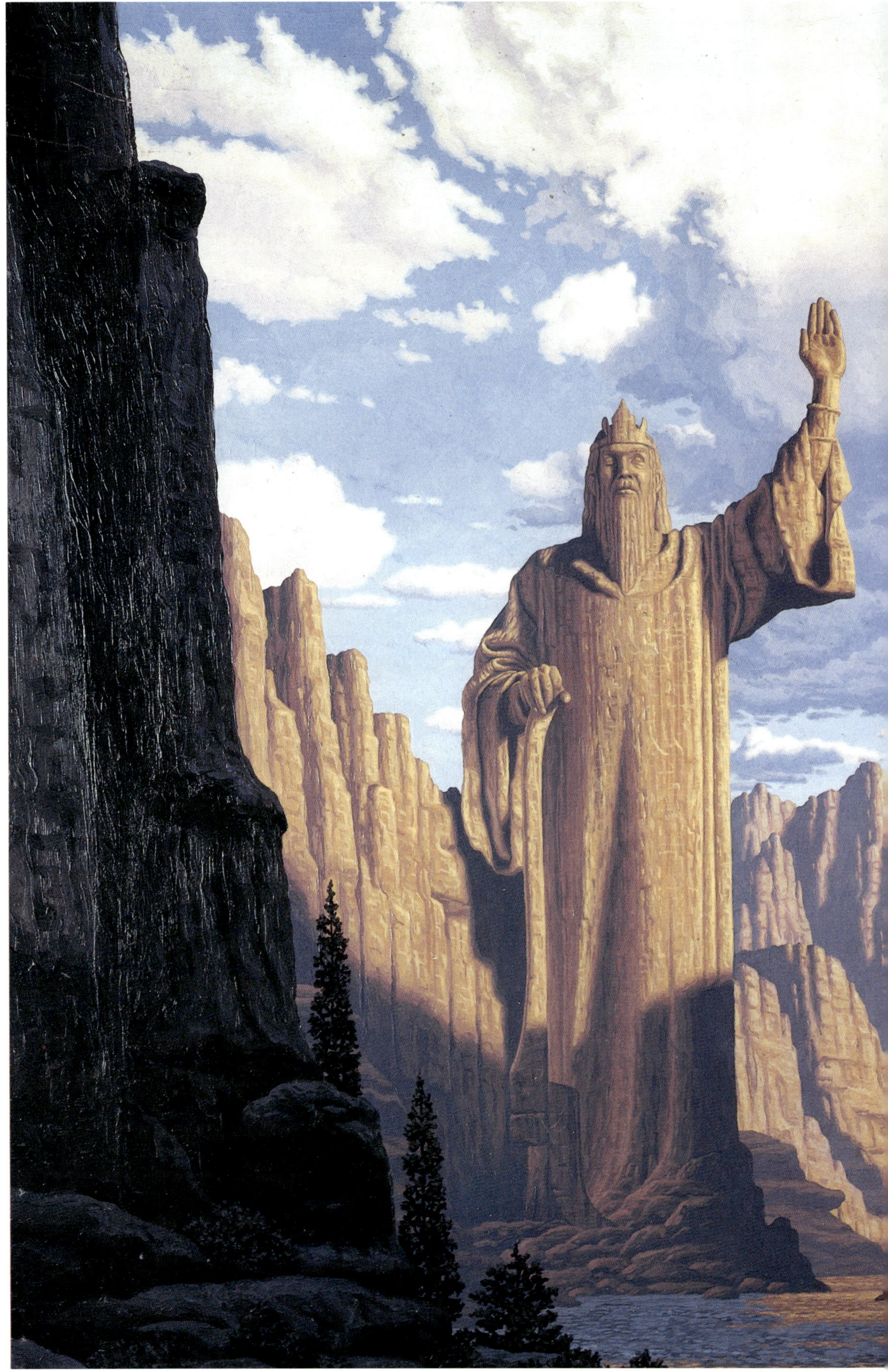

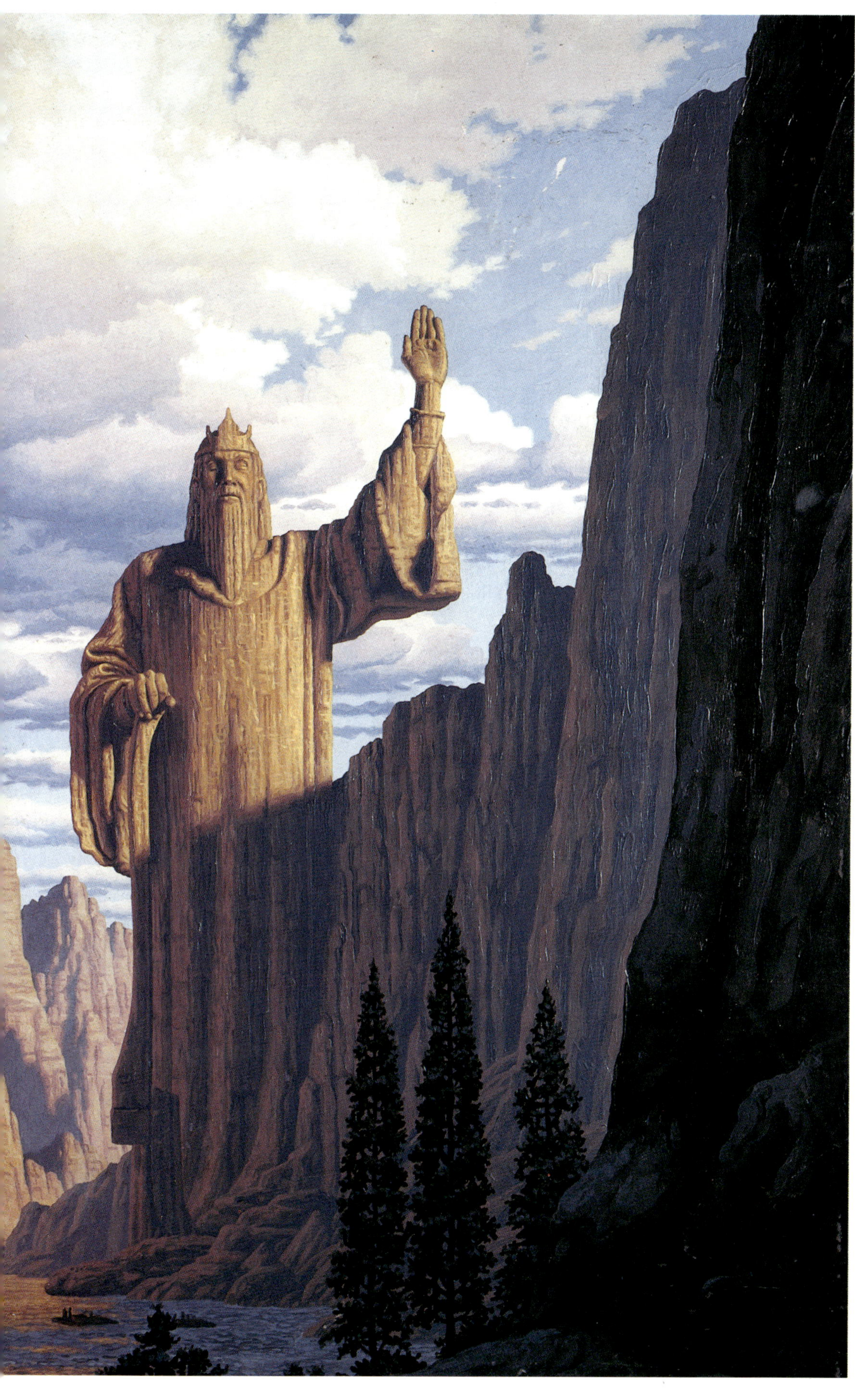

Equally important to Tim's development as an artist was his passion for films and special effects. The films of George Pal during the 1950s had an enormous impact on Tim's work, and continue to do so today. Of particular interest are Pal's *Destination Moon* (1950), *When Worlds Collide* (1951), and *War of the Worlds* (1953). During this time, Tim would completely forget about drawing and animation, and focus all of his energy and talents on recreating the special effects he had seen on the screen. Working closely with Greg, Tim would spend months working on miniature sets of cities and planets. Alien ships were built, modelled closely after the tripod machines made famous in Pal's movies, and constructed so that they could be pulled on rollers down the streets of the set. Miniature explosives were placed in the buildings and under the streets, and the entire set was wired to a control box. Once everything was in place the brothers would begin filming, the tripod machines would roll down the streets, and the set would be systematically destroyed.

Tim's interest in special effects was always balanced by his love of art and animation, and usually followed his heart for direction. He would often spend six months at a time building sets and blowing them up, then suddenly find himself animating again after watching the latest Disney production. His mixed interests served him well, as he discovered that not only were these two art forms compatible, but essential to each other. All of the disciplines learned during this period contribute directly to his work today: the realism, lighting, action and composition involved are trademarks of the art of Tim Hildebrandt.

Despite these diversions into filmmaking, however, Tim remained determined to become one day a Disney animator. Throughout his high school years, Tim often corresponded with the people at Disney Studios. While some of the material they sent him was helpful in developing his craft, the bottom line was always the same: all Disney animators must have attended some sort of basic art course. This prompted Tim to enrol in Meinzinger's Art School following his graduation.

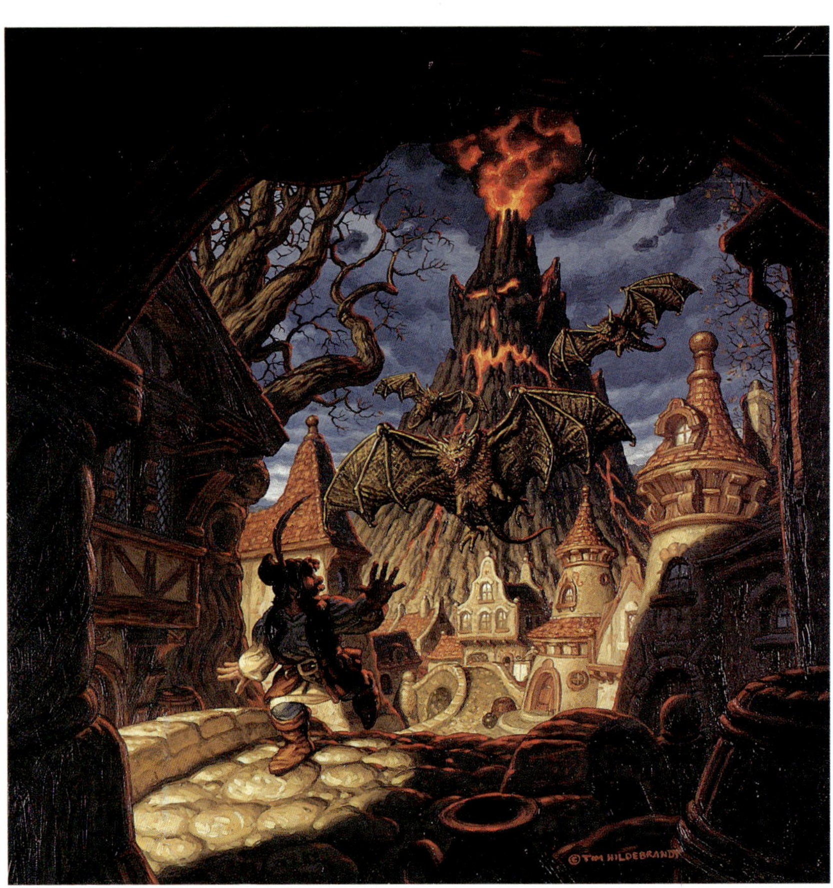

Messengers of the Dragon Lord
From the *Realms of Wonder* calendar, TSR, 1983, acrylic on masonite. Published by TSR.

RIGHT **The Amazon Fire Crystal**
From *Urshurak* by Tim and Greg Hildebrandt and Jerry Nichols, Bantam, 1979, acrylic on masonite. Tim and Greg initially built a model of the device and made the costumes.

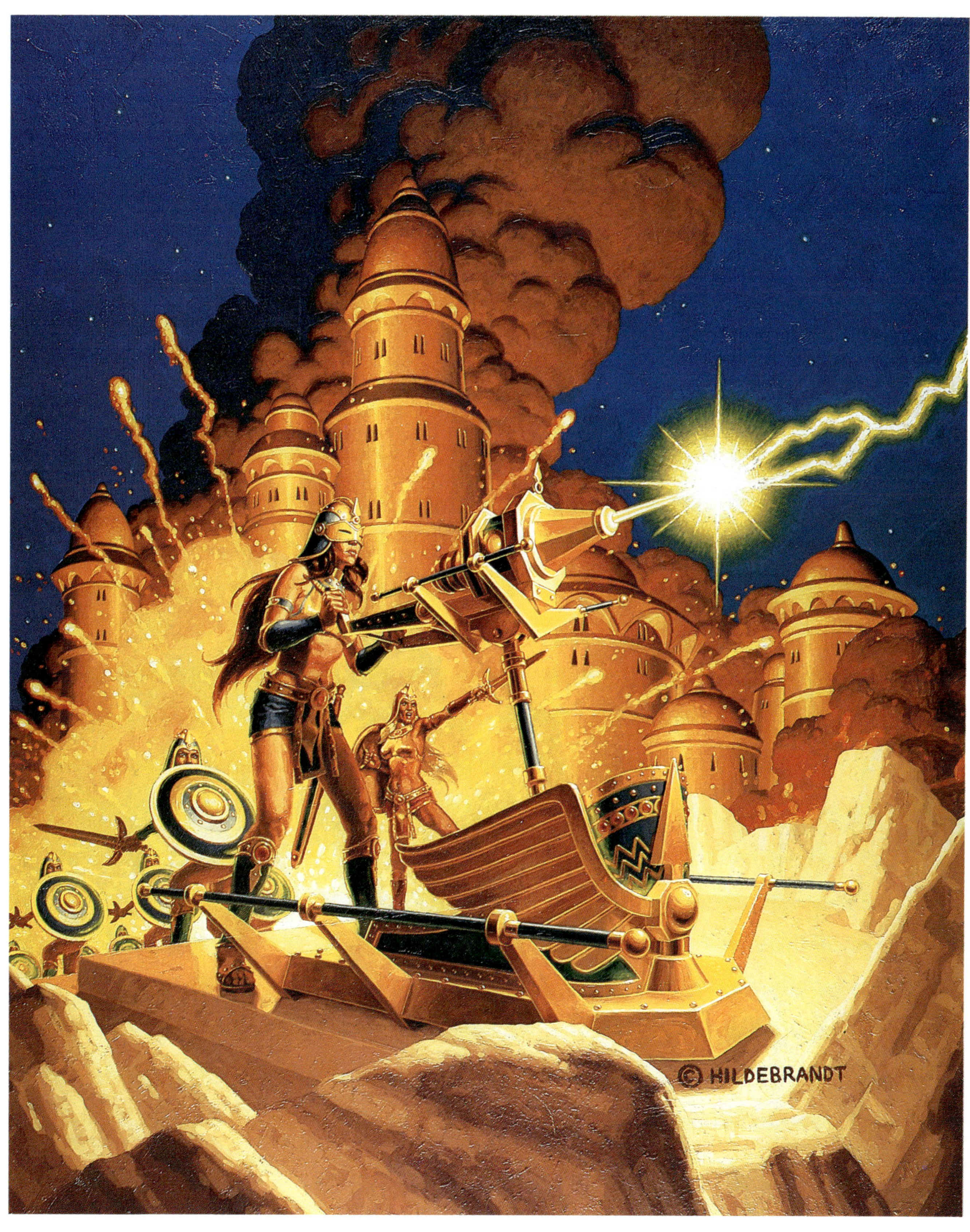
© HILDEBRANDT

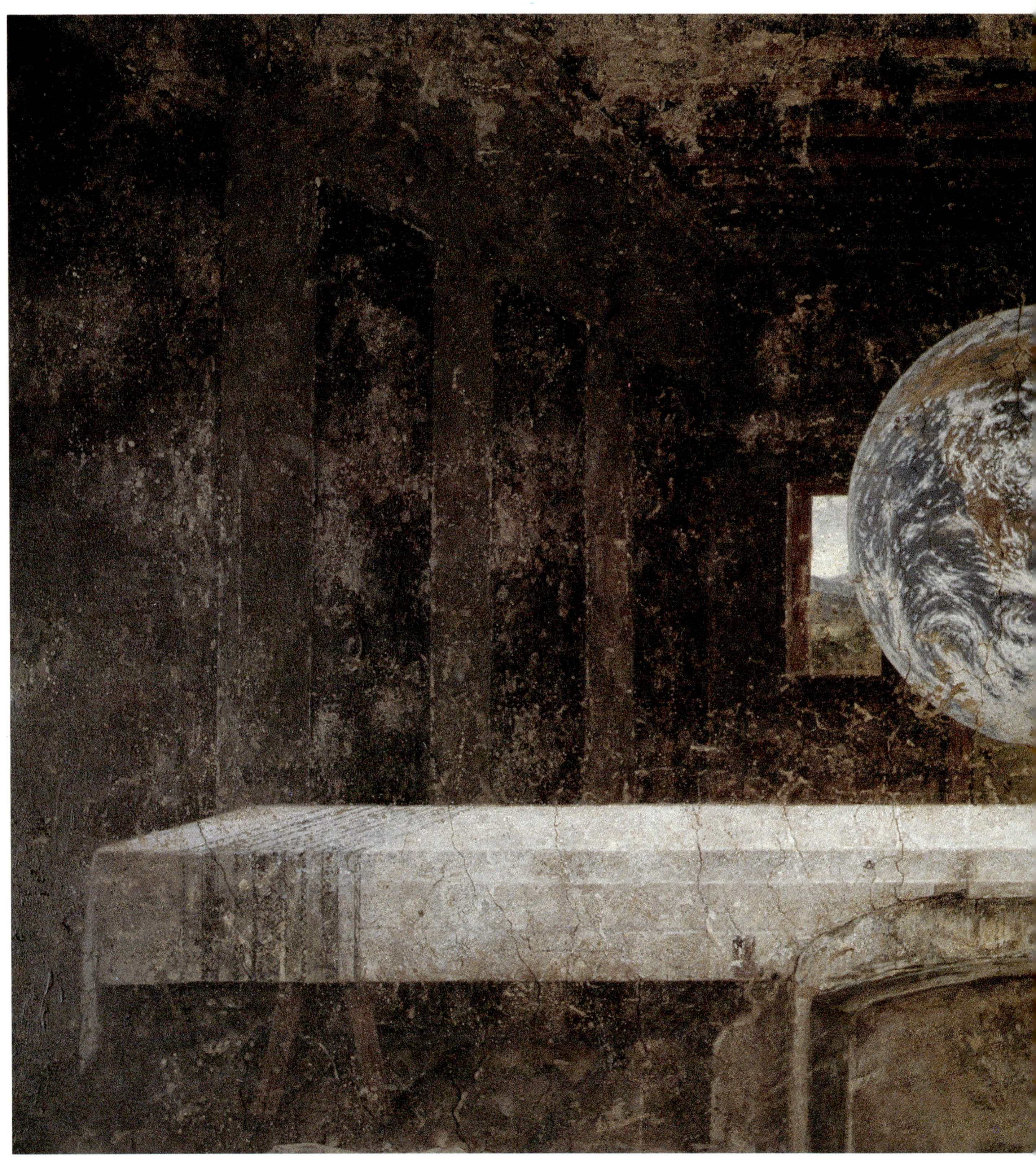

A Study in Earth Tones – The Bleeding Earth
Acrylic on masonite, 1990. Tim: 'The New York Society of Illustrators in
conjunction with the United Nations invited 150 artists to participate in
a show called *The Artist and the Environment*. This painting was my
contribution. I had to sum up in a sentence why I had chosen to paint
this particular picture. I said that all great art in a state of decay is
worthy of restoration. What greater work of art is there than the Earth.'

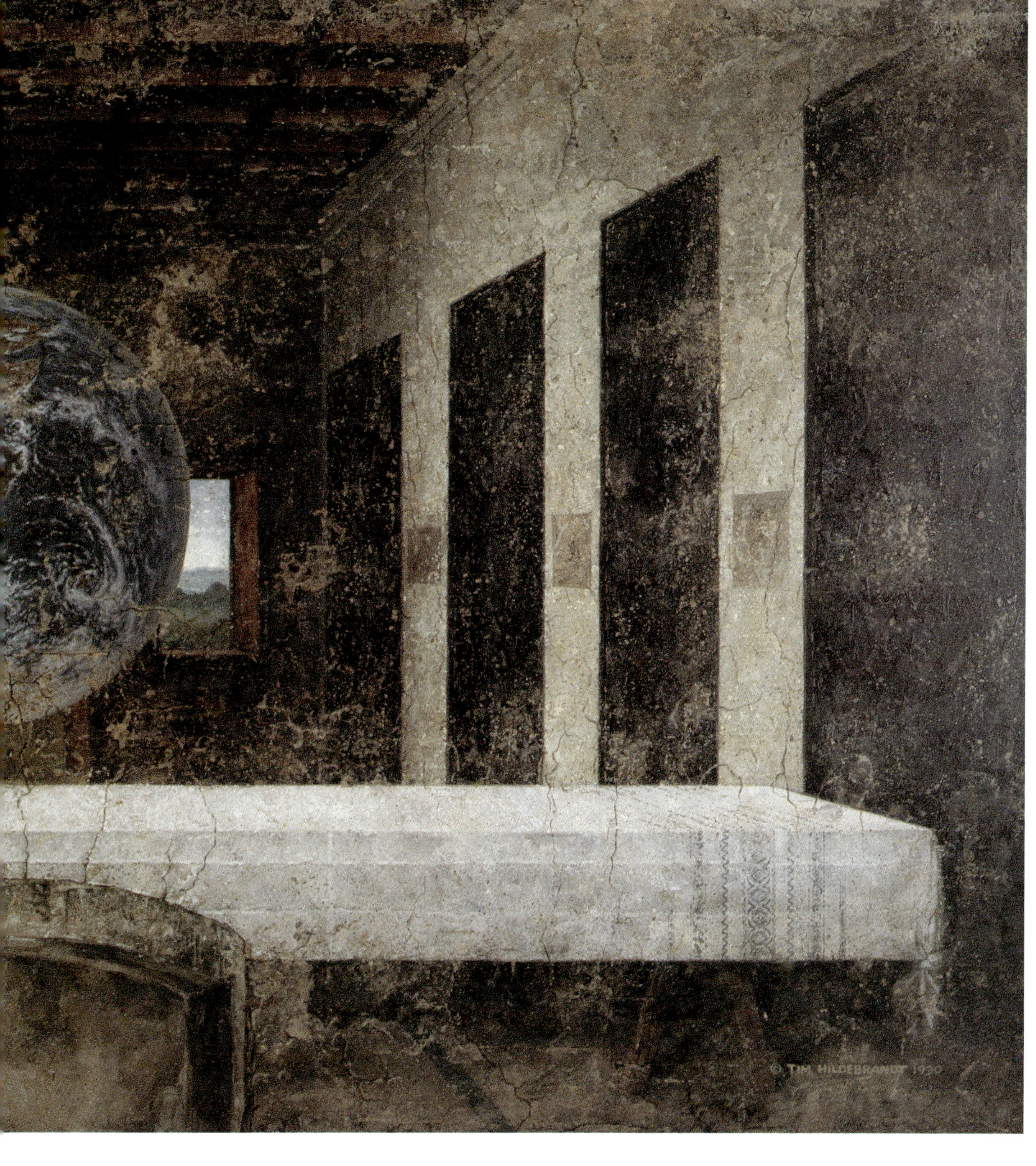

Meinzinger's was a small school in Detroit, Michigan, located on the second floor of a building on Woodward Avenue. Tim attended there for only a short period of time, but learned much about life-drawing, anatomy, perspective, colour and design. One of the most important things that Tim learned was to go against the grain. He learned that art schools teach their students to specialize; in reality, it is best not to specialize. Art schools will teach you not to copy; Tim learned to copy everything. By learning as much as you can from as many sources as you can, developing an individual style will follow naturally. Above all, question traditional teaching. Innovation is as fundamental in art as anywhere else in society.

Tim's father was instrumental in helping him land his first job as an artist. Tim was nineteen when his father arranged for an interview at Jam Handy, an organization that, among other things, made films for Chevrolet. Both Tim and Greg applied for the job. They arrived at the company together, showed some samples of their work, and were hired on the spot.

The lessons learned at Jam Handy were far more important than the wages earned, which started at one dollar per hour. Tim often fondly refers to this time as his 'college education'. There he learned such basic animation skills as storyboards, background painting and stop-motion animation. He also learned to use the airbrush, and worked on set design for their live action films.

The brothers left Jam Handy in 1962, after having been with the company for four years. They headed for New York to begin work with a religious organization headed by Bishop Fulton Sheen. For the next six years they made documentary films depicting poverty, oppression and hunger. During this time, the brothers basically stopped drawing. They returned to New York in 1968 with a portfolio, feeling that their artistic talents had been wasted. Tim felt that it was like starting over, relearning how to draw. But with determination and confidence in their abilities they found work with Holt Rinehart and Winston. Their job was to illustrate several

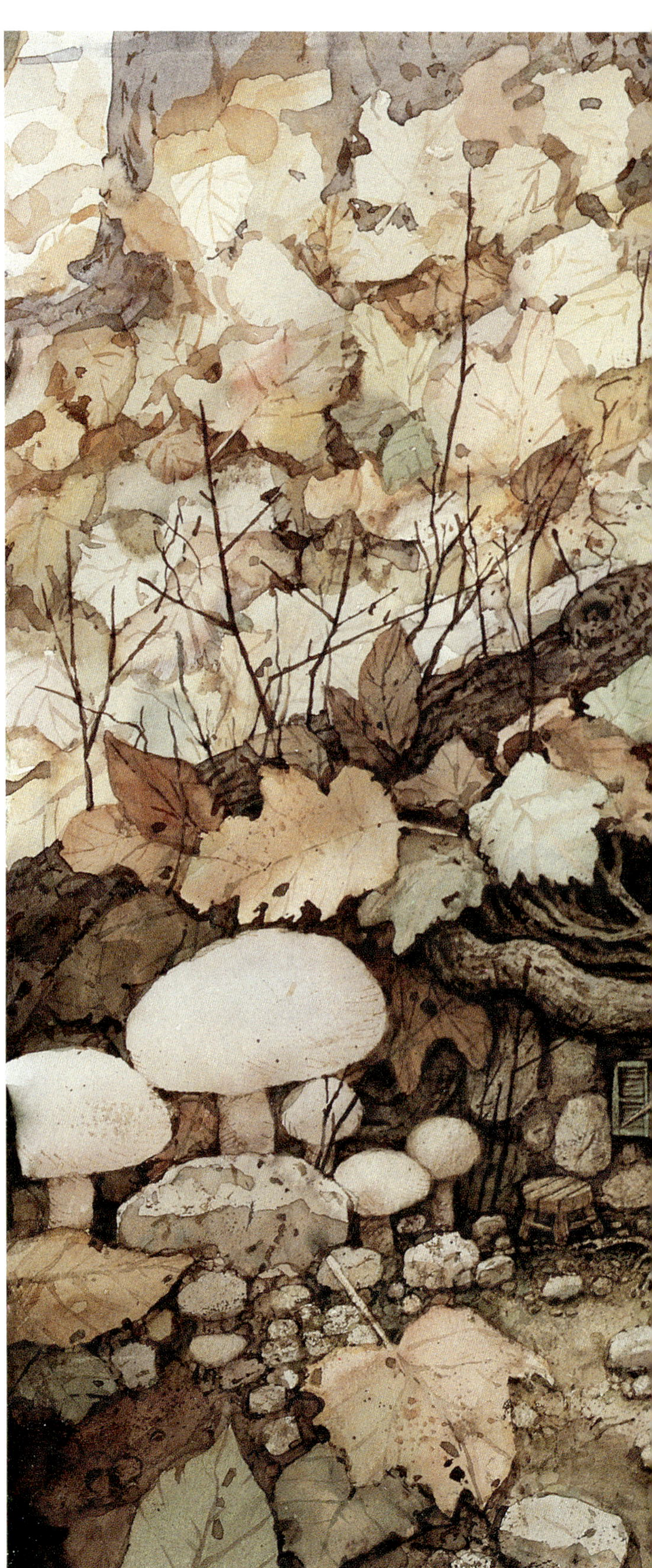

Henry David's Place
Portfolio piece, 1969, watercolour on illustration board. Tim painted this picture to show to various children's book publishers. If they liked it, perhaps they would offer him some commissions.

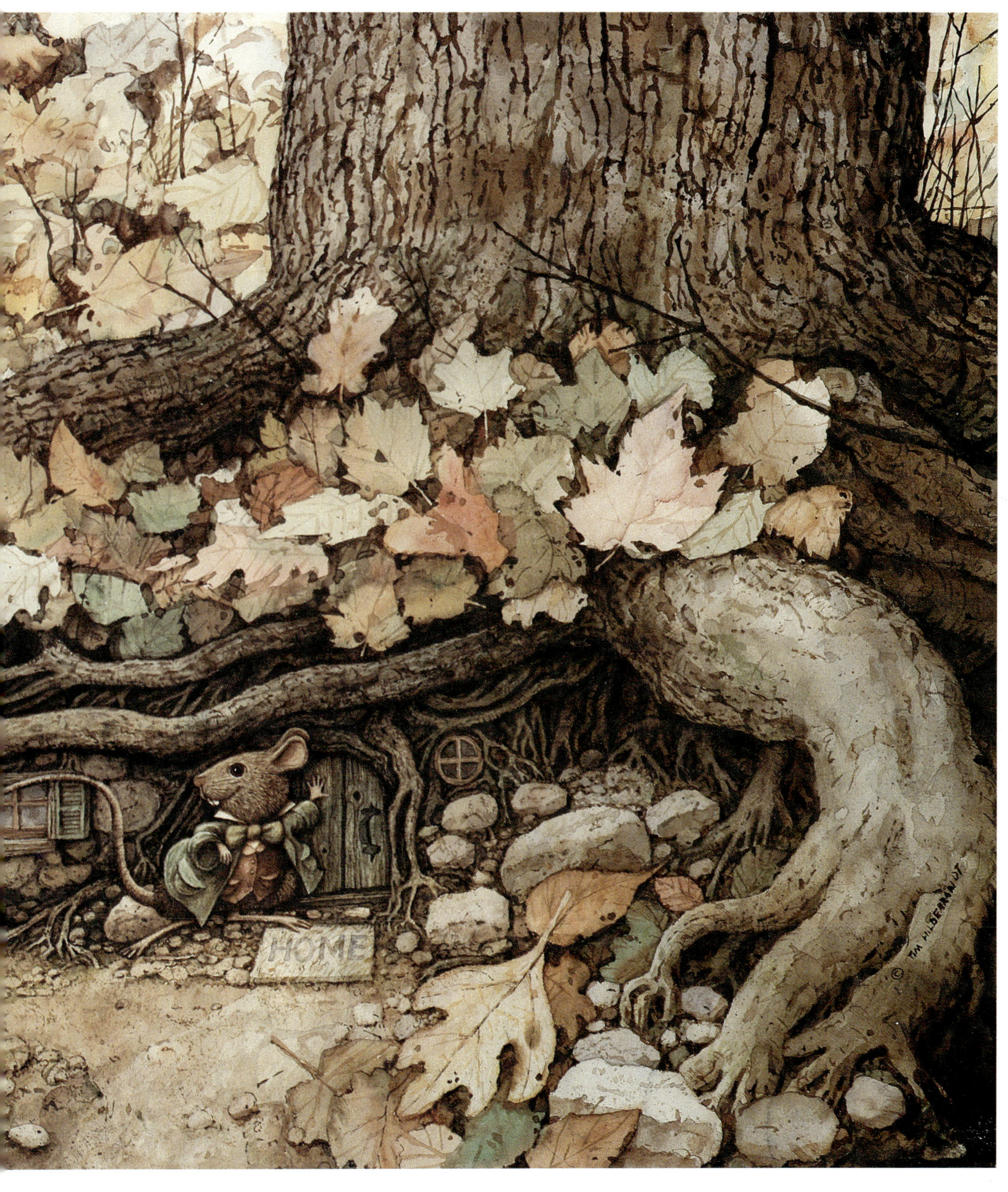

HOME

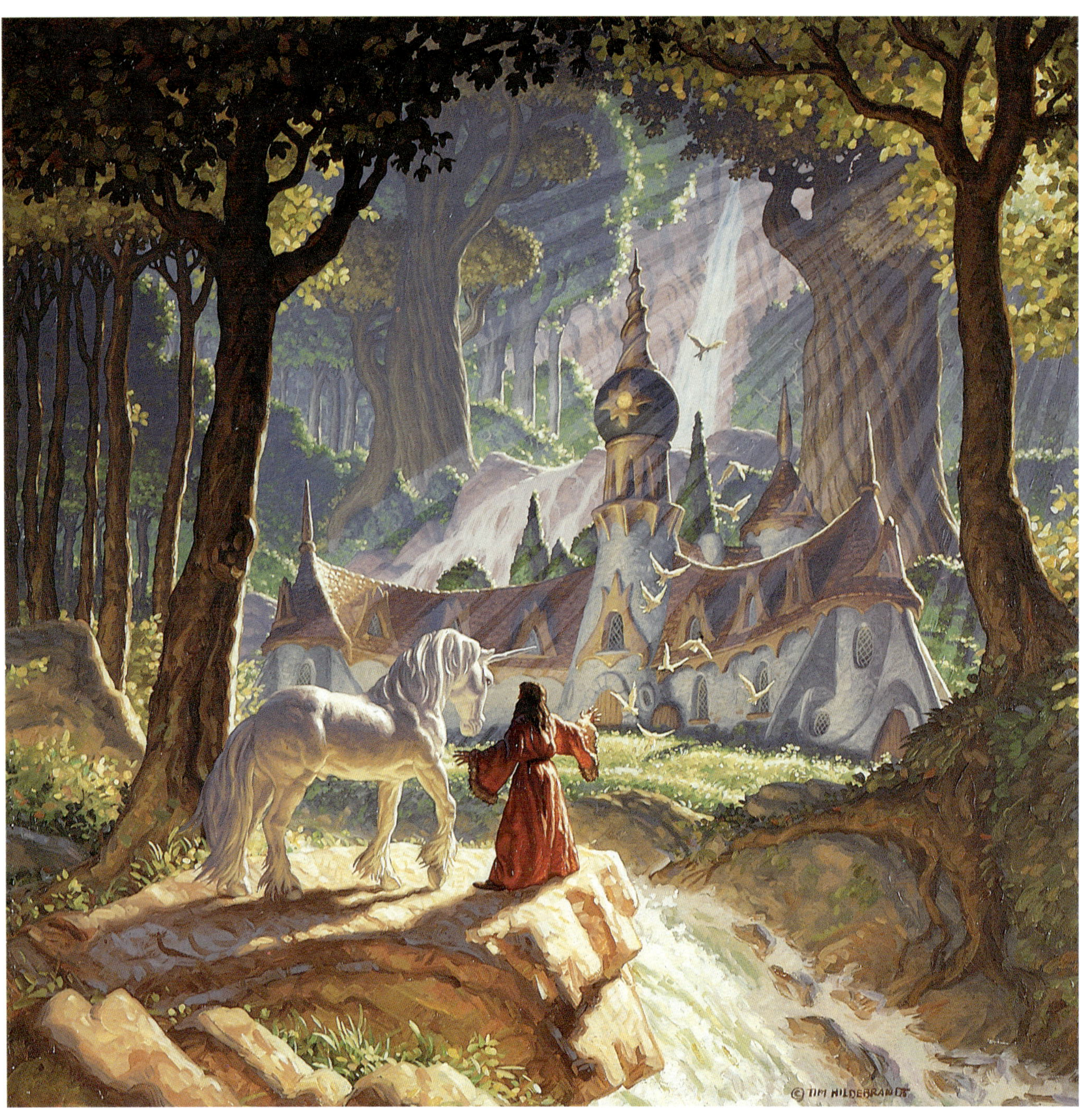

The Wizard Glade
Calendar illustration, 1983. Tim: 'The trees on either side help to frame the composition. The light source is high and is placed behind the subject, thus creating an edge light. If you look carefully you will notice that the scene is lit also by a strong light bouncing from the ground.'

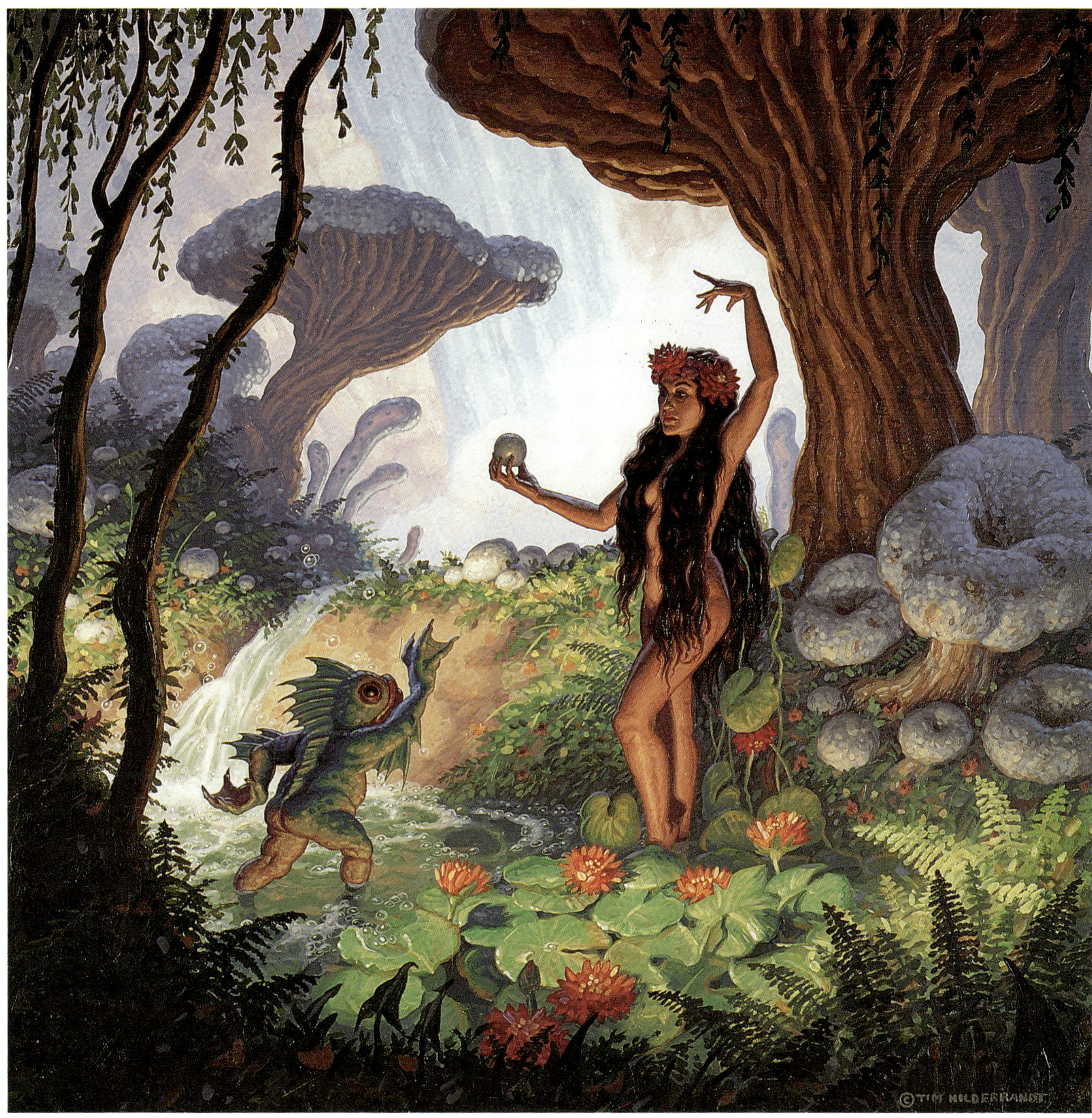

Water Nixie
From the *Realms of Wonder* calendar, TSR, 1987,
acrylic on masonite. Notice how all the lines in this
composition lead to the centre of interest; the
vines in the foreground, the mushroom behind
the central figure.

children's textbooks scheduled for re-release. The brothers also kept busy doing advertising work, and painting album covers for RCA and Victor. They had found their niche as freelance illustrators.

It was, of course, the paintings for the Tolkein calendars that first made them famous. Tim had read *Lord of the Rings* years before, and had decided at that time to somehow illustrate those books. At that time, however, he had no idea what form that would take. In 1975 Tim's wife, Rita, gave him a Tolkein calendar illustrated by fan artist Tim Kirk. On the back in fine print was an advertisement, asking artists who were interested in illustrating the calendar to contact the publisher. The brothers responded and were asked to paint a cover for another Tolkein book, *Smith of Wooten Major & Farmer Giles of Ham*. This trial painting landed them the job of painting the Tolkein calendars, which made them both instant celebrities in the world of fantasy art. The assignment of the *Star Wars* movie poster came the following year, topping off the careers of possibly the most celebrated illustrative teams in history.

Following their success as illustrators, the brothers decided to design a fantasy of their own. Together, they created *Urshurak*, a fantasy world envisioned by the brothers and brought to life by the words of an old friend, Jerry Nichols. The book was illustrated throughout by the brothers and was a huge success. They then decided to take the concept one step further: make *Urshurak* into a film.

For the next two years, the brothers made the rounds in Hollywood, trying to find someone to produce their story. They spent thousands of dollars preparing elaborate presentations that would make the sale and, several times, it seemed as though they were close. It wasn't until their finances were almost depleted that someone informed them that the bottom line was *Urshurak* would simply be too expensive to produce.

During this time they had literally put themselves out of the art market. It seems that the key phrase for professional illustrators is 'out of sight, out of mind'. And the brothers had been out of sight for over two years. They

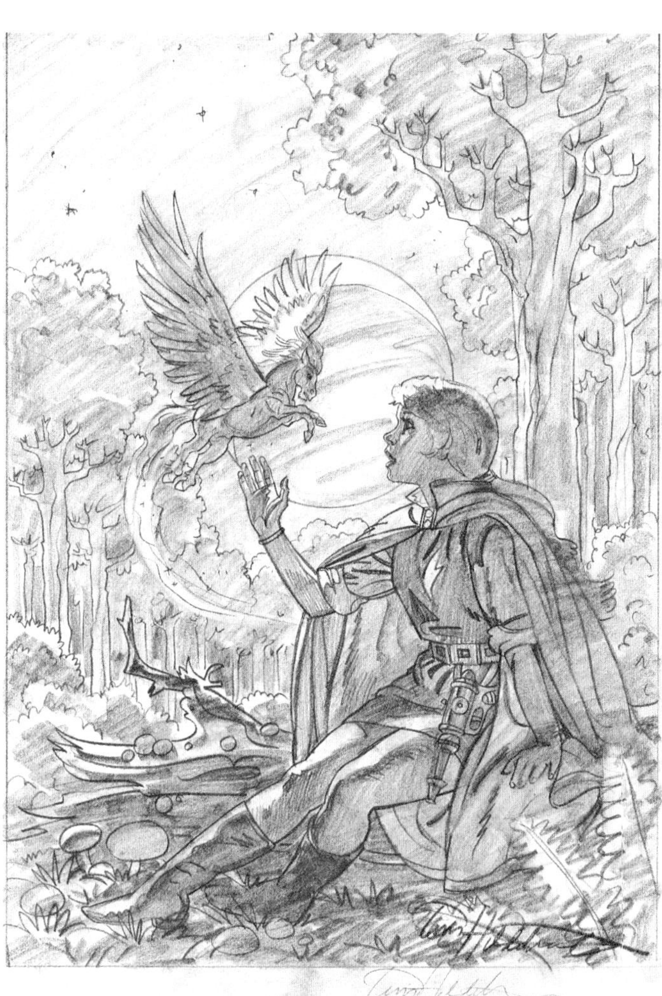

Unused cover sketch for *Vendetta* by M.S. Murdock, 1987. Tim: 'The book was a mixture of fantasy and science fiction. The publishers wanted the latter to be emphasized.' (See page 65 for the final version.)

RIGHT **The Amazon City of Zandura**
Finished pencil drawing from *Urshurak* by Tim and Greg Hildebrandt and Jerry Nichols, Bantam, 1979. Tim: 'I crossed Egyptian and Assyrian architecture in this composition.'

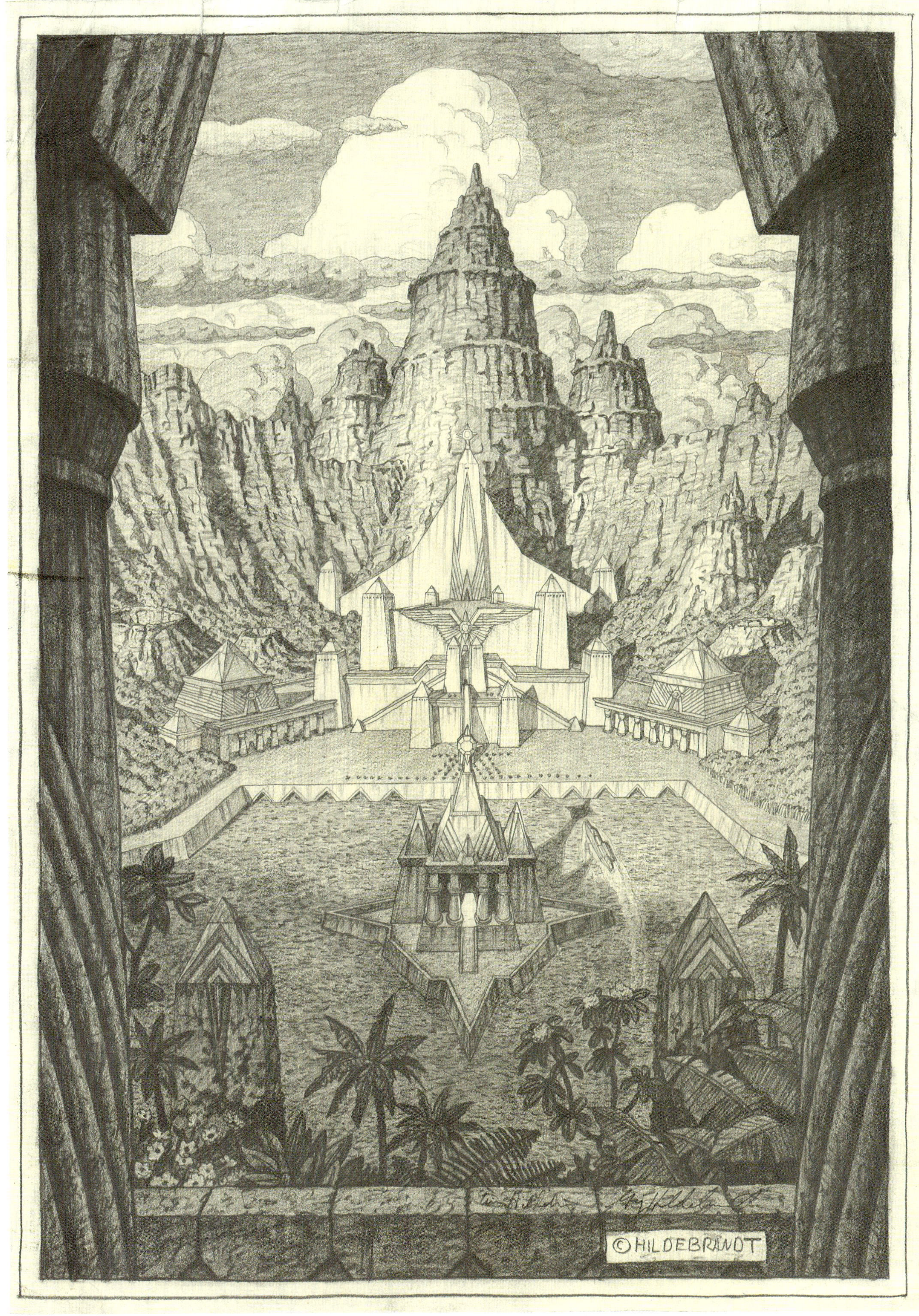

©HILDEBRANDT

tried to regain some recognition by first producing an *Atlantis* calendar, then children's books, but there simply wasn't enough money to get by. Due largely to the constant stress of the previous two years the brothers split apart, and began working on projects as individuals.

In 1982, Rita Hildebrandt helped Tim land a job producing calendars for TSR, and it seemed that Tim was finally back on track. Tim painted two calendars for TSR's *Dungeons and Dragons* series, and moved on to painting fantasy book covers and advertising material. His most recent works can be seen on book covers for such authors as Alan Dean Foster and in the Landmark calendar series *Visions of Other Worlds*. In addition, he has continued his interest in film by becoming the executive producer for a low-budget thriller titled *The Return of the Aliens: The Deadly Spawn*, and is currently working with special effects artist John Dodds on an animated short titled *The Dinosaur Rag*.

As for the future, Tim sees no end in sight: his love for illustrating is a major reason for his continued existence. He is interested in spending more time creating art for his own satisfaction, or expressing his opinions more through his art. He is particularly interested in painting subjects that reflect his environmental concerns, and continues to pursue his interests in special effects filmmaking. Whatever the subject, it is certain that we will be able to enjoy Tim's work for many years to come.

The Deadly Spawn
Movie poster, 1980, acrylic on masonite. Tim: 'The producer, Ted Bomus, got in on the act – this is him from the back fighting off the monster.' Tim was the art director of this low-budget science fiction film and is shown below painting the miniature set which was built in the barn. The film was shot in the house.

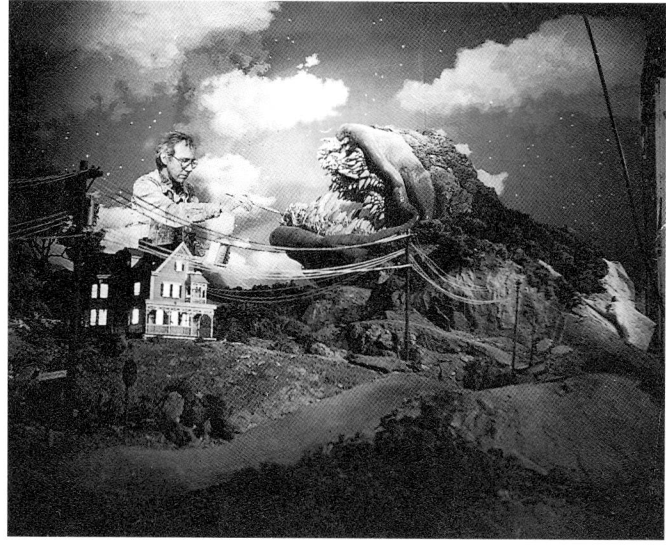

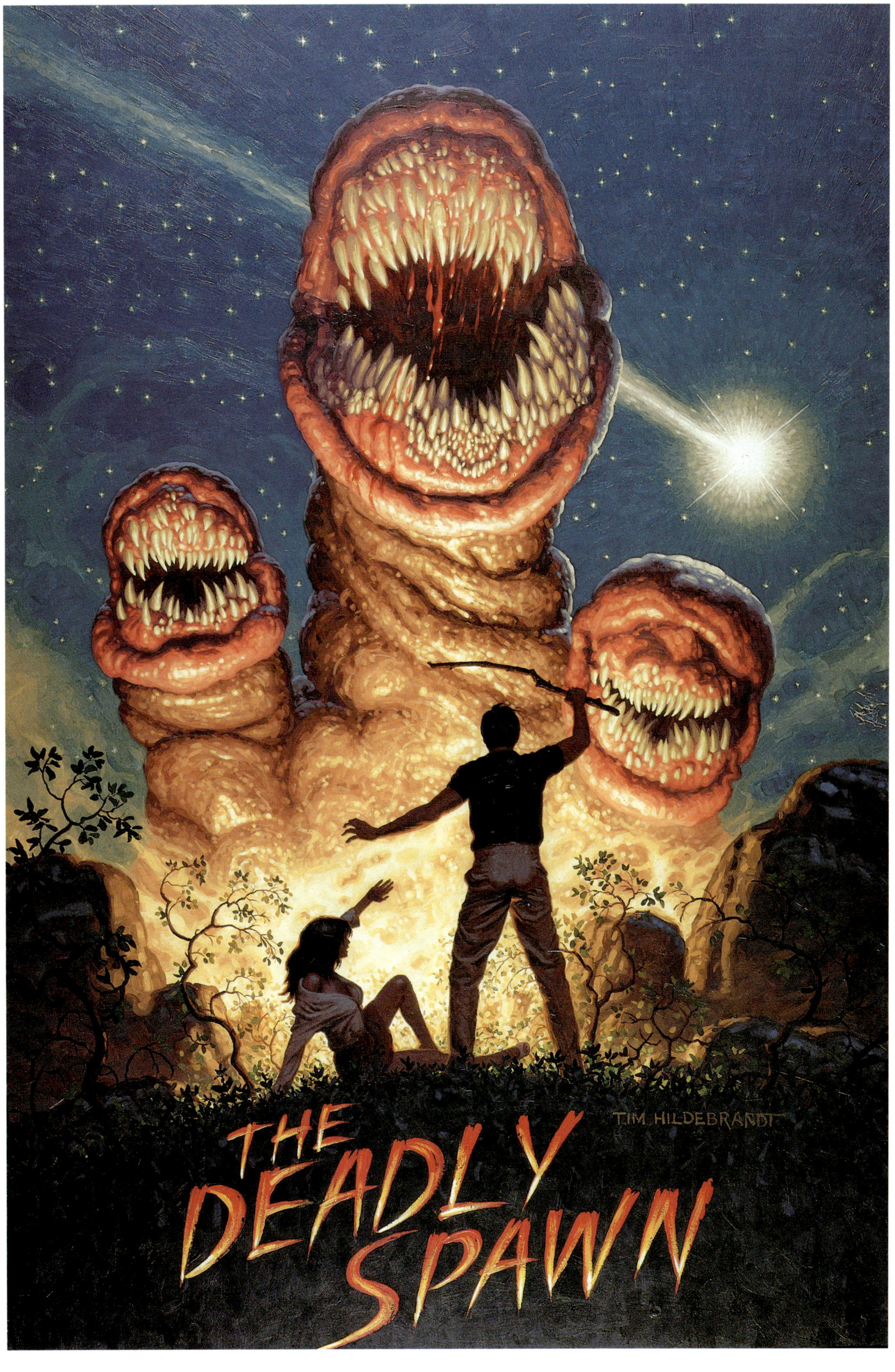
TIM HILDEBRANDT
THE DEADLY SPAWN

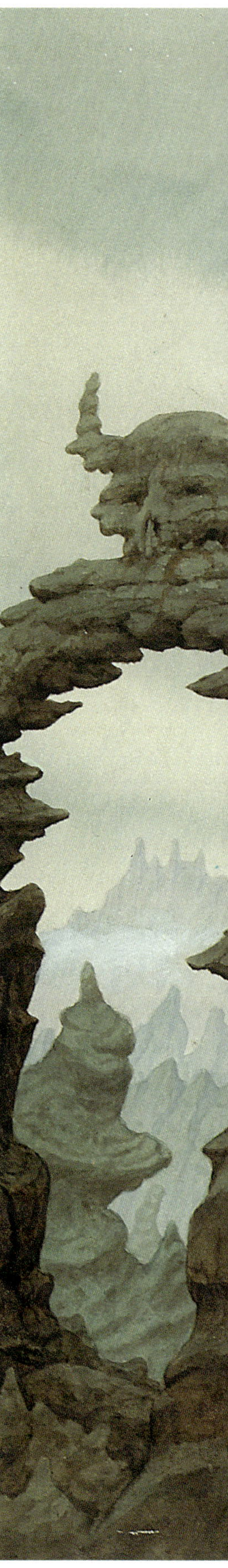

Zormena's Castle
From *The Fantasy Cookbook*, 1983, watercolour and acrylic on illustration board. To achieve a sombre mood this painting is lit with an overcast light. This creates cool highlights and warmer coloured shadows.

Section One
Influences & Resources

To some extent every artist is influenced by some other artist whose work they respect and admire. These unseen forces can surface in the artist's work in any number of ways. The influence can be very specific, as in a borrowed technique, or it may be more general in nature, as in a particular style. More often than not the effects of these influences are somewhat subtle in nature, but are present nonetheless.

By far, the most singular influence on the art of Tim Hildebrandt can be summed up in one word: Disney. Tim only half-jokingly refers to his fondness for Disney art as an obsession, and feels that the impact it has had on his life is largely responsible for his career today. This attraction for Disney began at a very early age, and has remained with him all of his life.

Of course, the word Disney by itself is rather generic, and in this case refers to the hundreds of artists who worked as Walt Disney Studios between 1937 and 1955. The animated classics *Pinocchio* and *Sleeping Beauty* played an enormous role in molding Tim's career, and he would spend countless hours trying to duplicate the art from these films.

From the hundreds of talented men and women who worked on these films, there were a special few that stand out as having had the greatest effect on Tim's work: Eyvind Earle, Gustav Tenggrin and Claude Coates. These men may have been referred to as 'background artists' or 'layout designers', but their contributions to the art community managed to transcend the simplicity of their titles. They were the role models from which Tim learned much of his craft.

Eyvind Earle was reponsible for creating the sweeping, stylized backgrounds for Walt Disney's *Sleeping Beauty*. These enchanting, though sometimes frightening designs were actually based on early Renaissance paintings. The fact that the characters of this film were designed to blend in with the backgrounds speaks for the quality and intensity of Earle's art. Tim would spend countless hours trying to capture their essence.

Gustav Tenggrin was another Disney background designer that greatly influenced Tim's art. He was responsible for creating the backgrounds for *Pinocchio*, and ultimately contributed to the entire look of the film. His line-and-wash studies possess a unique dreamlike quality, yet are rich in detail. They portray the same feeling of quaint antiquity that is apparent in many of Tim's own paintings. His powerful compositions, creative use of lighting and shadow, and his close attention to detail are all readily apparent in Tim's own work.

Although Gustav Tenggrin may have designed the backgrounds for *Pinocchio*, it was an artist by the name of Claude Coates who actually painted them. Like many of the Disney artists, Coates had the ability to render a scene that lay somewhere between fantasy and photo-realism. Coates pioneered the use of opaque pigments as the preferred medium for backgrounds at Disney, and his work on *Pinocchio* set the mood for what many consider to be Disney's finest film. Like Earle and Tenggrin, Coates possessed an incredible sense of composition and detail that later would provide a wealth of inspiration for Tim Hildebrandt.

Not all of Tim's childhood heroes came from Disney, however. Some of the other artists who shared in this role were Howard Pyle, N.C. Wyeth, and Hal Foster.

Howard Pyle was one of the earliest pioneers of fantasy art, and was very influential in making it the genre that it is today. His paintings are wonderful studies in composition, and display a unique dramatic elegance. His figures are an interesting combination of line and tone, often poised, and somehow larger than life. Much of the drama from his paintings stemmed from his knowledge and use of light and shadow.

N.C. Wyeth is perhaps best remembered for his fantastic illustrations of the story classics *Treasure Island*, *Robin Hood* and *Mysterious Island*. As a former student of Howard Pyle, Wyeth incorporated into his own work many of the qualities that made Pyle famous. Like Pyle, Wyeth's figures are imposing. His mastery of composition and light were also learned from Pyle. However, Wyeth's paintings contain a more childlike quality, and are often

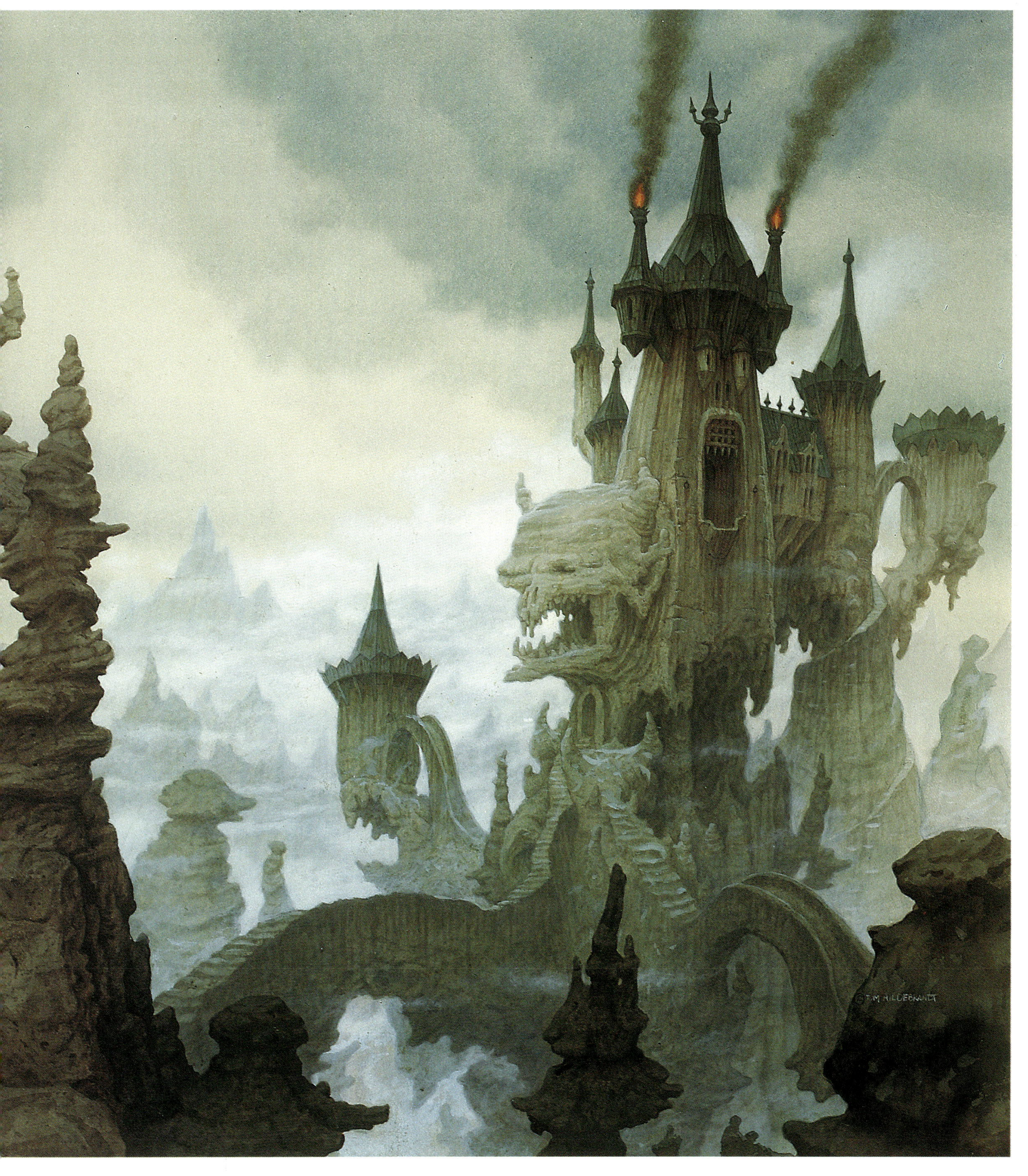

more energetic and forceful.

Hal Foster was another non-Disney illustrator who Tim gives credits for his development as an artist. Foster created the original *Prince Valient*, a weekly comic strip depicting the adventures of a prince in medieval times. The association is obvious; many of Tim's own illustrations are set within this period. Also apparent is the same mastery of composition and human form that Tim has captured and used within his own art.

While other artists were instrumental in shaping Tim as an illustrator, his most important daily source of inspiration comes from the creative manipulation of his resource material. Throughout his years as a professional illustrator, Tim has amassed a huge collection of reference photos, costumes, books and three-dimensional models that all contribute to the execution of his paintings. By combining bits and pieces of this reference material with his own skill as an artist he is able to render any scene he is apt to imagine.

For many purists, the thought of using a photograph to aid in drawing or painting is somehow cheating. The fact is, most professional illustrators today use photos for reference. It is probable that if photography had existed during the days of the old masters, most of them would have used it. A professional illustrator today must often work very quickly to keep up with important deadlines, and photos are simply a tool that enables them to do that.

In addition, keep in mind that photographs are merely a point of departure for the artist. They provide him with information concerning essentially three things: shapes, highlights and shadows. Very rarely, if at all, are the photographs copied exactly. And it is extremely unusual if the colours from the photographs are actually used in the scheme of the painting. Some may still argue that live models could be used to achieve the same thing, but professional illustrators are notoriously practical people, and live models simply aren't practical once you consider the alternative.

Many artists strive to achieve the maximum amount of detail in their photography as this can translate to more

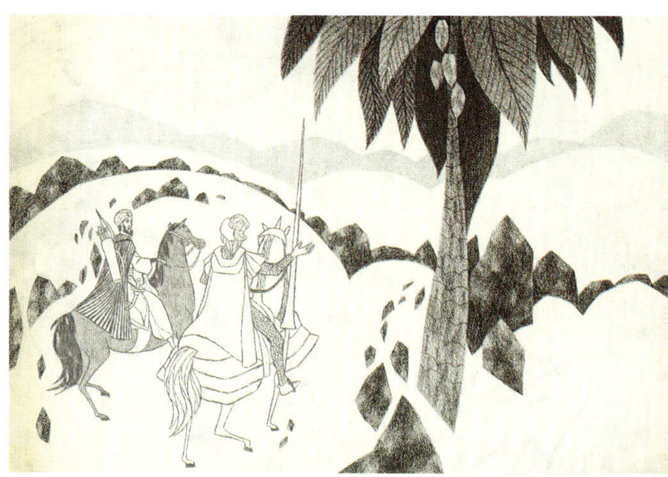

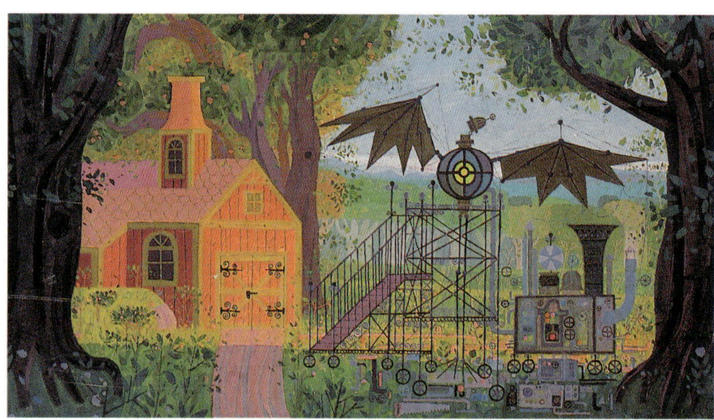

ABOVE, TOP A 1959 pencil drawing from an unpublished book. Tim: 'When I saw Disney's *Sleeping Beauty* in 1958 the thing I was most taken by were the elaborately detailed background paintings by Eyvind Earle. I tried to copy his stylized compositions and ended up with paintings that were even more stylized. This is evident on all four pictures shown here'; ABOVE Early animation background, 1962, casine on drawing board.

OPPOSITE PAGE, ABOVE **The Quest** Casine on illustration board, 1959.

OPPOSITE PAGE, BELOW Early animation background, casine on illustration board, 1964.

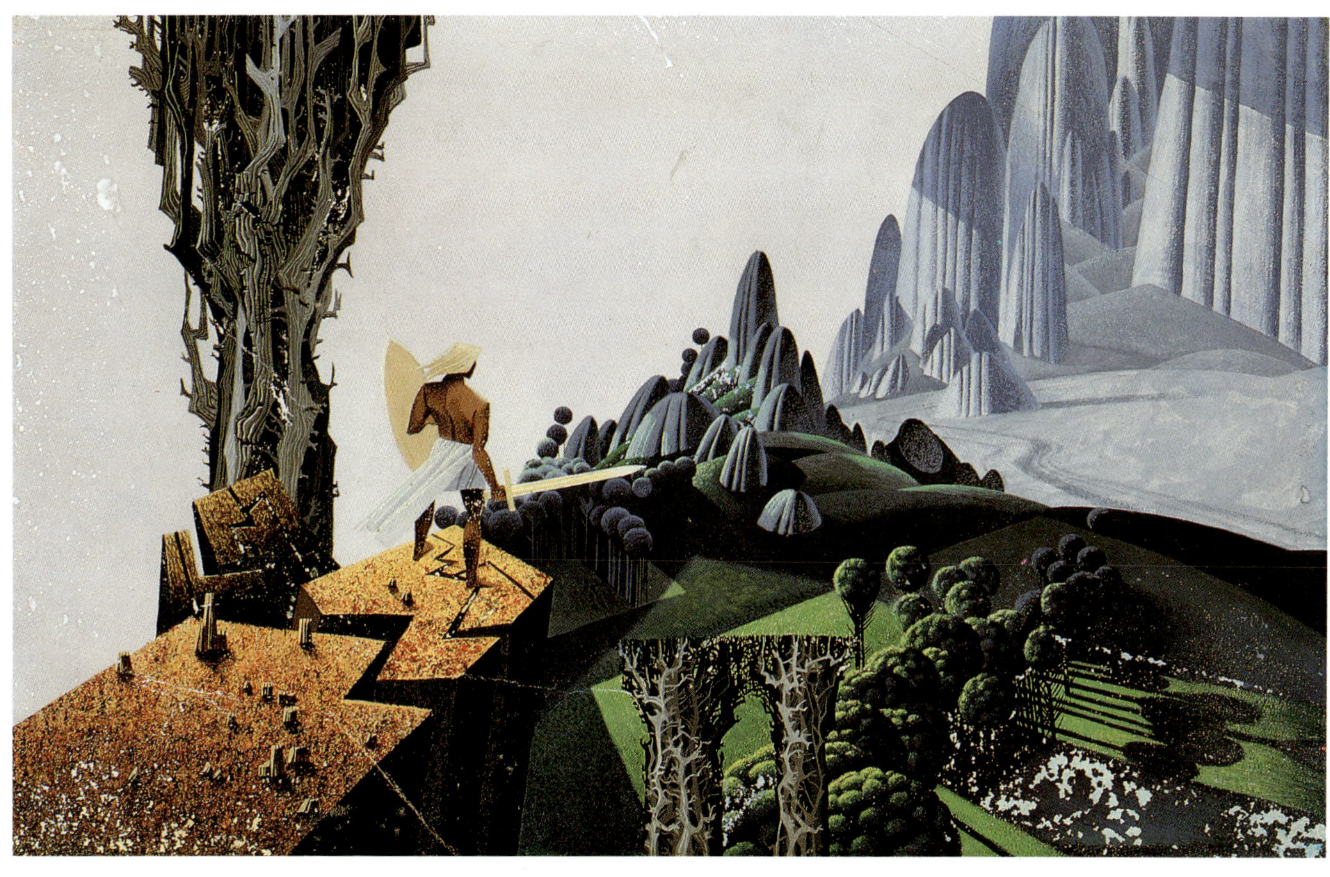

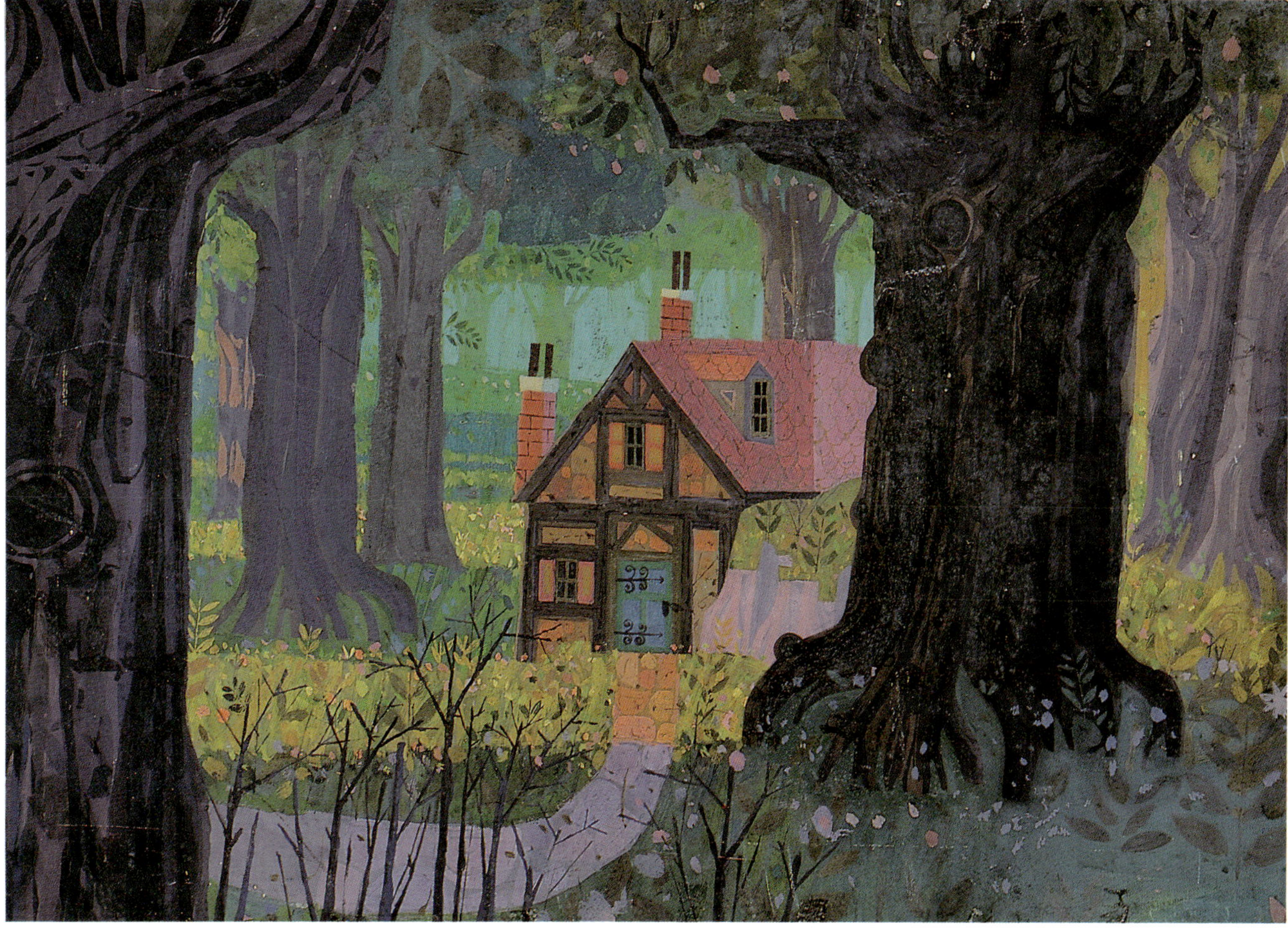

detail included in their paintings. Tim's approach is quite different. The only thing that he is interested in from a photograph is shape, shadows and highlights. He uses a simple Polaroid SX–70 camera for most of his photos as the small format tends to diminish the amount of apparent detail. This might seem quite surprising, since many of his paintings have a quality that approaches photo-realism. However, this is only an illusion. It is created by combining technique with a vast knowledge of how objects are perceived, rather than how they actually are. Nevertheless, it is difficult to tell what details have been left out without a side-by-side comparison of the photograph and the painting.

One of the dangers of including too much detail from a photograph is that your figures may become awkward and lifeless. If you are not careful, you can easily achieve a waxwork look that is strangely realistic, but totally lacking the illusion of life.

Tim uses friends and family members to pose for his photography sessions. As models, they are categorized by type. Each individual has certain traits that make them ideal for modelling certain characters. For example, Tim might select someone who is short, stocky and bearded for a picture of a dwarf. A giant would possess certain qualities of a giant, such as sinewy arms and large hands. Those individuals with more delicate features usually pose for elves or faeries. Asking someone to pose for a picture of a troll often requires a bit of diplomacy and a sense of humour, but most of the time, people will gladly model for the character.

Even the most suitable models will usually require some manipulation of artistic technique to make them become the character. Photos are a beginning, not an end in themselves. For example, to make a centaur appear realistic, the human half should still display some horse-like characteristics. To do this you could simply extend the face, making it jut out to exaggerate his features. The ears could become longer, protruding from beneath a flowing mane. The illusion of realism is then suggested by the artist, rather than copied in detail from a photograph.

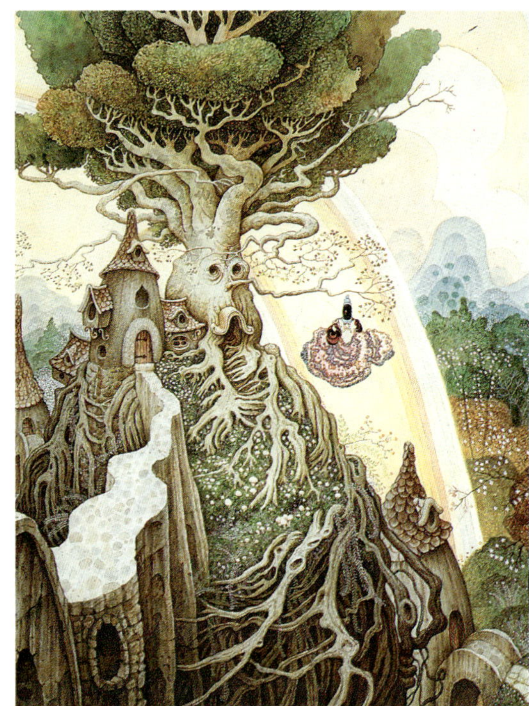

Portfolio piece, 1969, watercolour on board.

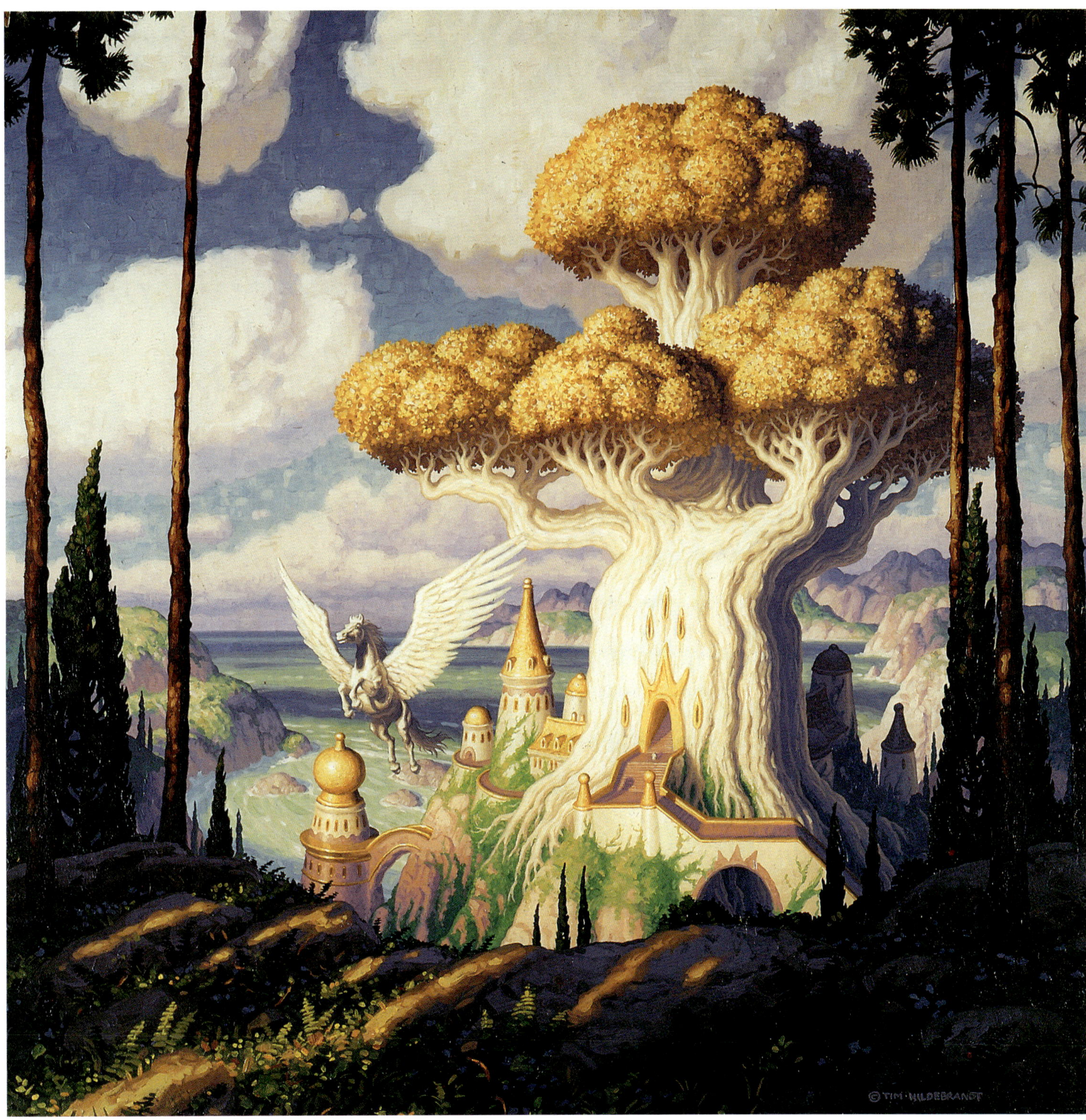

The Elven Fortress
From the *Realms of Wonder* calendar, TSR, 1983.
Tim: 'I came up with his idea after we had had
broccoli one night!'

Before Tim can begin to photograph the model, he must consider the costume that the model will wear. Costuming can be an art in itself, and is an integral component of photography. It is not necessary to prepare a costume in great detail; the important thing is to create the general shape of the costume. In order to 'fake' this effectively, though, you must know how the costume should appear. This knowledge can be developed through a personal interest and study of period costuming.

You needn't worry about the exactness or authenticity of every detail. Since you are creating a fantasy setting, you can combine pieces from different periods to develop something really unique. Most of the time, the simplest designs work best, and can be coordinated differently with other costume pieces to create the one you need.

You may design the costumes yourself, or check out a book from the library that has period or cultural costumes in it. Most of these designs are very simple to make, and can be produced at home in very little time. Some pieces can be bought, such as boots or belts, but before you invest a lot of time and money shopping check out a local flea market. If you absolutely cannot find the costume you need, and you live near a large city, you may be able to rent one. Costumes don't have to be elaborate or expensive, but they should be fairly accurate in depicting the shape required by the figure you are painting.

Costumes are important in that they give the artist information that otherwise would be difficult to place. Clothing has a tendency to flow in a certain way, revealing certain characteristics about the character and hiding others. Folds and wrinkles produce highlights and shadows that are extremely difficult to reproduce without reference. However, as with all reference material, costuming is a means to an end, rather than an end in itself. You should reach a compromise between what you have and what you actually need. The artist shouldn't get so caught up in accuracy of the costume that it detracts from his primary job of painting.

After the models are selected and properly clothed, the studio is then made ready for photography. The most

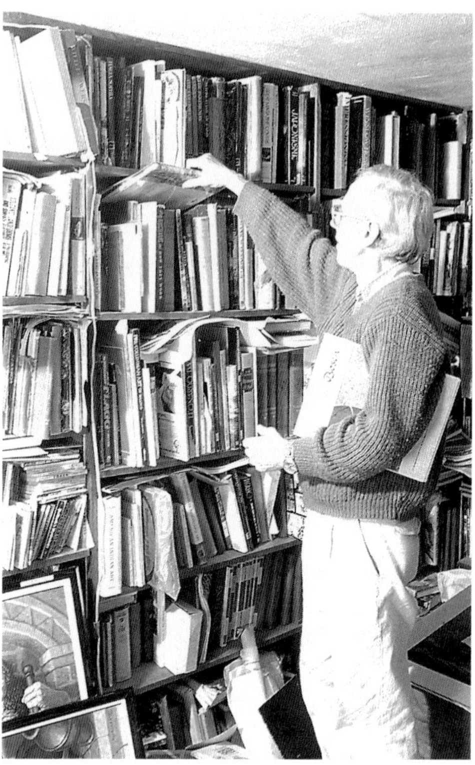

The artist's reference library: 'You can't collect enough reference,' he says. The various models shown Tim has collected over the years. 'Plastic models of animals come in very handy – at times I have made my own models out of clay.'

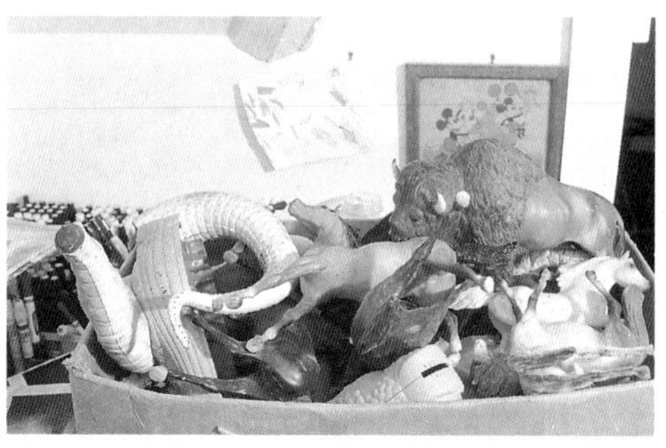

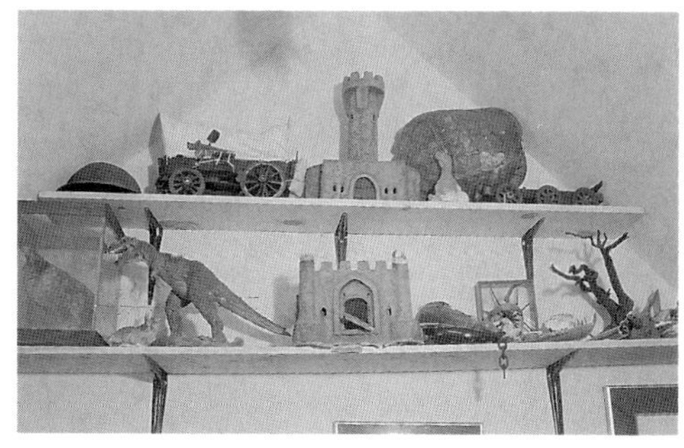

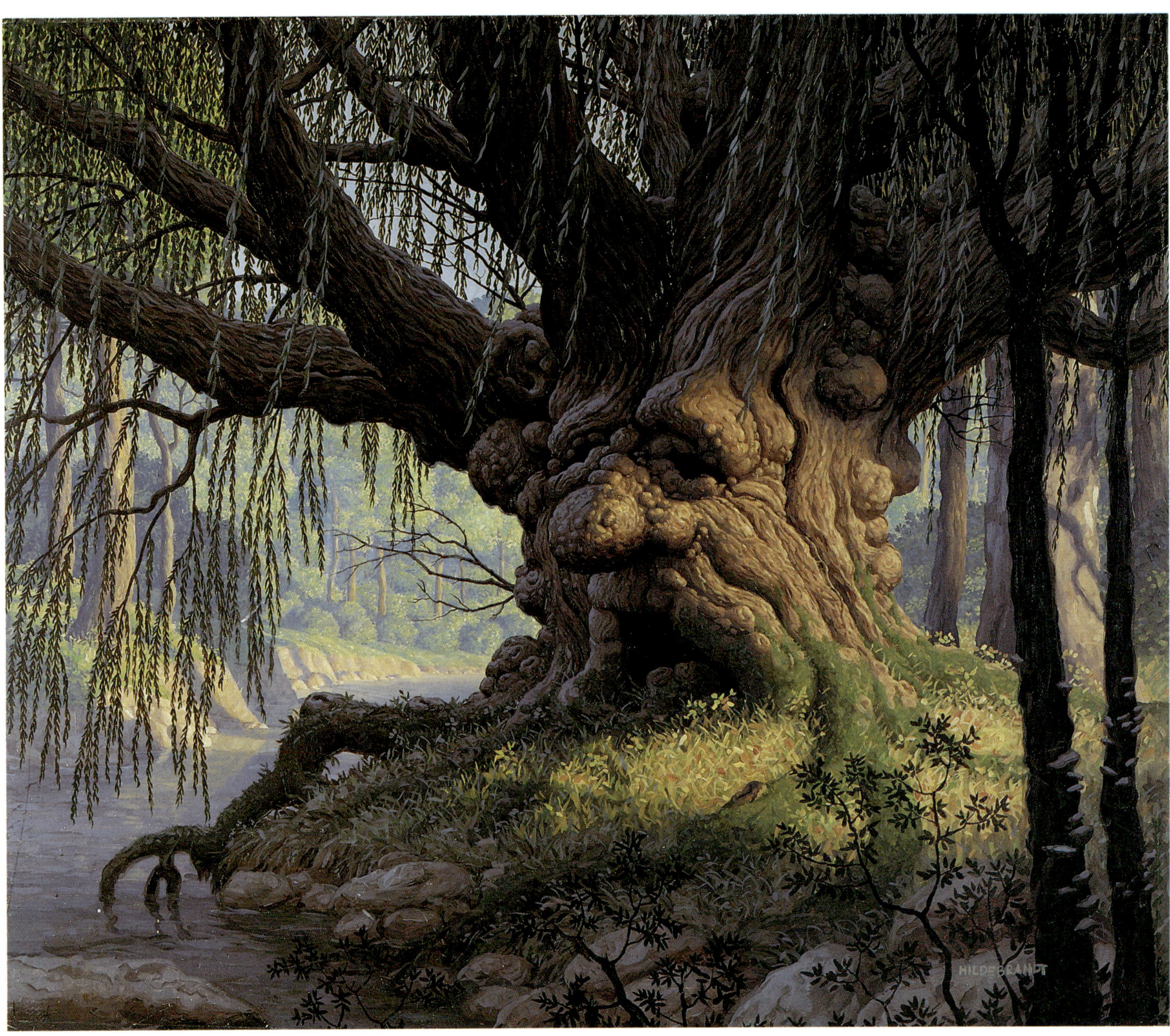

Old Man Willow
From the 1978 J.R.R. Tolkien calendar, Ballantine
Books, acrylic on masonite. Tim: 'Lots of
photographs of willow trees were taken for
this picture.'

crucial ingredient here is the lighting. Tim uses two different types of clamp-on photofloods to light the scene, depending on what type of film he is using. Daylight lamps are used to light figures that will appear outdoors under sunlight, while Kelvin lamps are used to light indoor subjects. To some extent, the lights might be used to differentiate between sunlight and moonlight. Daylight lamps produce a very harsh light, while Kelvin lamps provide a softer, more bounced light.

Tim almost always includes two light sources. A single light source will usually give reference that leads to a monochromatic scene, which he tries to avoid. Two light sources are ideal for most scenes, making them more interesting in regard to light and shadow. More rarely, he may light the scene with three or more sources, though too many light sources can have a tendency to clutter the picture. Therefore, Tim tries to keep his lighting as simple, yet interesting, as he can.

The number and positioning of the lights is derived from the rough composition. The comp is the blueprint, and for the picture to work the lighting arrangement must be followed precisely. Initially, the lights are set up close to where they should be; if a composition calls for moonlight streaming over the character's shoulder, the light is placed up high. The models are then positioned according to the composition, and the lights are adjusted with final precision.

Once everything is perfectly in place, the photography begins. Tim chooses angles that match the composition, and usually shoots several photos. At least one of these is an overall shot, while the others are various close-ups that are needed for detail that might otherwise be obscured. He uses no flash with his camera, as it would destroy the delicate lighting situation that he has created.

Most of Tim's reference material is photographed with the Polaroid camera, although he has used colour and black and white 35mm. His use of 35mm is extremely rare, however, since most of the time he is attempting to minimize the amount of detail in a photograph. Generally, the most important elements of a photo are shape,

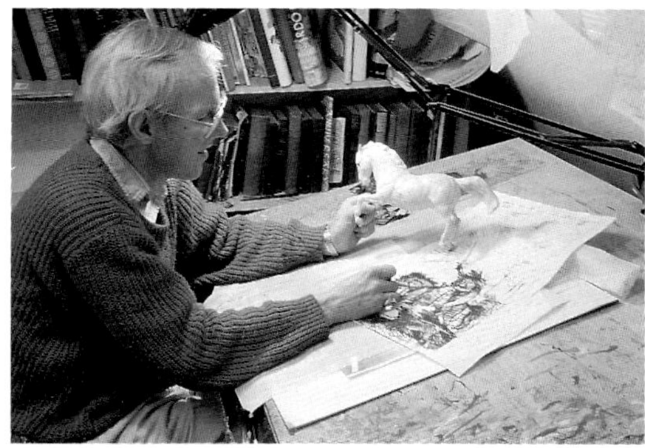

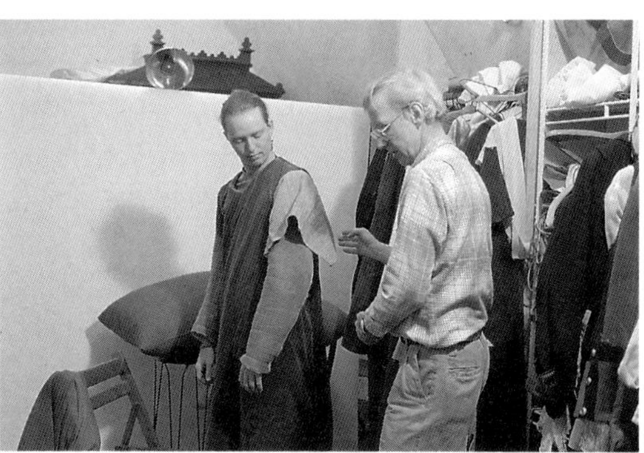

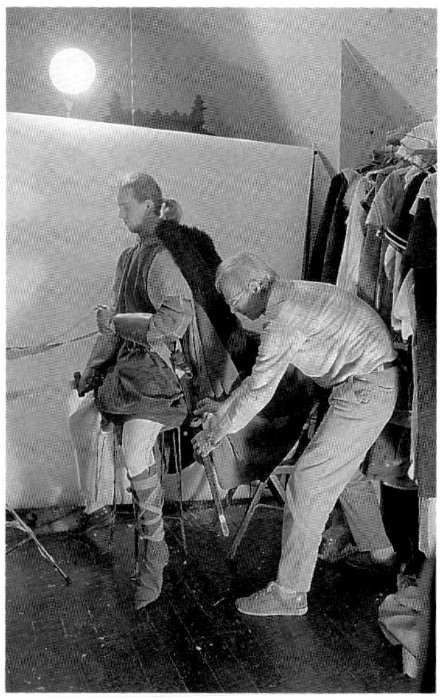

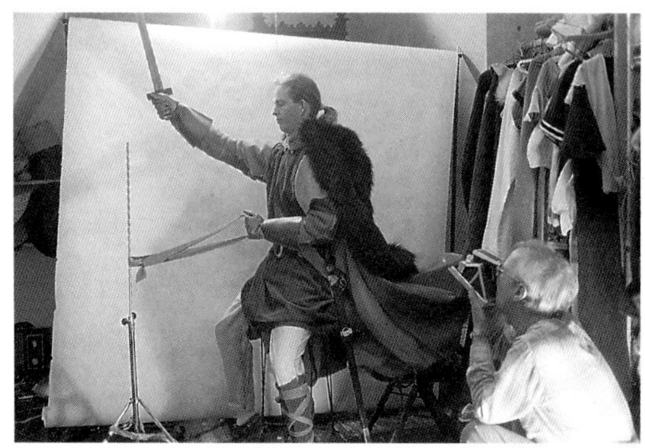

TOP The artist at work on a development sketch for *Lord of Chaos* in the Realms of Wonder studio. 'I keep those books I use most often within easy reach'; BELOW Posing session. 'After I draw the rough sketch and decide where the light source is to be, I pose the model and light him that way.'

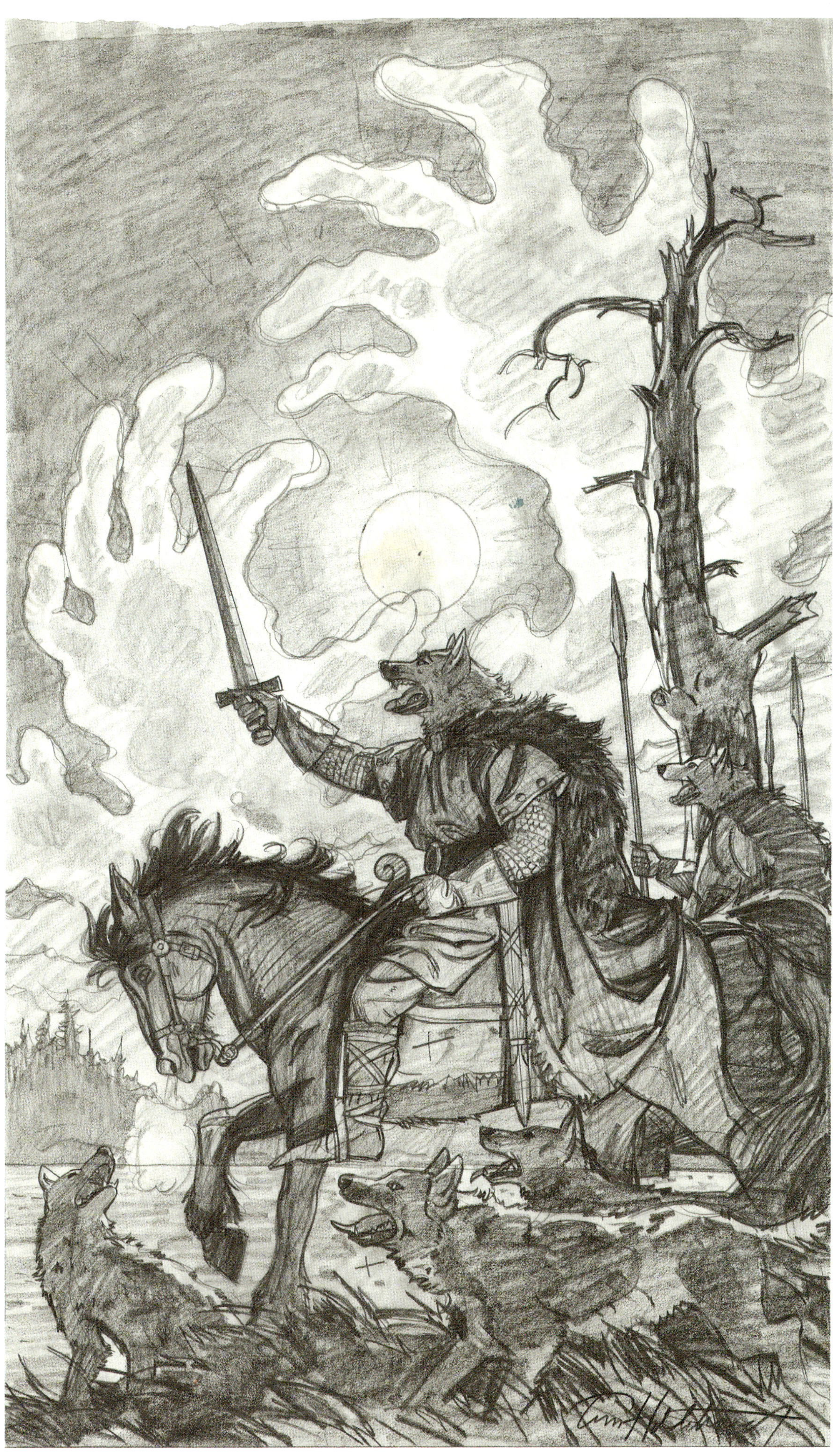

Lord of Chaos
Finished cover sketch for the book by Elizabeth Boyer, published by Del Rey. Tim: 'I usually present an art director with a sketched idea taken to this level of completion. I don't really have to draw it this detailed for myself.'

38 highlights and shadows.

Another value of a photograph lies in the fact that it never changes, and that it might be useful at some other time. Tim keeps all of his photos, and as a result has amassed a huge collection of reference photographs that he can call upon any time they are needed. In addition, he collects photos of strange and unusual items from friends and family, depicting scenes such as the recent capture of a squid during a family vacation. The rule here is, 'when in doubt, store it with the others'. Any photograph could potentially be the inspiration for a future idea.

Along with photos, Tim has assembled a huge reference library that he can use when looking for ideas. Through the years, he has put together a collection of books that deal with every conceivable aspect of art, history, design, architecture; to list them all would take a chapter by itself. A young artist might take notice of the value of books, and begin a reference collection of his own. Their uses are endless. For example, while designing a dragon Tim might be stuck for reference concerning wings. Since bat wings closely resemble a general conception of what a dragon's wing might look like, Tim can simply turn to a book on bats. Designing an incredible building may be as simple as looking through his books on architecture, and combining elements of various cultural or period designs. And a difficult compositional design problem may be solved by studying texts on composition, the published work of other artists, or both. A good reference library is a must for a fantasy illustrator, although if you are just starting out, the public library works just fine.

Three-dimensional models and toys are also an important part of Tim's resource material. Plastic figures of horses and dinosaurs, miniature castles, figure armatures, and a stuffed iguana make up part of this collection, but he is constantly in search of more. Some things are borrowed from nature, while other items are gleaned from flea markets and toy stores. These models and toys have the advantage of not moving; for instance, getting a real horse to pose in just the right position and lighting situation can be difficult at best. Plastic models or toys can also

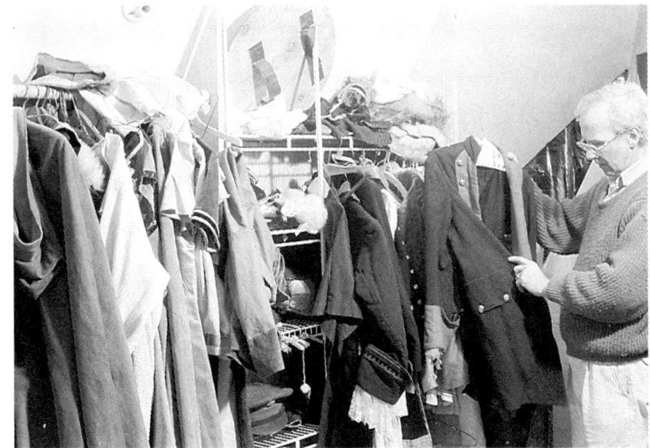

The costume shop. Tim: 'My wife Rita makes most of the costumes – some come from flea markets.'

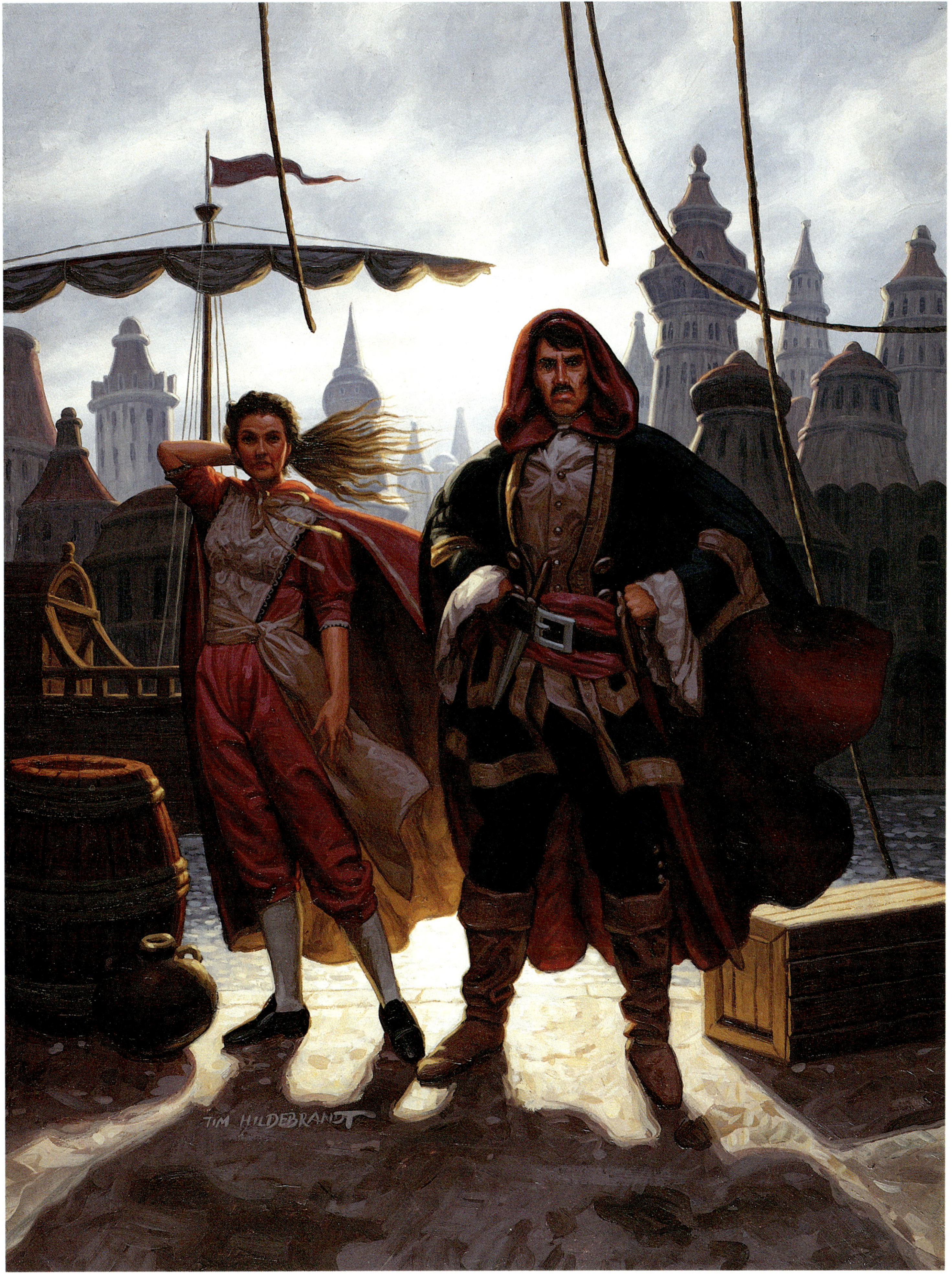
TIM HILDEBRANDT

help solve difficult problems in perspective. Keep in mind that you can never accumulate enough reference material, and must constantly be on the look out for it.

In your search for reference material, do not be afraid to copy or borrow from nature. There are countless astounding creations that exist within our own world. Keep your mind open to combinations that could exist, and constantly ask yourself the question, 'what if . . .?' The possibilities are limitless. What would happen if you crossed a beetle with a man? Can a creature exist that is both eagle and a lion? Imagine a spacecraft with grasshopper wings – anything and everything is grist for the fantasy artist's mill.

Tim Hildebrandt is, out of necessity, a modern Renaissance man. The world's short supply of dragons and other fantasy creatures have forced him to creatively manipulate his reference material to simulate those characters and scenes he wants to portray. Aside from being an artist, he is often part scientist, part designer, engineer, photographer, costume designer and even philosopher. Depending on what his work calls for, he may take on other traits as well. For sometimes it takes all of these qualities to create an alien or fantasy world that lives with its own logic, environment and biology.

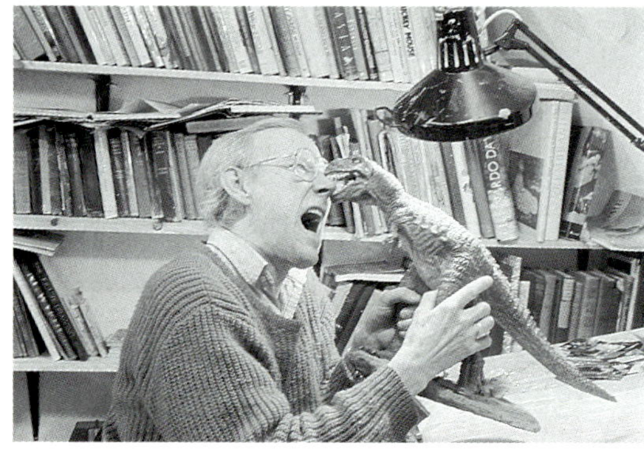

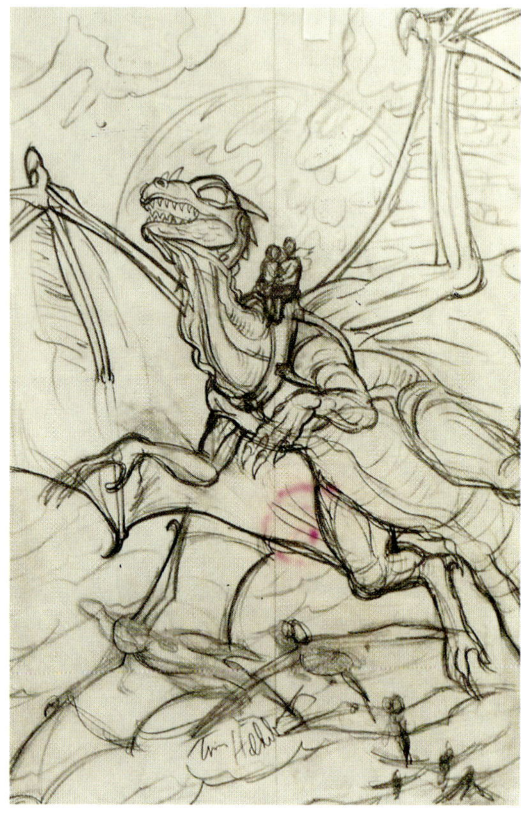

F'lar and Mnementh
From *The Dragonriders of Pern* calendar, 1985, acrylic on masonite. Tim: 'For reference I used a stuffed iguana and a model of Tyrannosaurus Rex acquired at a science fiction convention.'

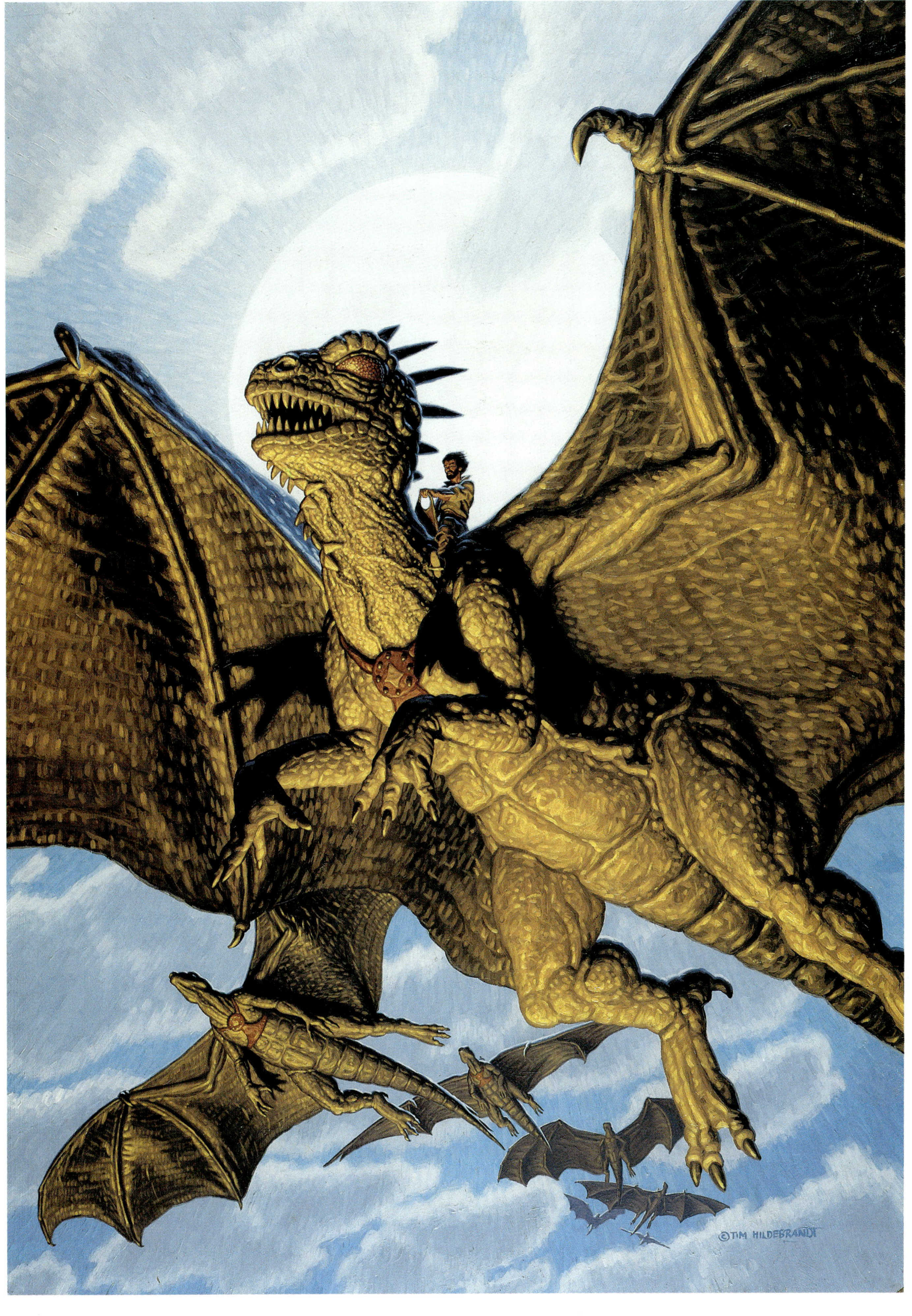
©TIM HILDEBRANDT

Section Two

Concept &
Composition

Perhaps the most commonly asked question a fantasy artist is presented with is, 'where did you get the idea?' The source of inspiration can be as varied as the art itself. Concepts can be derived from objects in the home, or an unusual experience, or from a dream. And provided the concept is executed in a realistic manner, there is no one to say that your perception is wrong. Even so, you may still have a difficult time coming up with an original idea. Don't worry. There is still another avenue you can explore.

As a professional illustrator Tim Hildebrandt has found that, for him, the only source of inspiration needed to develop an idea is in the material that he illustrates. For example, if he is given a book cover assignment he makes it a point to read the entire book. As he reads he makes notes of any scene that would possibly make an interesting composition. When he has finished reading he narrows his choices down to the scene or scenes that he feels most strongly represent the most important part of the book. If he isn't satisfied with any particular scene, he might combine two or more scenes to create one that describes the most important part. Or, the decision could be based on a more general feel of the text as a whole.

On more rare occasions an art director may have a very specific idea concerning what should be illustrated. This defines the subject matter instantly and is usually presented to Tim in the form of a rough sketch. In either case, once the subject for the illustration has been decided he then prepares to compose the scene.

The composition of the scene chosen to be painted is the single most critical step in the entire process. The analogy Tim often uses is that beginning a painting is comparable to building a house. First, you must prepare the foundation, making certain that it is strong. Without a solid foundation the house will collapse. Composition is considered to be the foundation of any illustration. If the composition is weak, no amount of technique or attention to detail will save it. On the other hand, if you have worked out a powerful composition, then the picture will hold together even if your painting technique needs

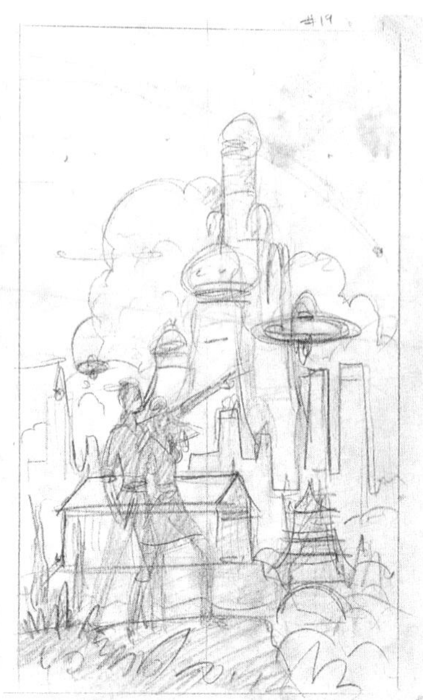

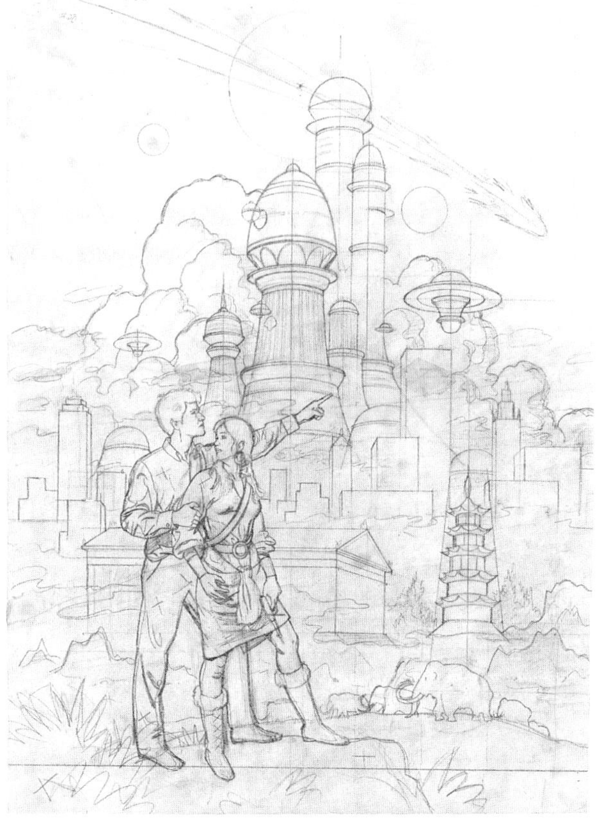

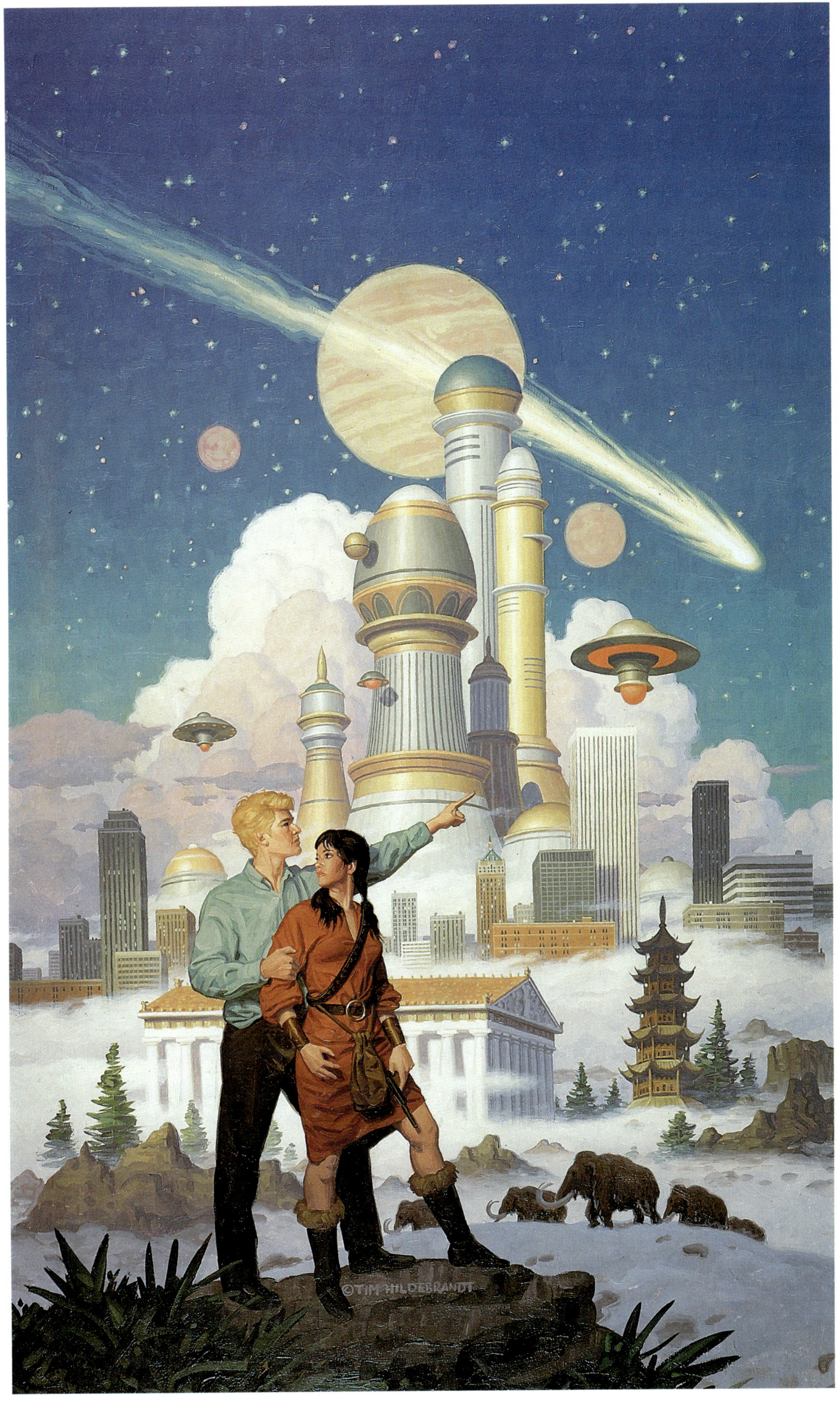
©TIM HILDEBRANDT

improvement.

One of the things Tim must consider before he can begin to draw is the type of composition it will be. There are two types of composition: formal and informal. Both types are heavily influenced by the subject that is being illustrated.

When everything in the composition is exactly balanced, and both sides of the centre line are equal in subject, weight, shape and size, the composition is said to be formal. This type of composition is best used to depict a formal or solemn occasion, or perhaps even a fantastic building. It is also the easiest type of composition to draw. When developing a formal composition Tim often draws only one half of the picture, then folds the drawing over to trace the other side. Of course, there are subtle differences such as the placement of blossoms or the details of figures, but essentially the two sides are identical.

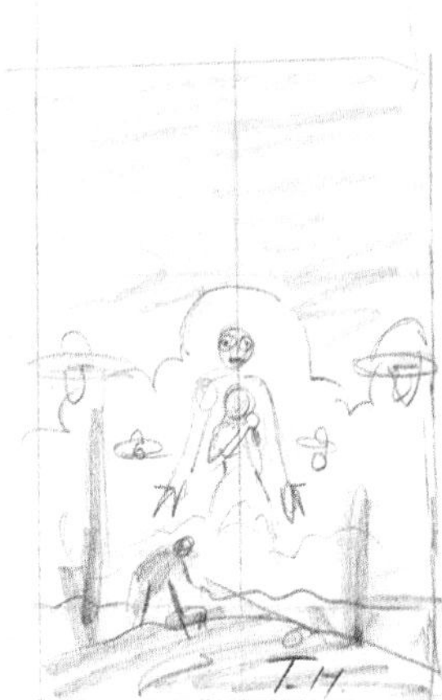

Any composition that is not formal is said to be informal. The word informal is a bit misleading, as the best informal compositions are carefully structured to have the greatest visual impact. One of the ways to bring structure to an informal composition is to consider our cultural heritage. In Western culture our eyes are trained to move from left to right, whether we are reading or viewing a piece of art. This fact can be useful in positioning elements of a picture so that the eye sweeps naturally to the centre of interest. A slight variation of this concept might be an illustration that has an oriental theme. In eastern culture the eye moves naturally from right to left, so the composition could be reversed. Either way, the eye should wind up at the centre of interest.

The shape the illustration will occupy is another important factor that must be carefully determined. This shape, referred to as the picture plane, is a vital consideration. If the illustration is to be used for a book cover it obviously cannot be composed in an extremely wide format. A possible exception would be if the cover were to wrap around both the front and back of the book. Usually, however, a book cover is a vertical rectangle. Paintings used for calendars are usually square, and illustrations

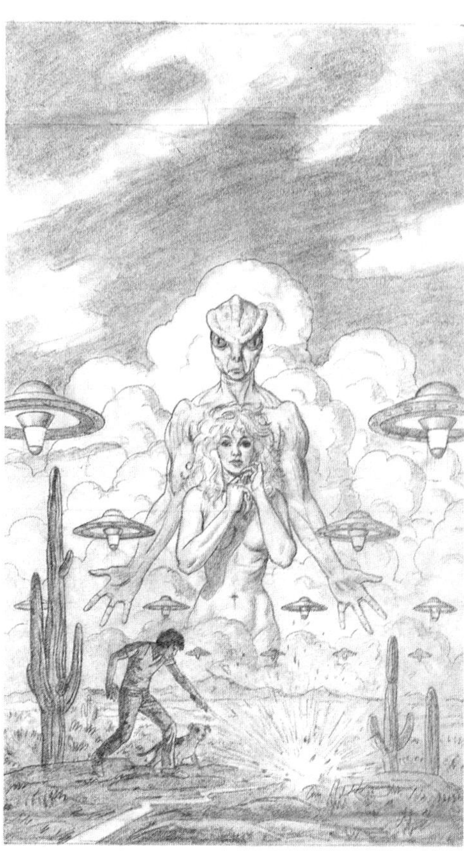

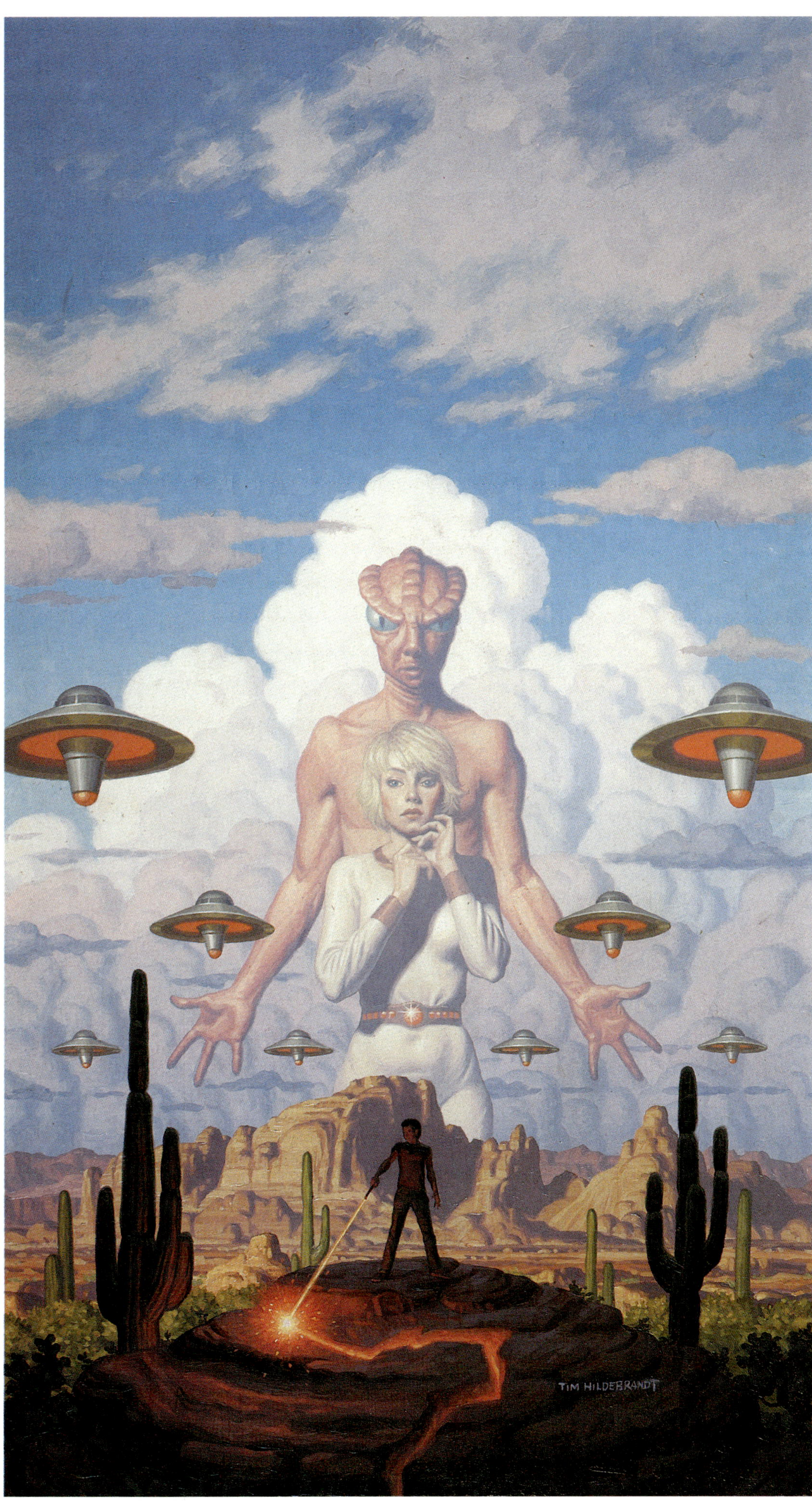

Those Who Watch
Cover illustration for the book by
Robert Silverberg, New American
Library, 1987, acrylic on masonite.
Tim: 'Note the addition of clothes on
the girl in the finished painting. The
publishers felt the sketch was a little
too suggestive. I also changed the
position of the boy to render a more
formal, centralized composition. Notice
the dominating one-point perspective –
the vanishing point is low, in the centre
of the horizon line.'

45

46 for children's books can be a very wide, horizontal
rectangle.

Once the picture plane has been determined the next
step is to locate the exact centre of the shape. This is done
by drawing vertical and horizontal lines down and across
the picture plane. Tim finds this a useful tool for placing
elements in the composition. It also serves to remind him
that he has a certain limited space to fill and that he must
stay within very specified boundaries.

Determining the picture plane and defining the spaces
to be filled is academic, and are not the only parts of the
compositional process. When planning the placement of
the elements in the picture there are further considera-
tions that require careful thought. These factors include
choosing, determining the position of the horizon line,
perspective of the main elements, and how you want to
light the scene. You should be concerned with all of these
elements simultaneously, as they all work together to
achieve the final result.

As mentioned before, the centre of interest in a formal
composition is located in the central area of the picture
plane. Finding the centre in an informal composition can
be just as easy. Using the principle of the cultural eye Tim
places the centre in the majority of his informal compositions just right to the centre line. The other elements of
the composition are then placed around the centre in an
arrangement that naturally leads the eye to the central
focus. If this sounds like a formula, it is. To see just how
effective it is, study some of the informal compositions in
this book.

The horizon line directly influences how the main subject will be viewed. As the name implies, the horizon line
is simply the horizontal line across the picture plane that
separates the earth from the sky. It also determines the
viewer's eye level. If the horizon line is placed low, the
implication is that you are viewing the scene from a low
point looking up. If the horizon line is placed high in the
composition, this implies that you are somewhere high
looking down.

This simple principle has enormous applications. For

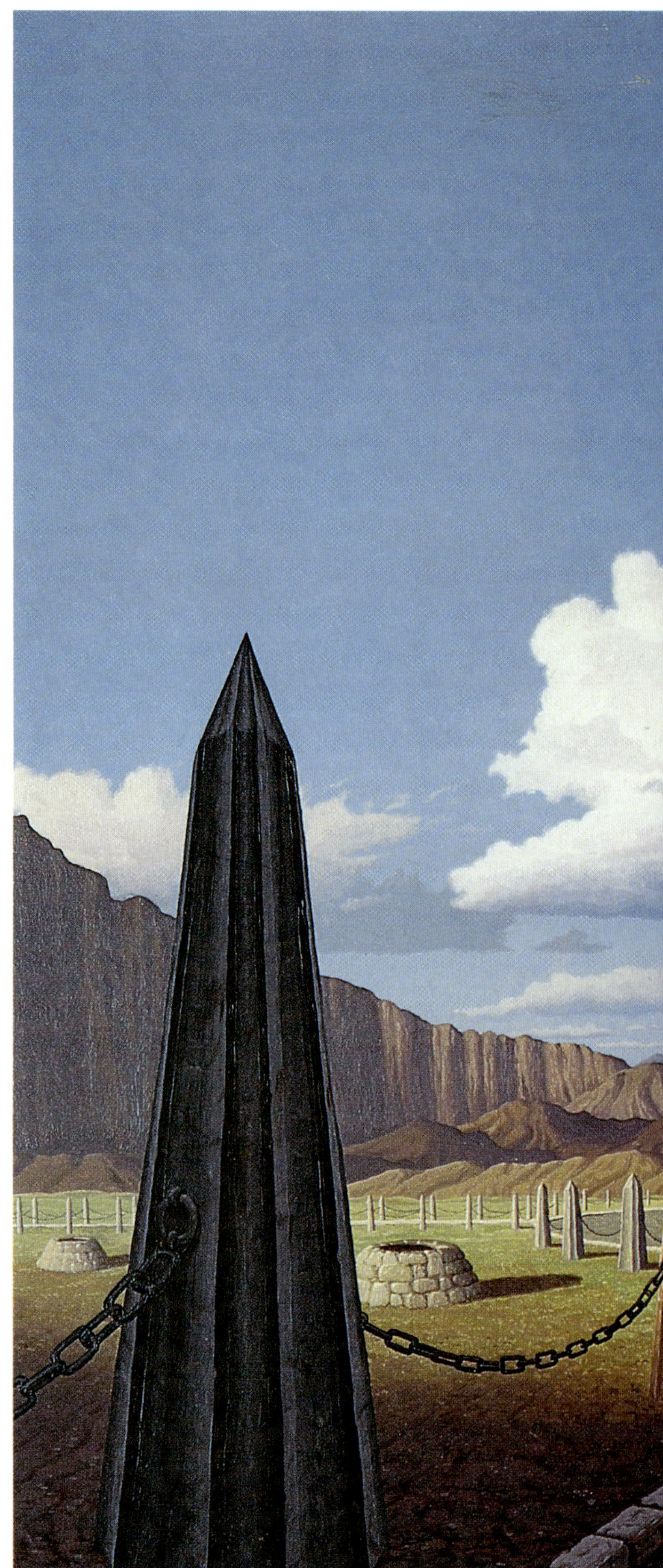

Orthanc
From the J.R.R. Tolkien calendar, Ballantine
Books, 1976, acrylic on masonite. Another
example of a formal composition and one-point
perspective. The tower was based on a piece
of coal.

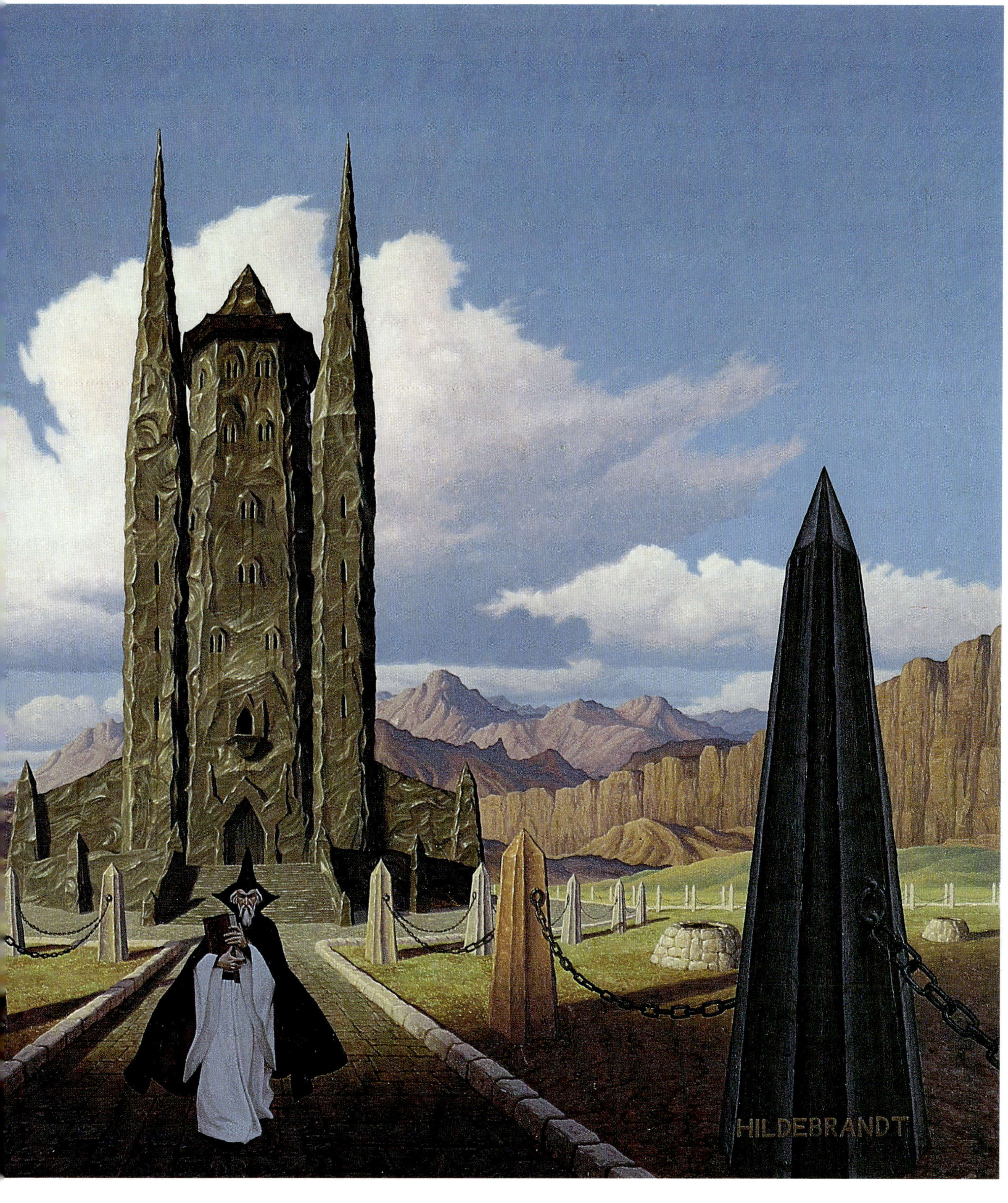
HILDEBRANDT

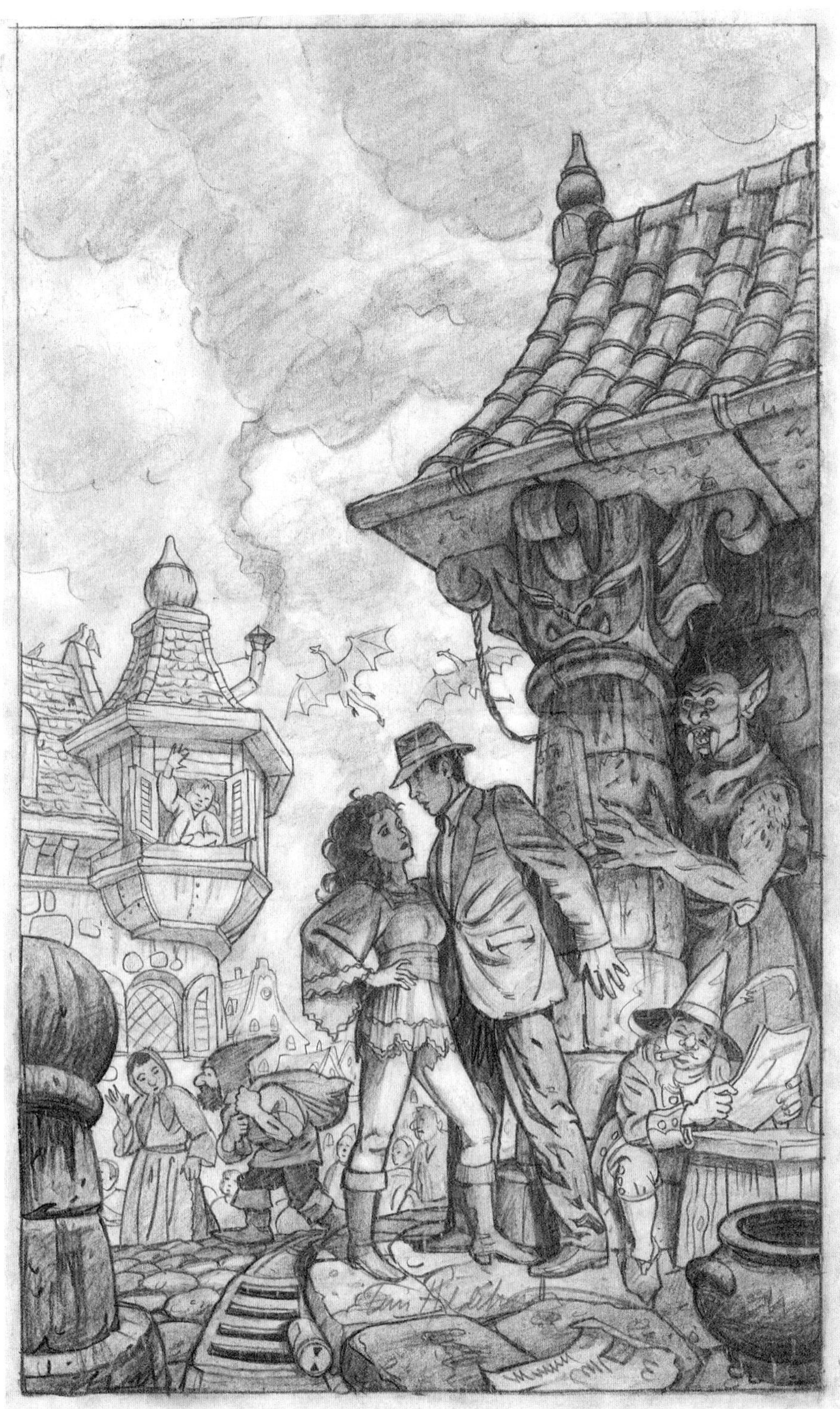

Dread Brass Shadow
Cover illustration for the novel by Glenn Cooke,
1989. Tim: 'If a line is drawn down the centre of
the composition the head of the man is just to the
right of it. He is the centre of interest, and all the
elements in the picture lead you in the direction of
his head.' The finished pencil drawing was
presented to the art director at New American
Library.

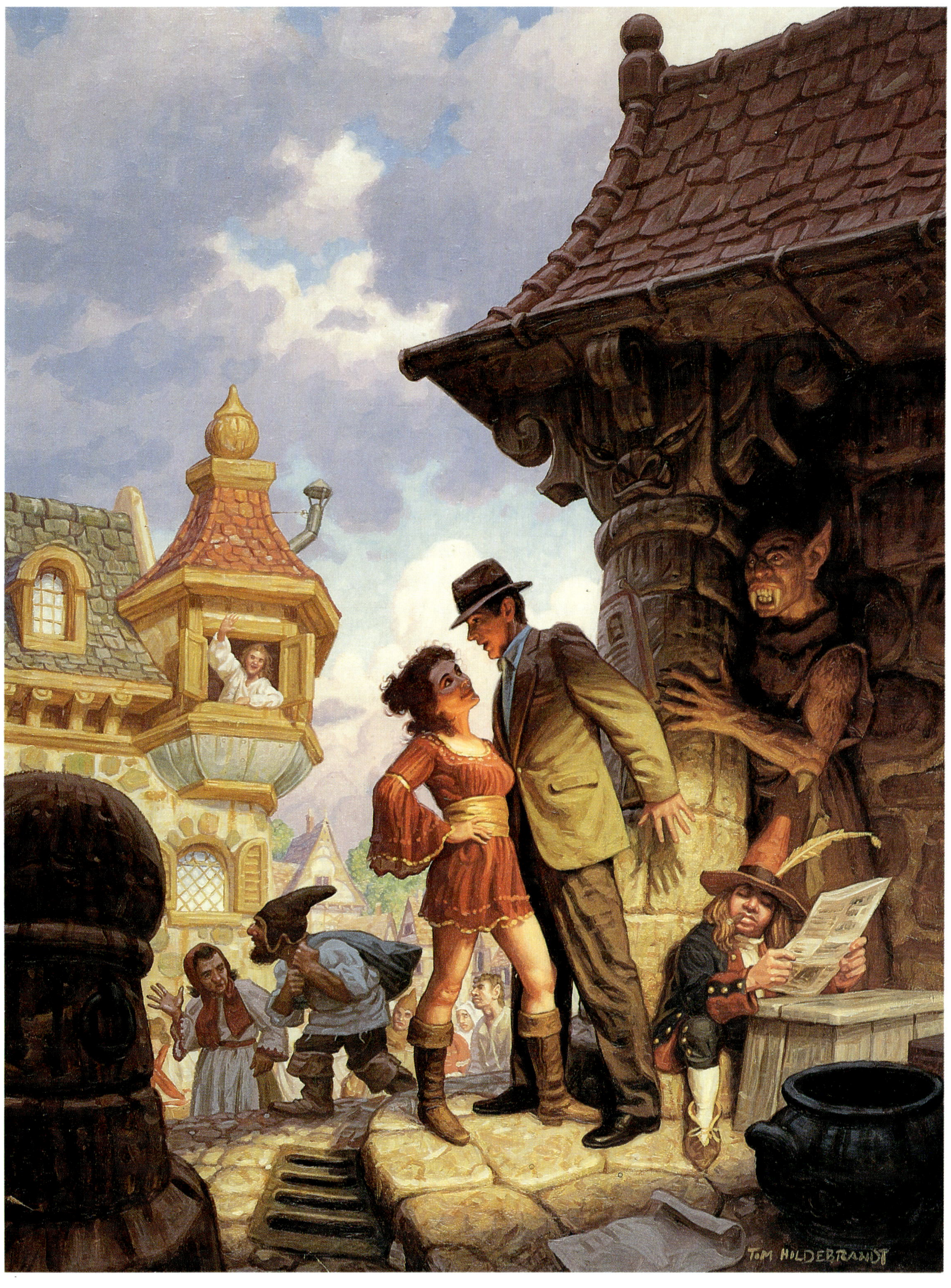

example, if you decide to compose a picture with a giant for the main subject, placing the horizon line low will give the impression of great size. If you are painting faeries a horizon line placed up high will give the viewer the impression that he or she is looking down on them and that the faeries are quite small.

When these principles are used in conjunction with the other principles mentioned in this chapter the development of the composition becomes much stronger. For example, if you have chosen a tall vertical format, and you wish to paint a dragon, you might consider a low horizon line to emphasize the dragon's great size. Utilizing the cultural eye principle, you might place the head of the dragon just to the right of the centre line in the upper portion of the picture. This would be the centre of interest. The bulk of the dragon's body might occupy the space in the lower left-hand corner. This arrangement would force the viewer's eye to move from the lower left to upper right.

Perspective is the tool that artists use to make the elements of a given composition appear to be correctly placed, from the most distant objects in the background to the closest object in the foreground. It also includes everything in between. Many books have been written on perspective, and given the space of this chapter, it would be impossible to describe all of the subtleties involved. Any serious art student should make a concerted effort to learn more about perspective by further reading as it is a crucial ingredient to realism.

Perhaps the easiest way to gain an understanding of perspective is to study some of the illustrations in this book. Notice how the objects in the foreground tend to diminish as they move toward the background. This is perspective. The point to which they recede to is known as the vanishing point. This point is somewhere either above, centred on, or below the horizon line. While this may sound complicated at first, it really isn't.

Single point perspective occurs when the objects in a composition recede toward a single point on the horizon line. Two-point perspective is where the perspective lines

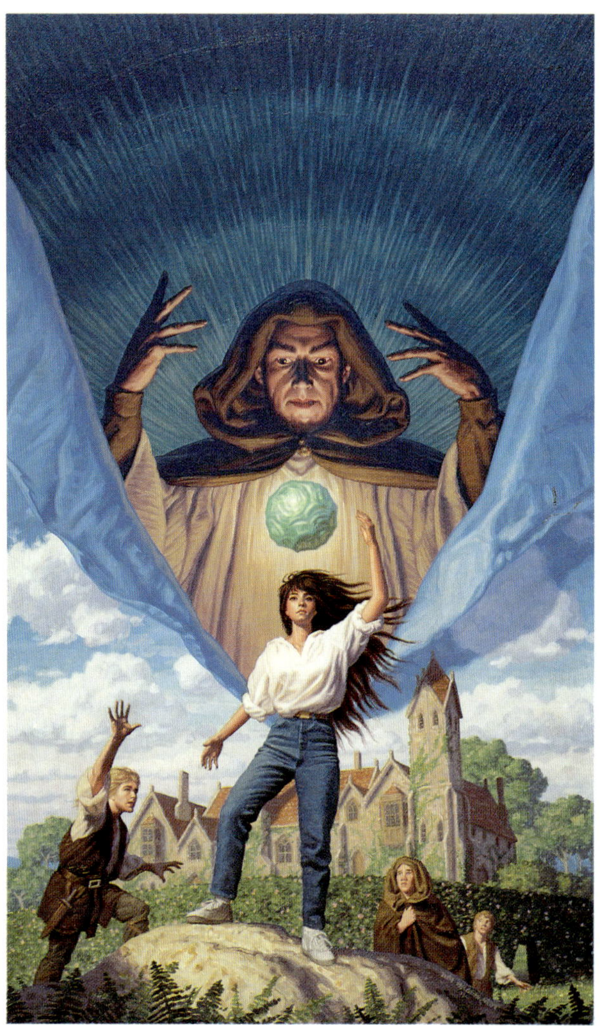

Worldstone
Book cover, New American Library, 1987, acrylic on masonite. Another formal composition.

RIGHT **Fang the Gnome**
Book cover, New American Library, 1988, acrylic on masonite. Here the girl is the centre of interest. The figures in the clouds drive the eye back into the picture.

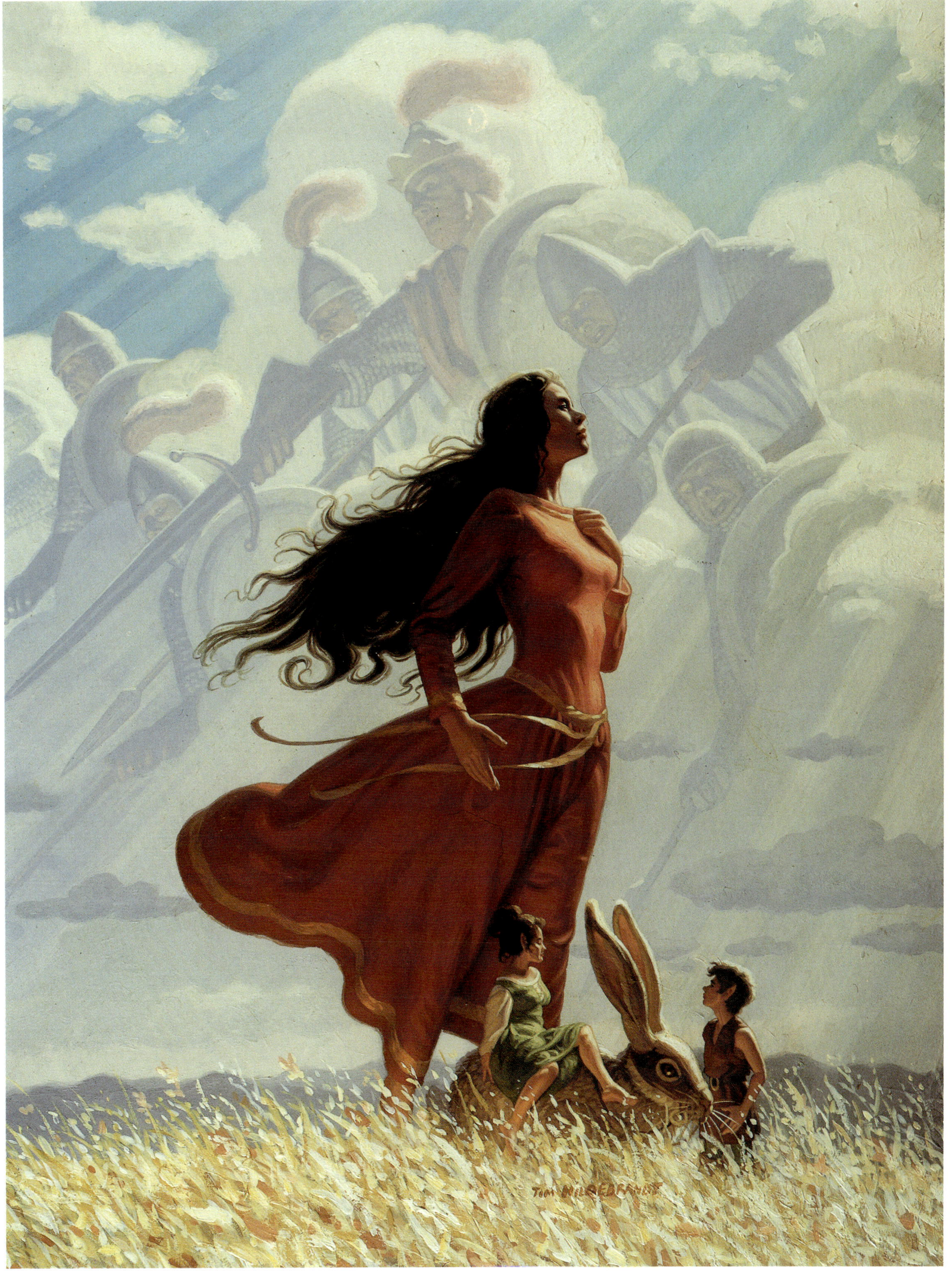
Tom NILREDFANCE

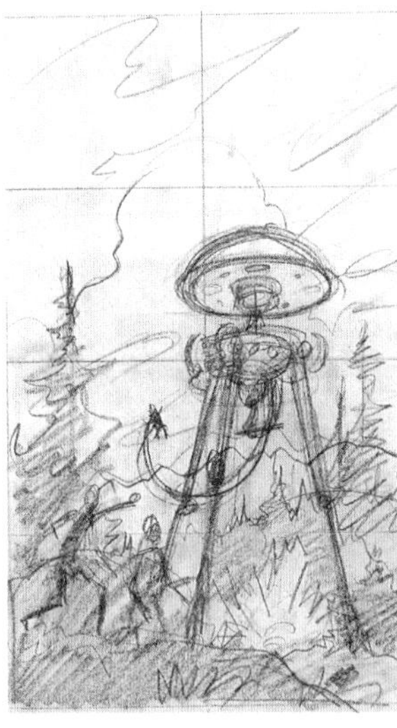

Tripods

Book cover, 1988, acrylic on
masonite. Tim: 'I wanted a subtle
insect appearance to the
machine.' In the finished sketch
the tall trees on either side help
frame the picture.

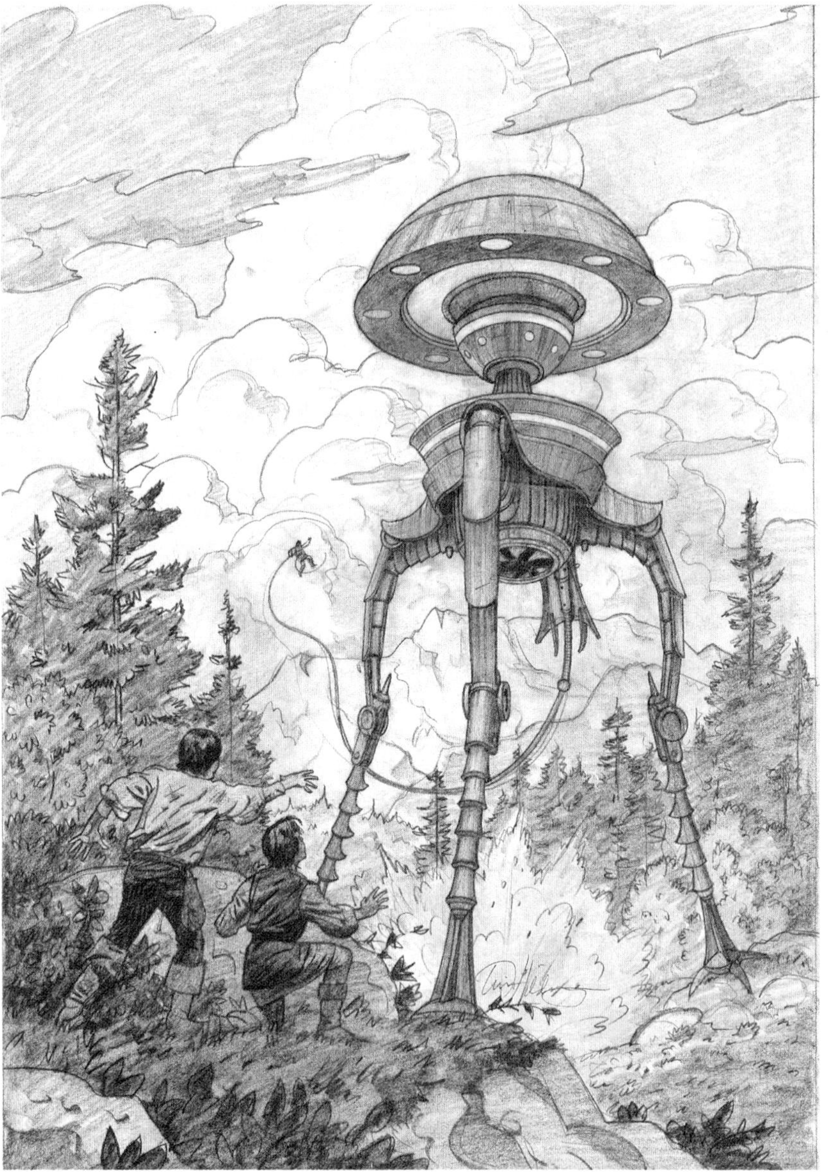

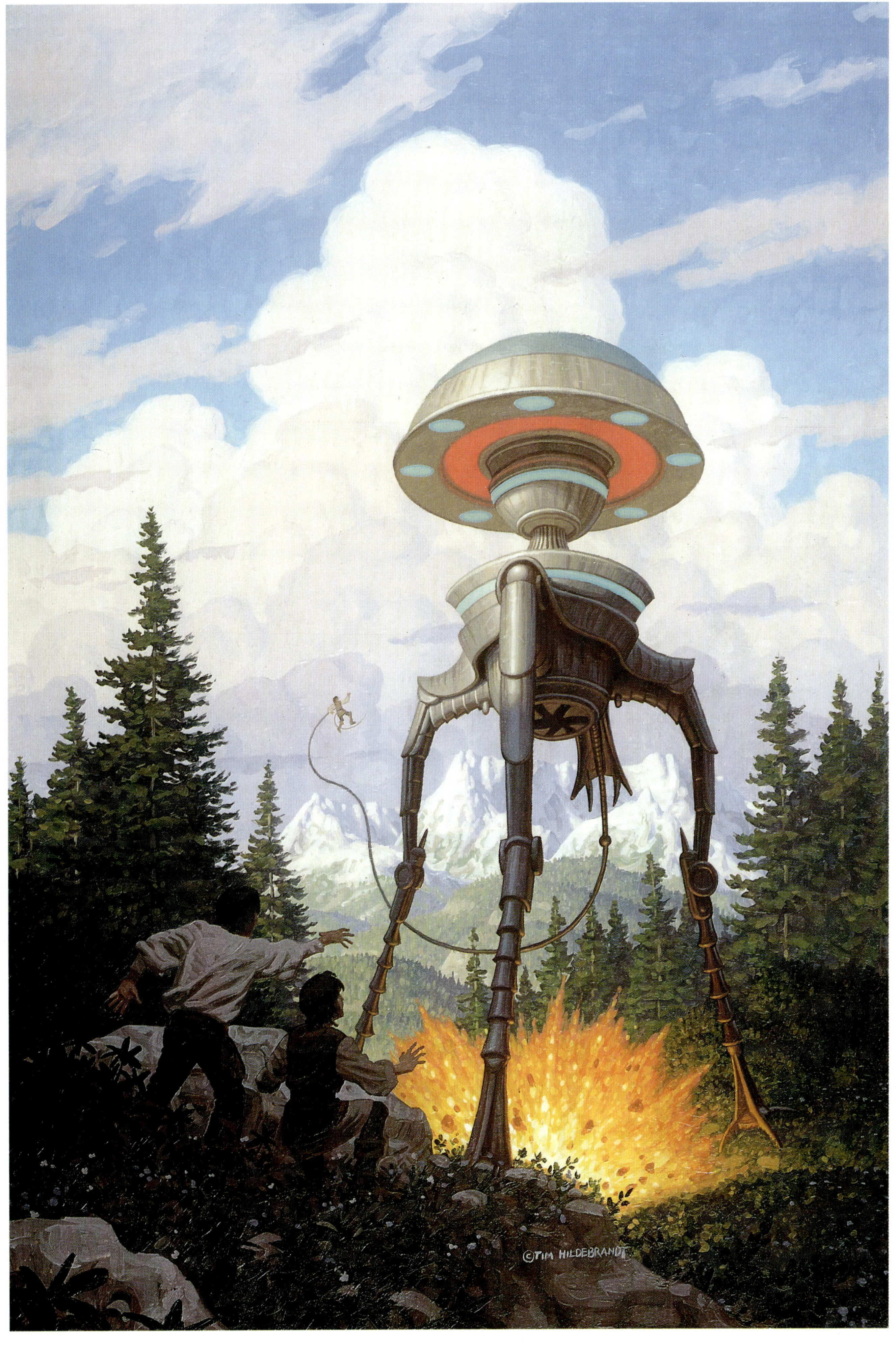

©TIM HILDEBRANDT

The Dragon's Carbuncle
Book cover, Del Rey Books, 1989, acrylic on
masonite. A variation on a formal composition. Of
the posing session Tim comments: 'The costume
here is quite simple. I just needed a basic shape.
To pose someone flying you have to lie them down
on the floor.'

54

converge at two different points on the horizon line, and,
of course, three-point perspective has three different
vanishing points. The number of vanishing points in a
composition is often determined by the complexity of the
scene.

The subject of perspective may sound complex, but
once you understand the basic principles involved you
will be well on your way to a more realistic composition.
Learn as much about it from as many sources as you can by
studying not only the theory behind it, but by observing it
within other artwork. The space given to perspective
here should only serve as a springboard for further study.
It is only meant to be an introduction to a creative tool
that will enable you to capture the realism you may desire.

One of the hallmarks of a Tim Hildebrandt painting is
his use of intense lighting and shade. Correctly applied,
the use of light and shadow create a remarkable sense of
realism that is often lacking in some illustrations. How
many paintings have you seen that are either flatly lit, or
have highlights and shadows arbitrarily placed throughout the scene? The key to success here is to simply determine what the source of light is in the composition, and
where it is located in the picture.

This is easier than it sounds. For example, a scene that
is set outdoors during the day would obviously be lit from
the sun. A secondary light source would be from the light
bouncing off the ground. Having decided on what light
sources to use, the artist must determine where these light
sources are located. They can be included in the scene,
but often a more dramatic effect can be achieved by keep-
ing them hidden. As a rule, Tim tries to include at least
two light sources to keep the scene from becoming too
monochromatic. And though he sometimes uses up to
three sources of light, any more than that would make the
scene too 'busy' or cluttered.

Experience has made it possible for Tim to 'see' all of
these elements of composition clearly from the moment
he chooses a scene. Everything discussed above is clearly
in his mind before he ever begins to draw. When he does
begin, he starts with very fast, loosely drawn thumbnail

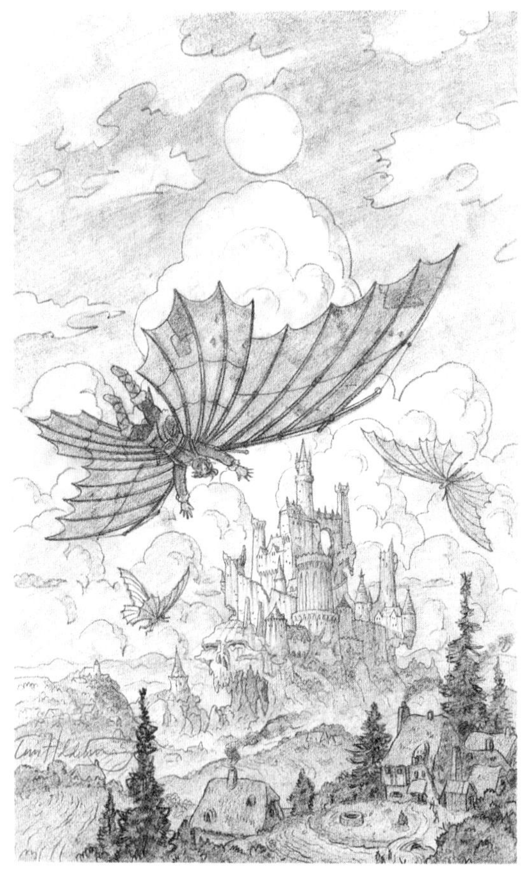

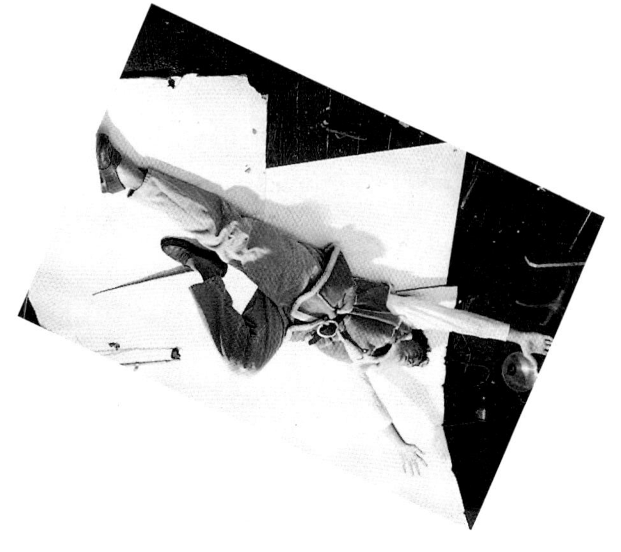

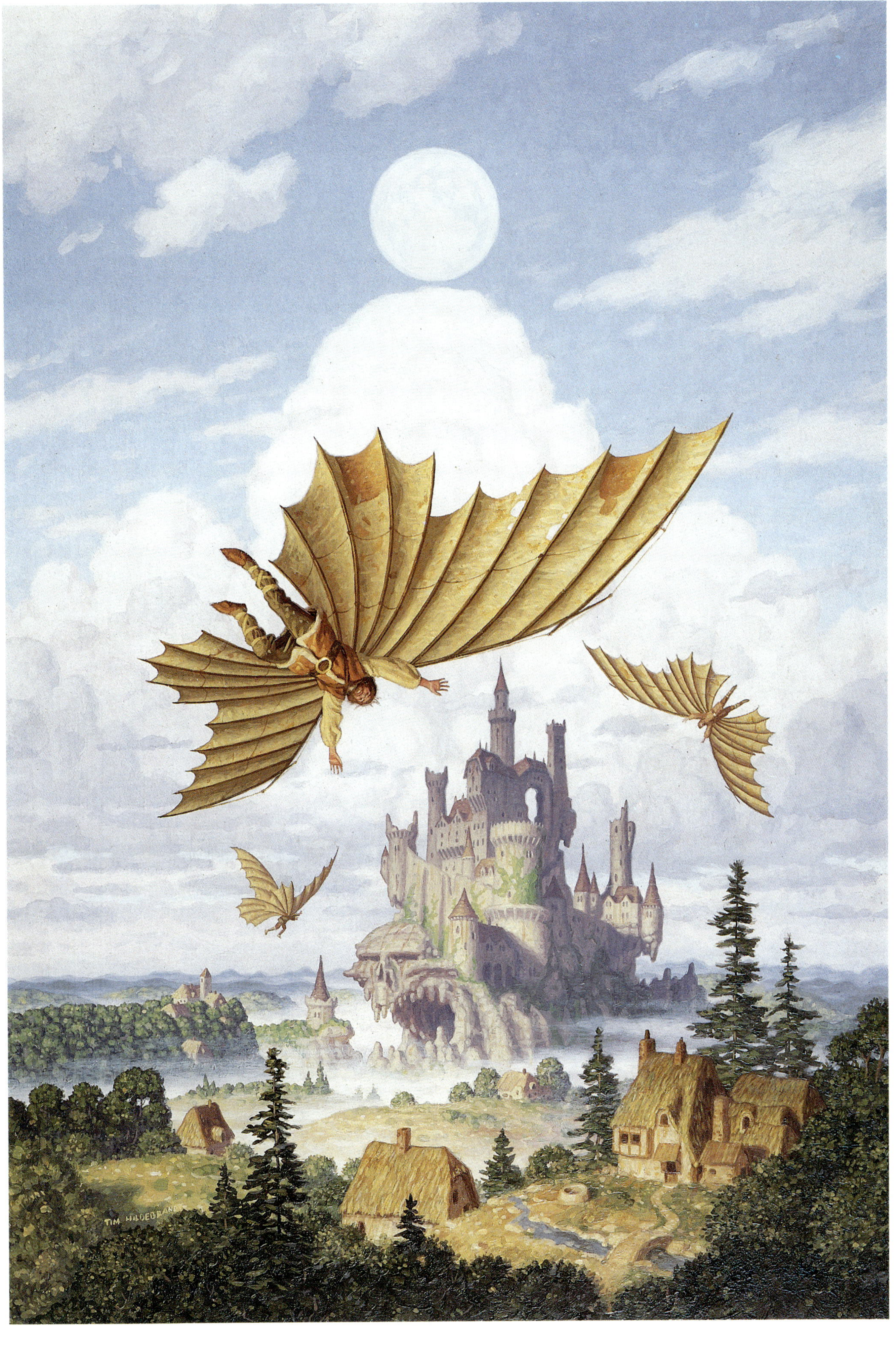

sketches. At this stage, he is only concerned with the placement of all of the elements. Once everything is placed to his satisfaction, he draws a rough comp, roughly four times larger. This larger drawing helps him to see clearly how all of the compositional elements are coming together and any problems in the composition are usually dealt with here. This drawing is also the one that is sent to the art director for approval. Once the drawing is approved, the process of refining and defining continues.

It is during this process that the compositional planning pays off. The scene, remember, is mostly derived from the material that is being illustrated. Many of the physical objects that are in the scene have already been determined. And knowing how the elements of the composition (picture plane, horizon line, etc.) are going to work together, the scene practically assembles itself. This allows the artist to concentrate more on rendering the scene realistically.

After the rough comp has been accepted by the art director, the photos of the models are taken. The most important consideration here is the lighting involved, and Tim is careful to light the models exactly as they are lit in the rough comp.

Through careful consideration of all of the compositional elements, it is then usually a simple matter of detailing. This is done by tracing the rough drawing, and adding the detail from photographs and other reference material. However, even now Tim is flexible enough to make changes that will enhance the final composition. It is much easier to change a pencil line on a drawing than to try to change a painting once in progress. Until the painting begins, nothing in the composition is beyond change – provided that change will improve the final design.

Creating a powerful composition may take an enormous effort on the part of the artist, but you should remember that it is the foundation for everything else that you do. Taking the time to determine all of the elements of a good composition may seem dry and tedious, but it is crucial if you hope to make a strong visual impact on the

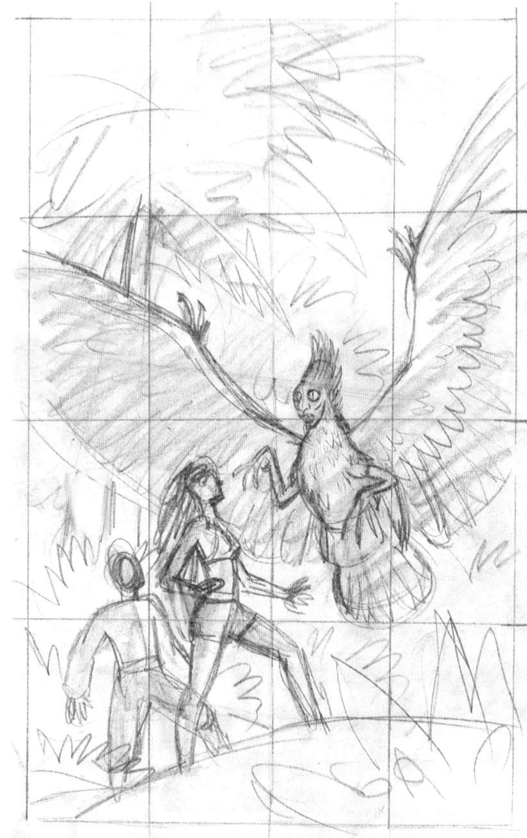

The Day of Their Return
Cover illustration and thumbnail sketch for the book by Poul Anderson, 1987, acrylic on masonite. Tim: 'Note the two light sources here; one from the sun high up behind, and the other from the sunlight bouncing up off the rocks.'

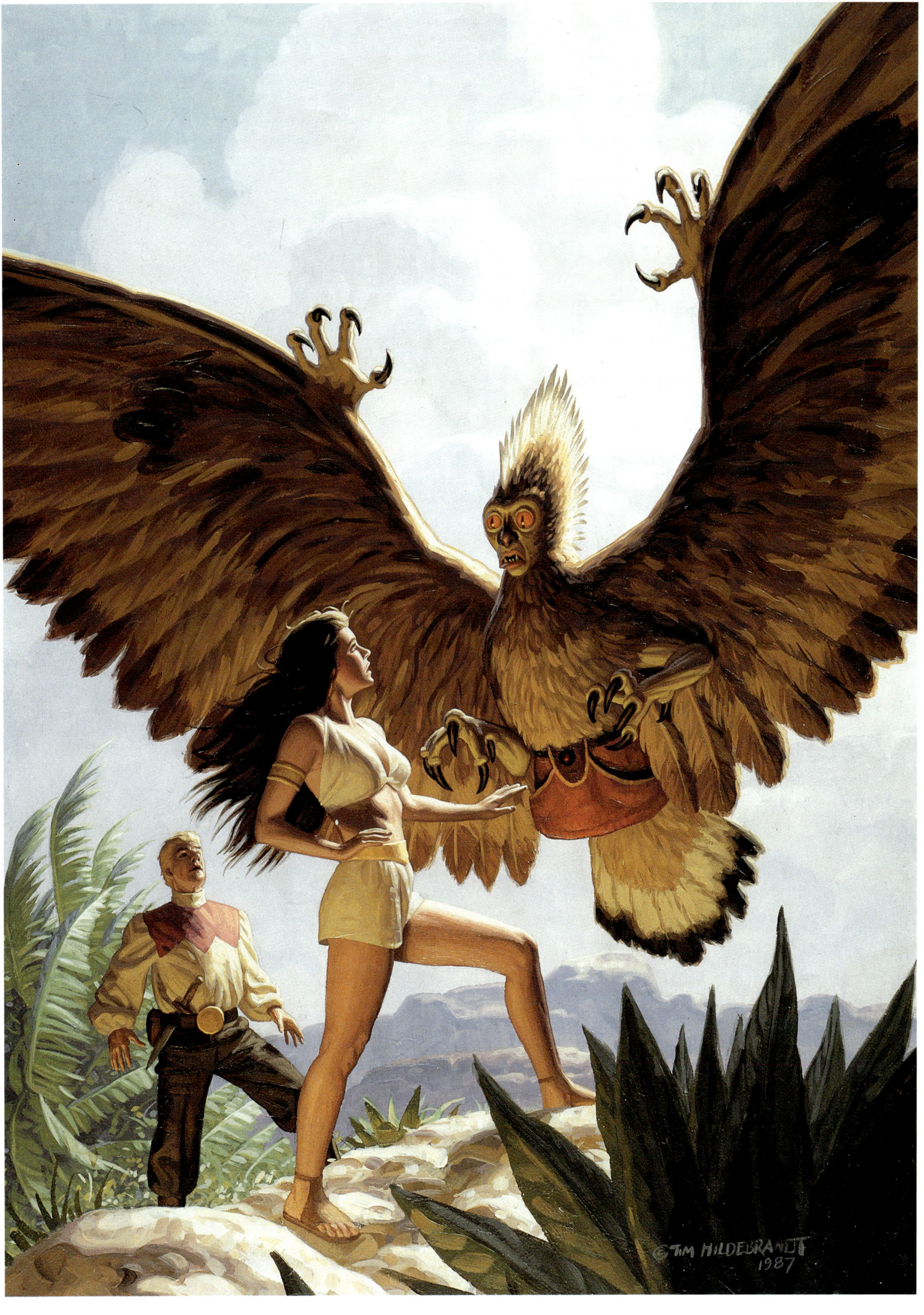

© Tim Hildebrandt
1987

58   viewer. In order to make the fantastic believable, the
artist must utilize all of these tools in order to convey a
sense of realism. In the real world, for instance, we see
everything in perspective. In order to make a scene believable, a fantasy artist must therefore depict things in
perspective. As a fantasy artist, you must constantly be
aware of how things appear in the real world, and how
nature operates. Only then can you make your fantasy
paintings convincing.

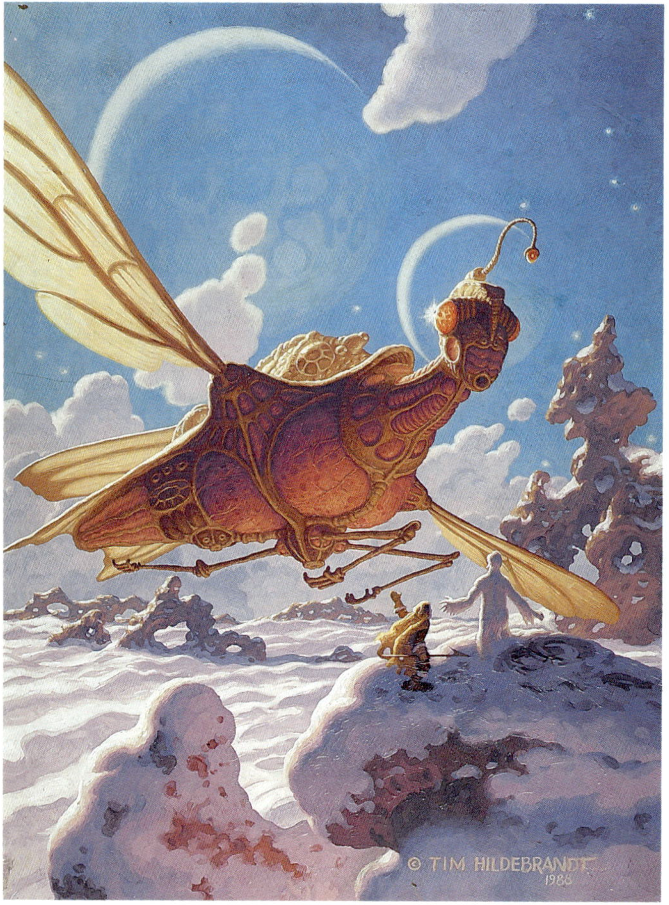

Poster, 1988, acrylic on masonite. Tim:
'Where do ideas come from? In this picture I
wanted to create a living machine so I
crossed an airplane with an insect.'

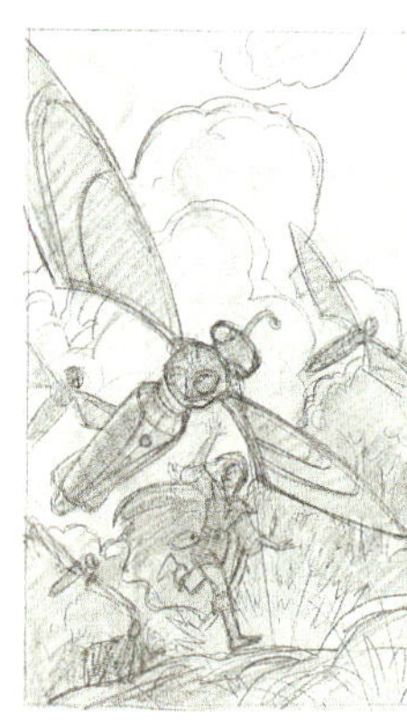

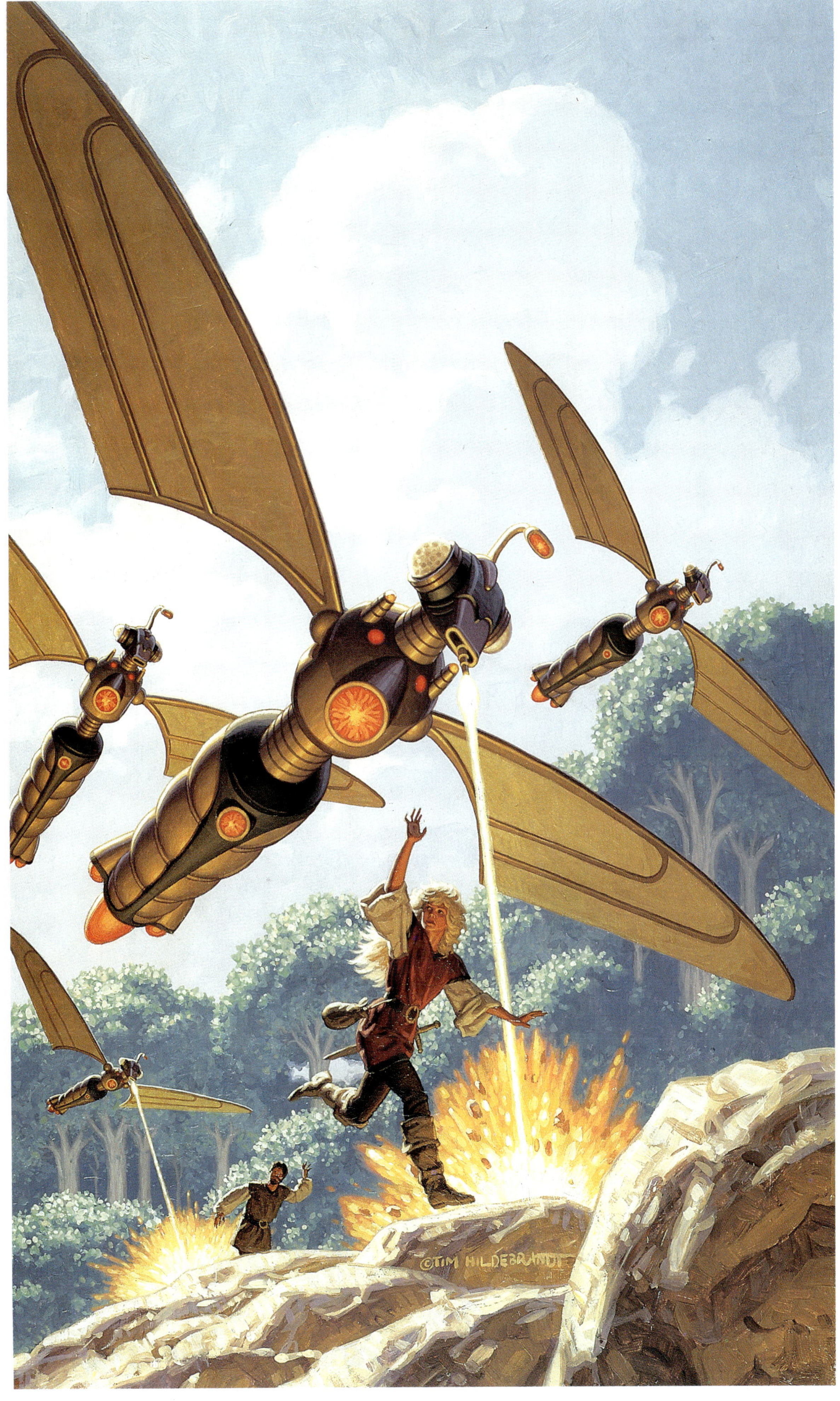
©TIM HILDEBRANDT

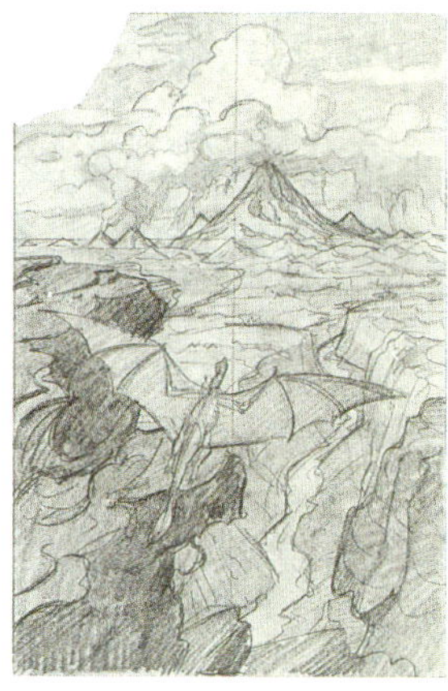

The Mountain
From *The Dragonriders of Pern* calendar, 1985, acrylic on masonite. Tim: 'You may think that the dragon is the centre of interest. Well, it isn't – the mountain is. This is an example of the use of a high horizon line.'

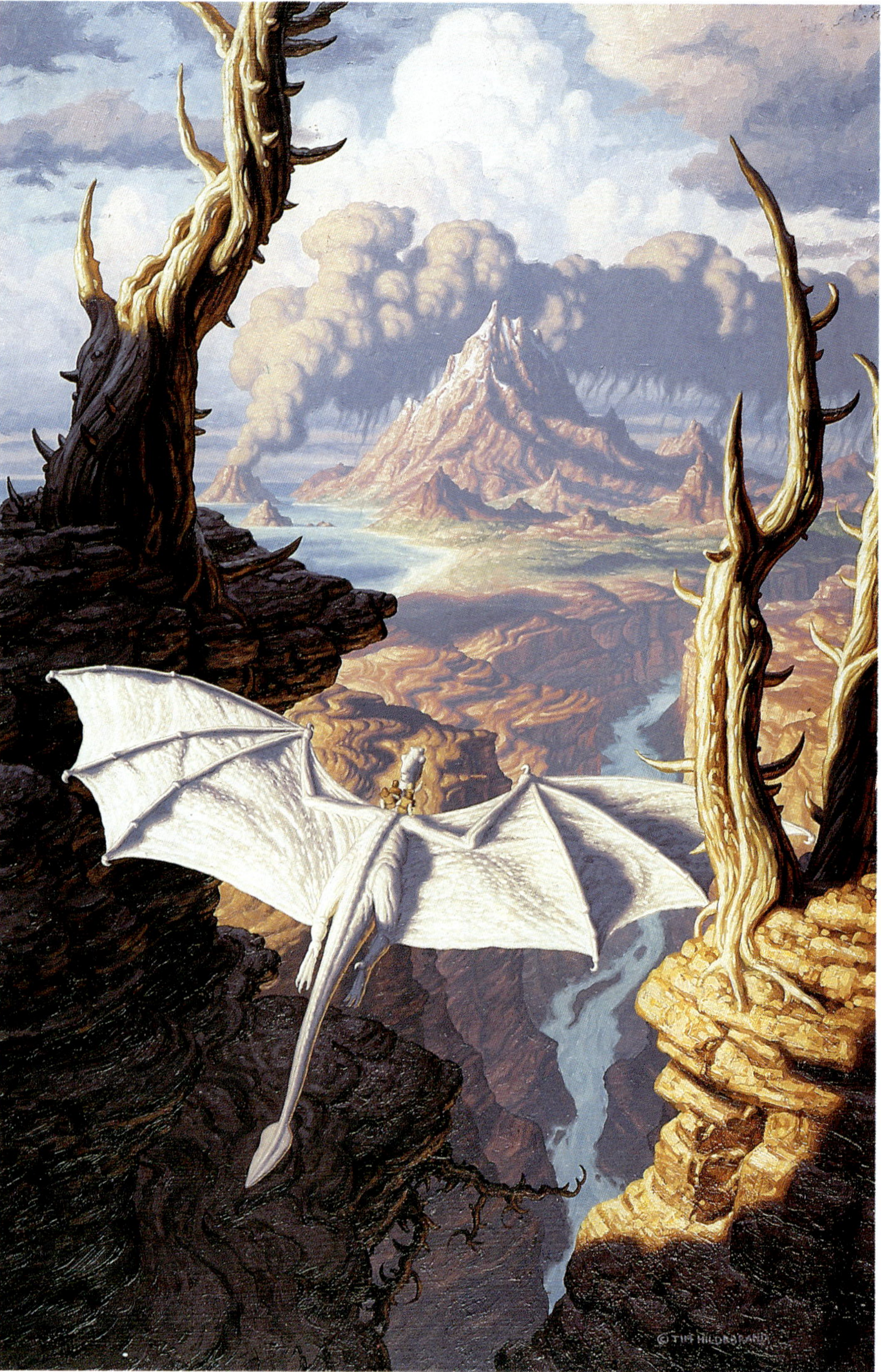

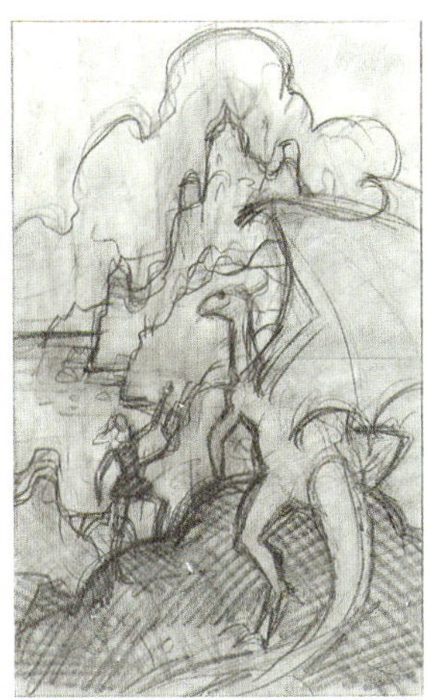

The White Dragon
Book cover, 1988, acrylic on masonite. Tim: 'I felt the high mountains behind the dragon detracted so I left them out of the finished painting.'

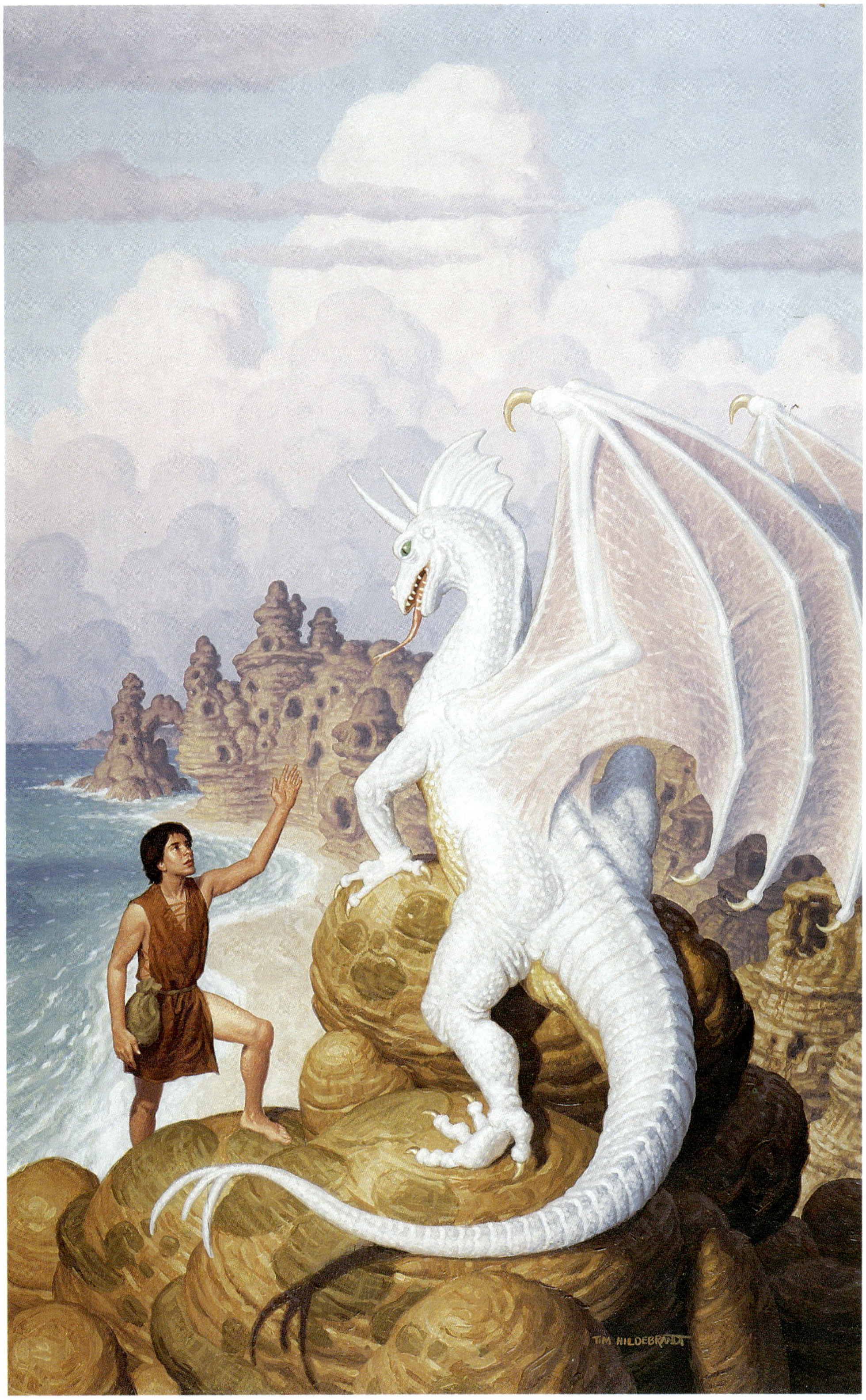

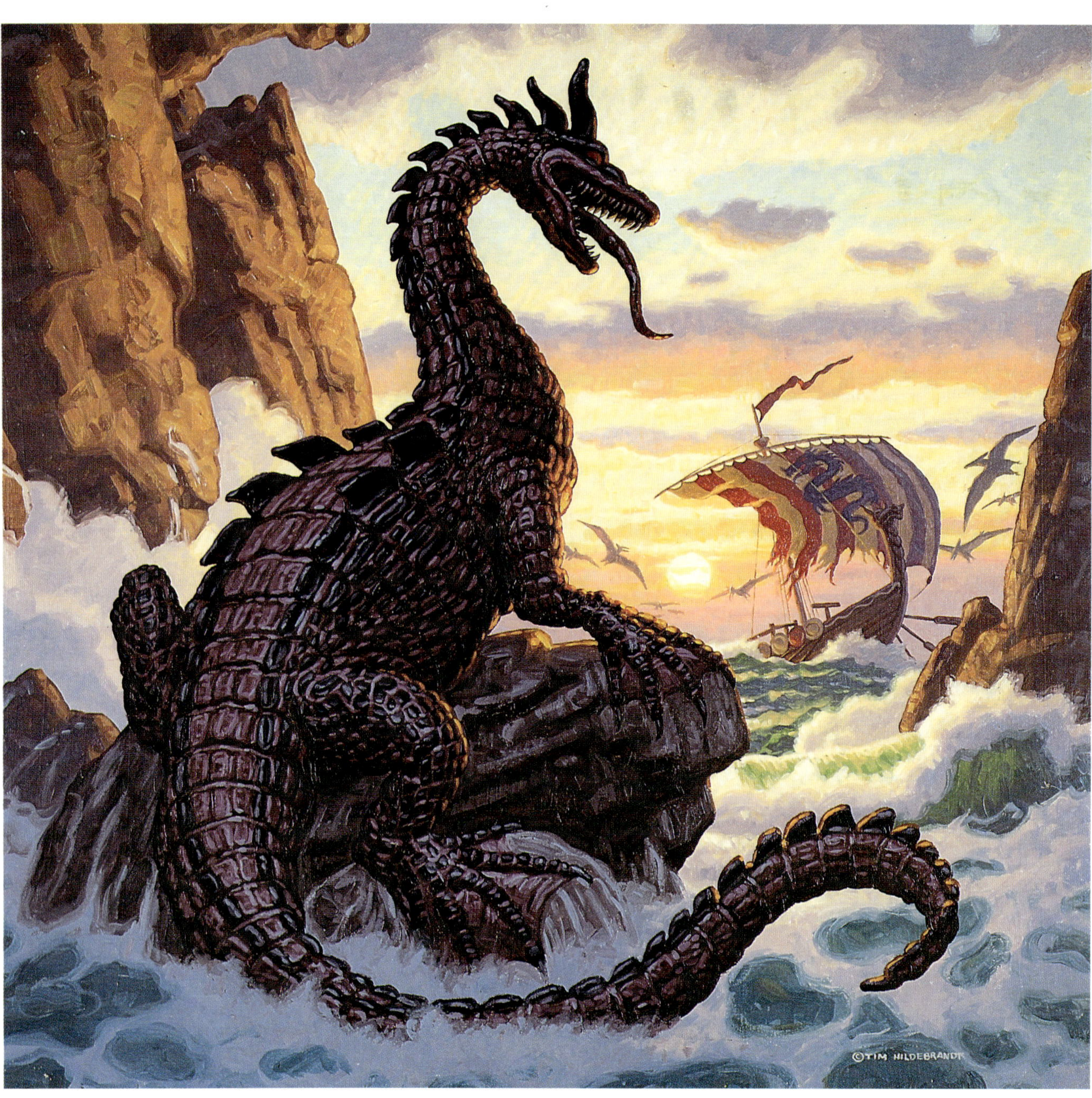

Sea Dragon
From the *Realms of Wonder* calendar, TSR, 1983,
acrylic on masonite. Tim: 'I used a stuffed baby
alligator for reference here. The centres of
interest are graded thus: sun, ship, dragon.'

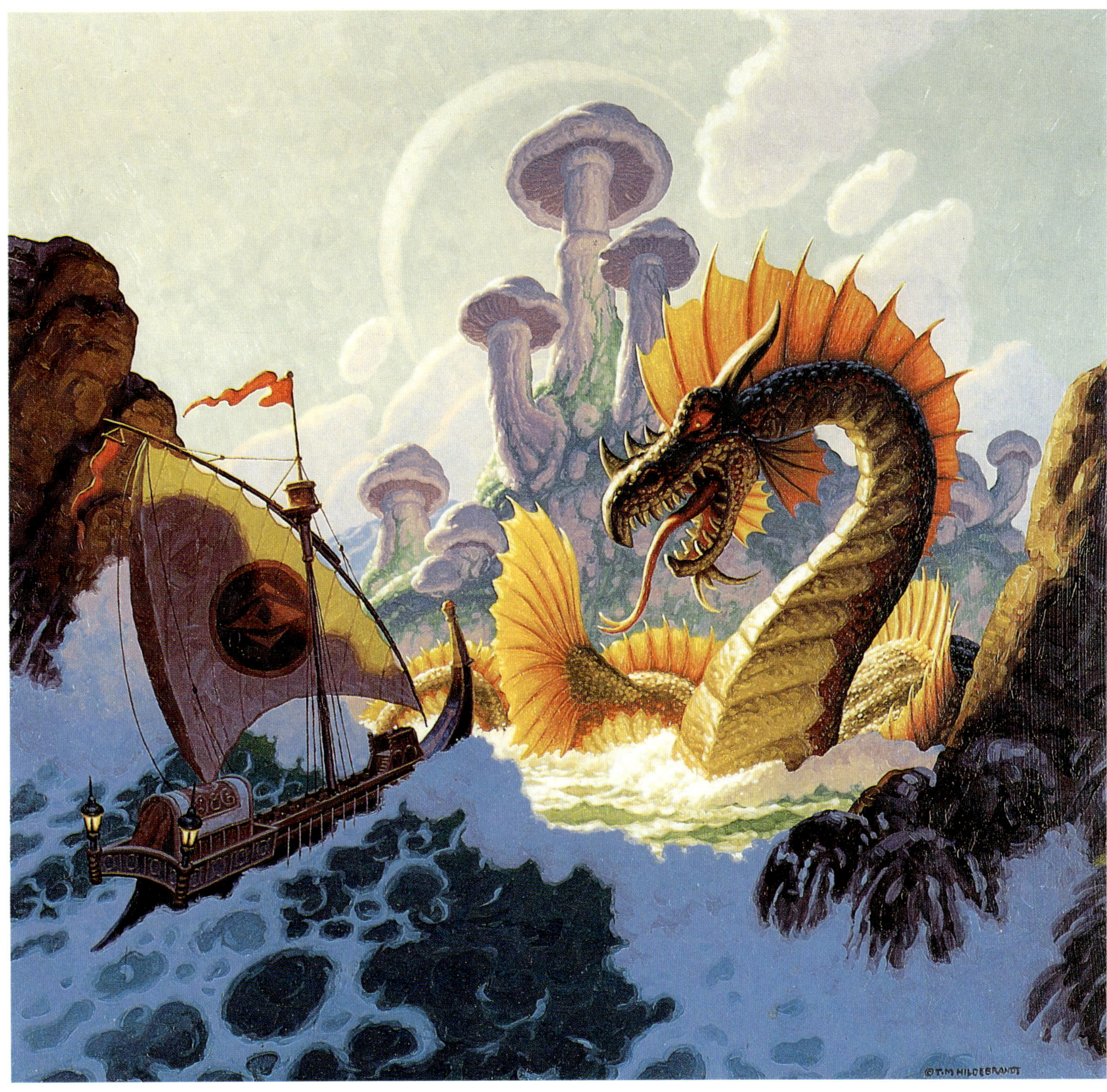

Cover for the *Realms of Wonder* calendar, TSR, 1982, acrylic on masonite. Tim used a plastic dinosaur head as reference here.

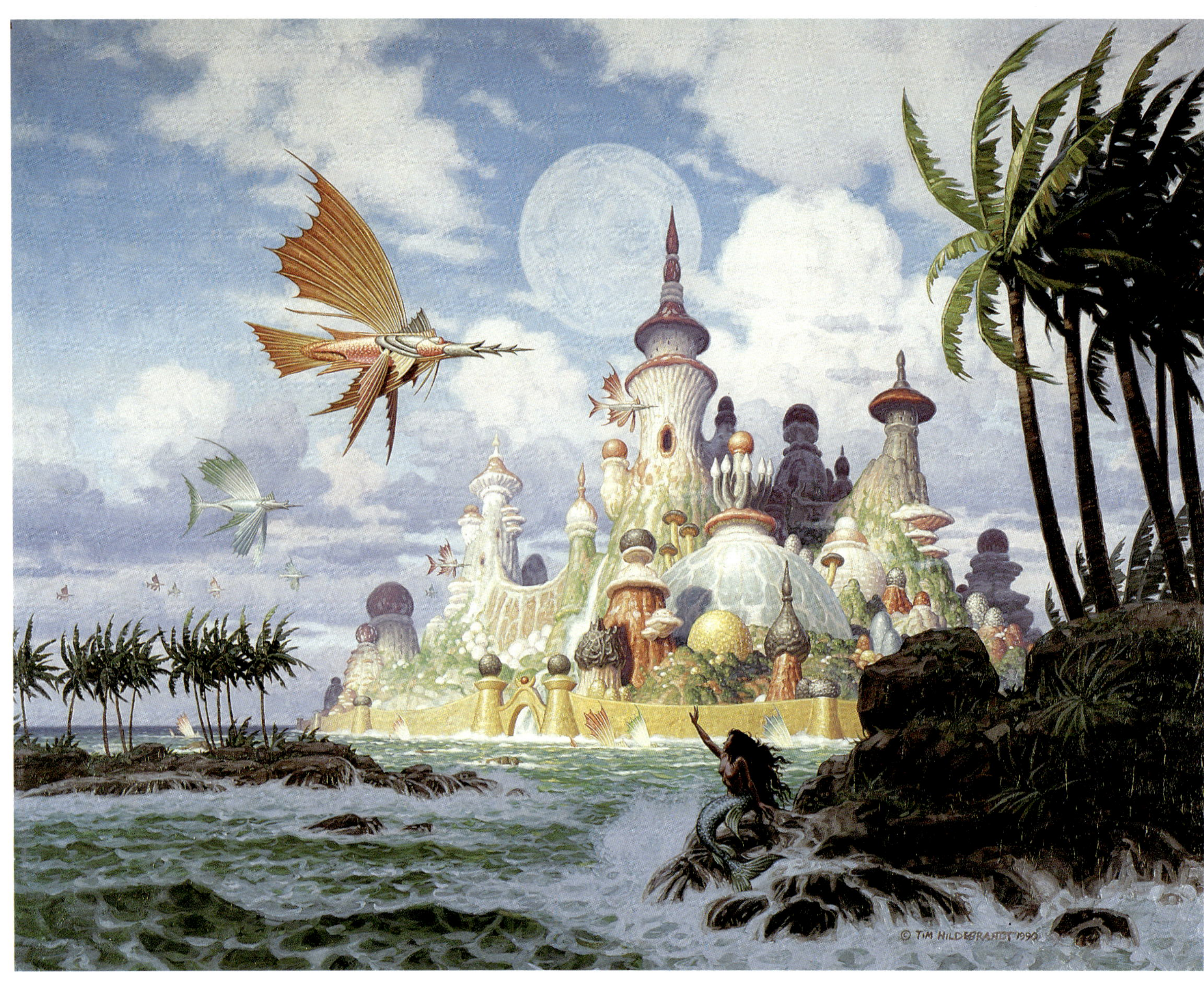

Fantasy Aisle
Private piece, 1990, acrylic on masonite. Tim: 'I chose a horizontal format to allow movement from left to right. This movement is emphasized in the movement of the palm trees, the water breaking on the rocks and the direction of flight. However, the upward thrust of the mushroom city and the trees do block this movement to a certain extent.'

RIGHT **Vendetta**
Final version of the cover for the book by M.S. Murdock, Warner Books, 1987, acrylic on masonite. Variation on a formal composition. Note the double light source.

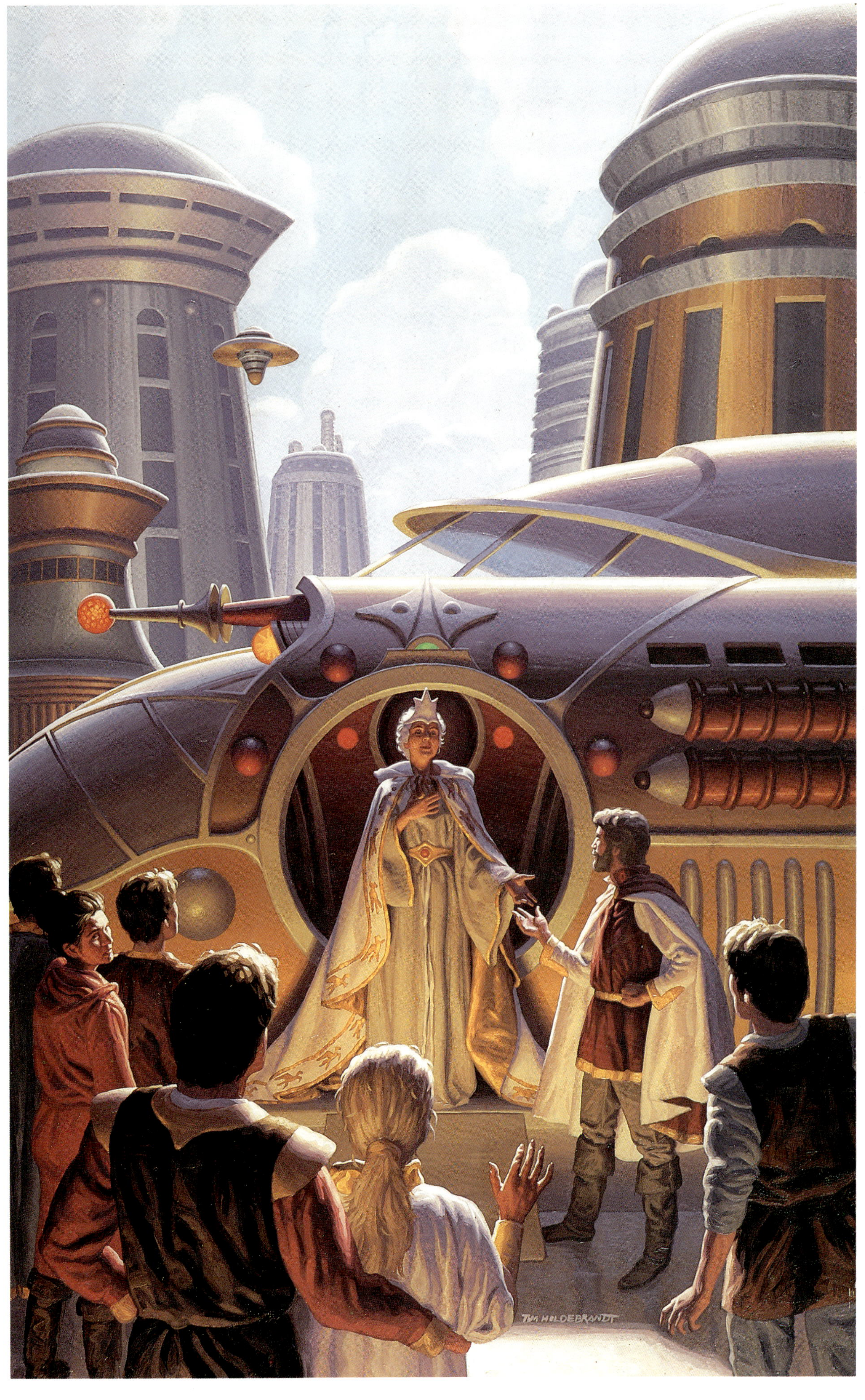

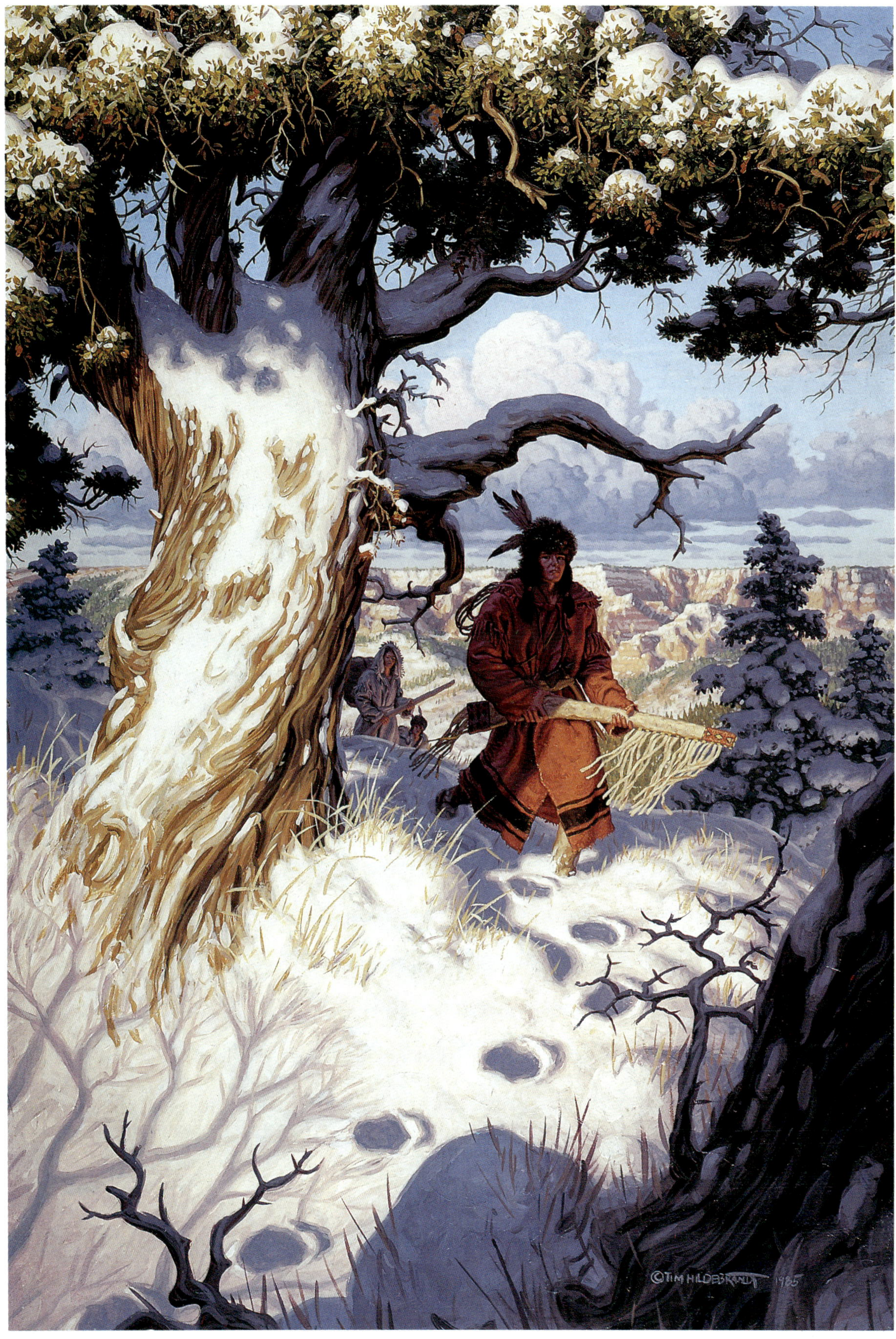

Blackfoot Indians Hunting Bear
Private piece, 1985, acrylic on masonite. Tim: 'I
like to challenge myself with something different
every so often.'

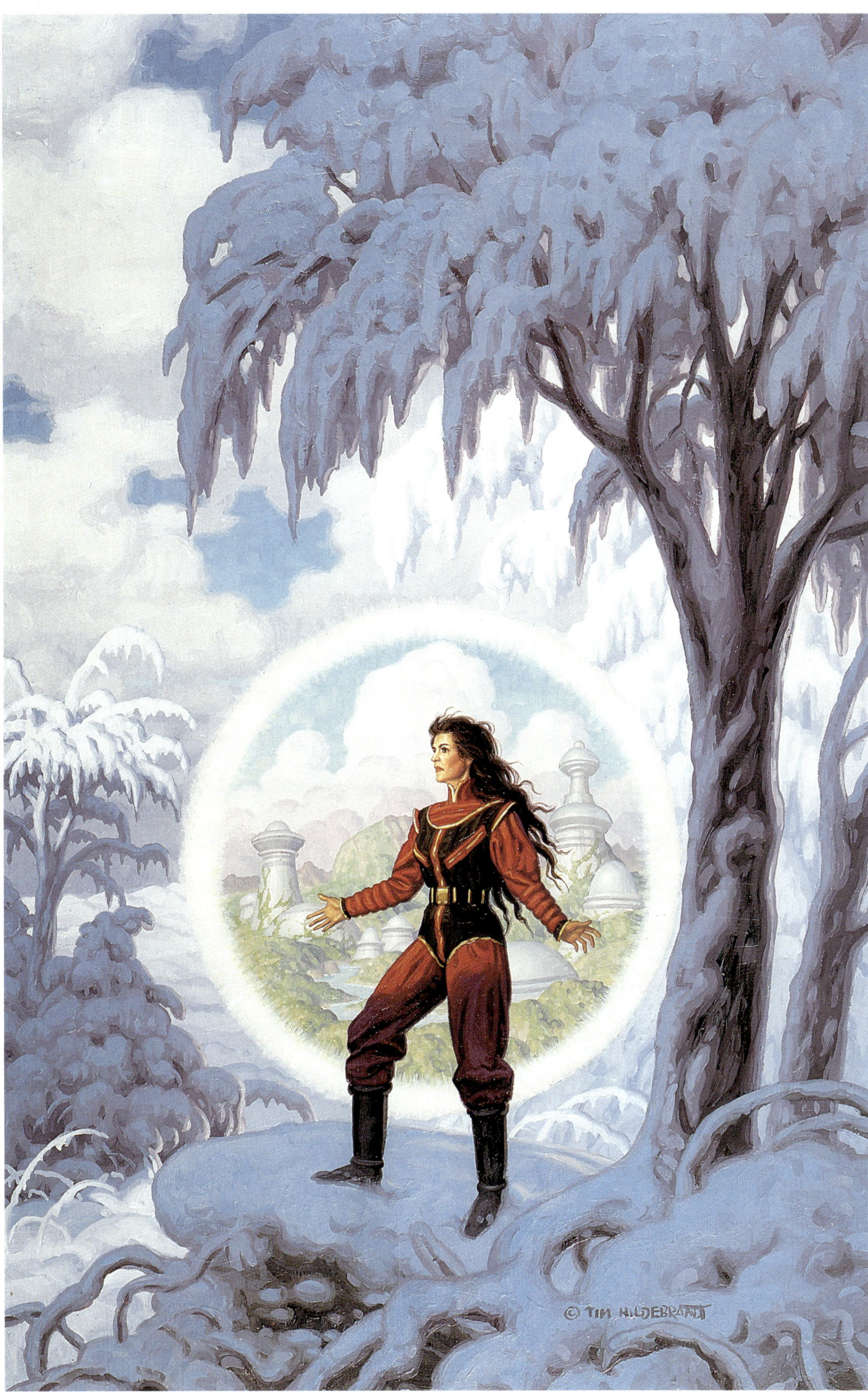

To Warm the Earth
Cover illustration for the book by David Belden,
1987, acrylic on masonite. Tim: 'For space suits
I sometimes use Air Force flying suits for initial
inspiration.'

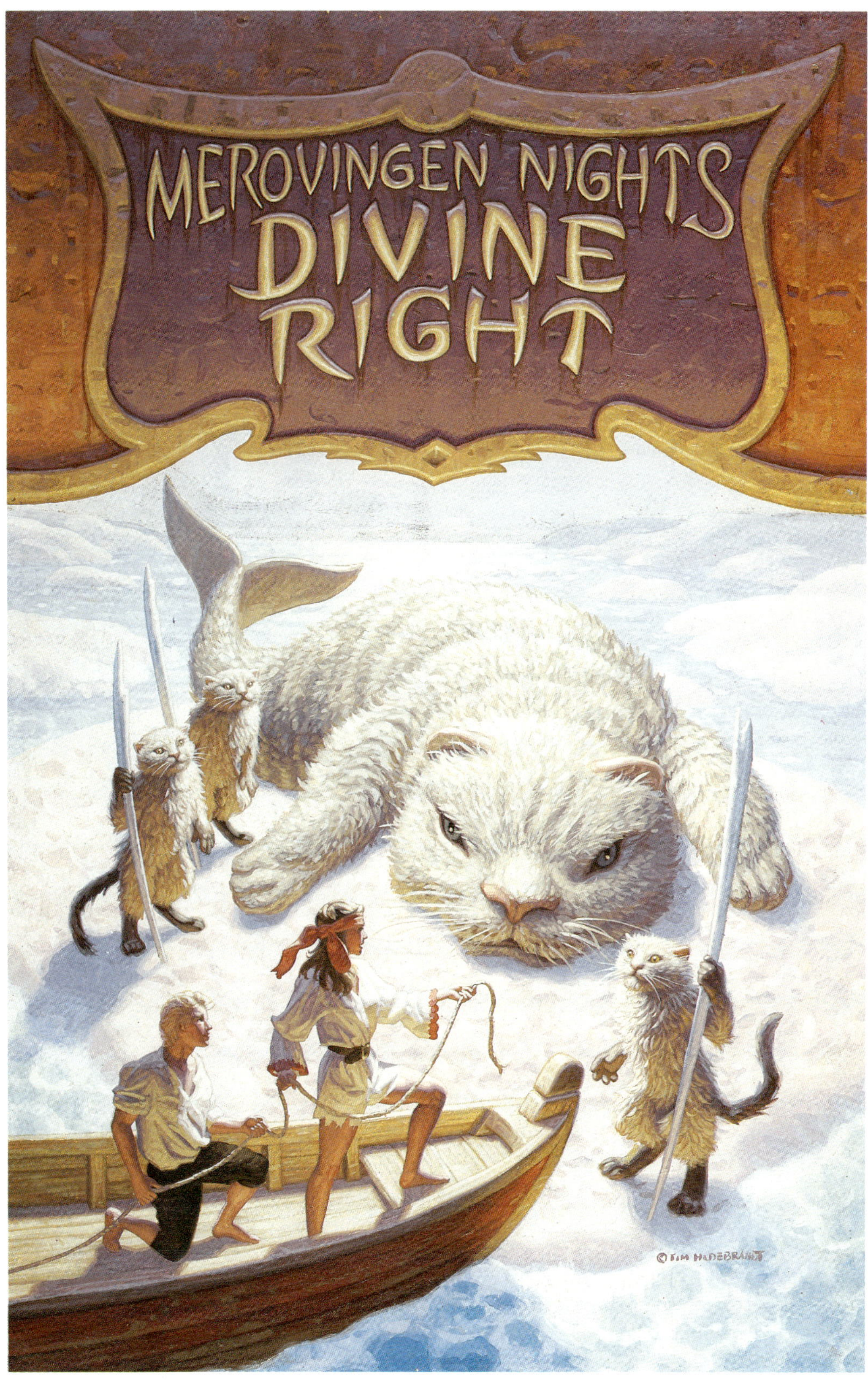

Merovingen Nights: Divine Right
Book cover, 1989, acrylic on masonite. Tim:
'Sometimes you have to include the book's title in
the illustration. My poor wet cat served as the
model in this one. She was not amused!'

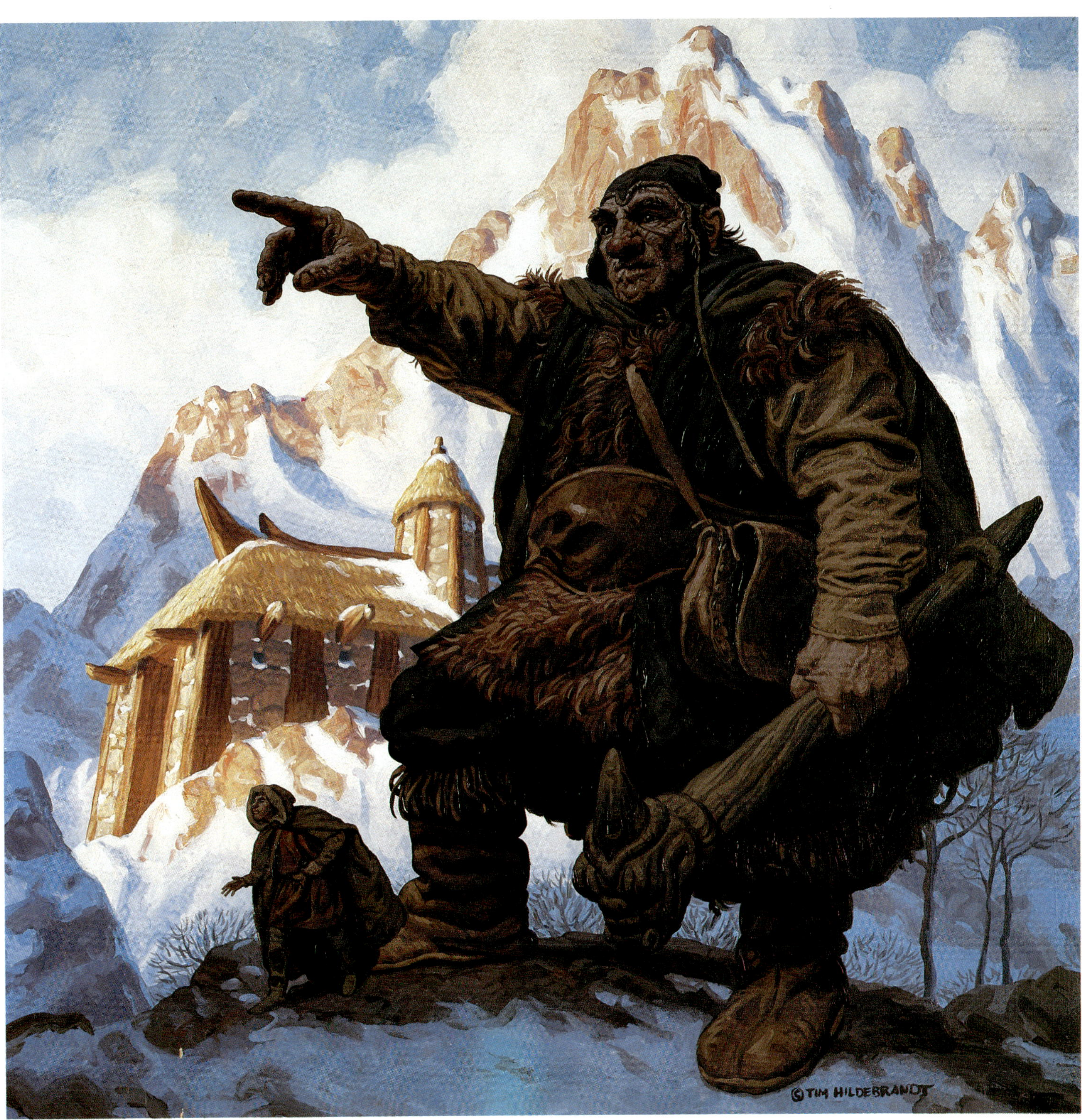

Snow Giant
From the *Realms of Wonder* calendar, TSR, 1983.
A low angle was used to emphasize the size of the
giant. Tim: 'My friend Bill poses for all my giants
and trolls. He enjoys it. He thinks he's beautiful!'

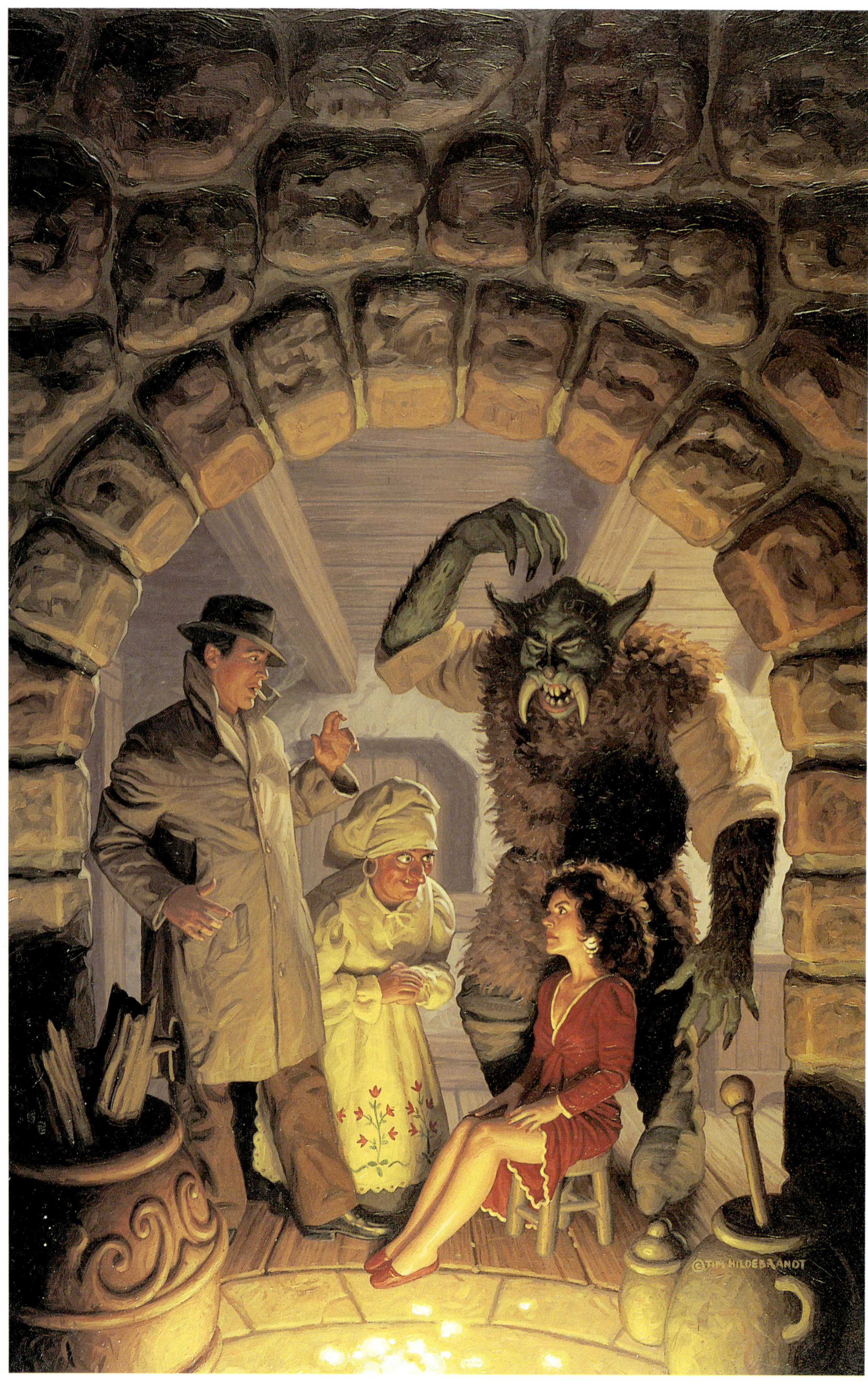

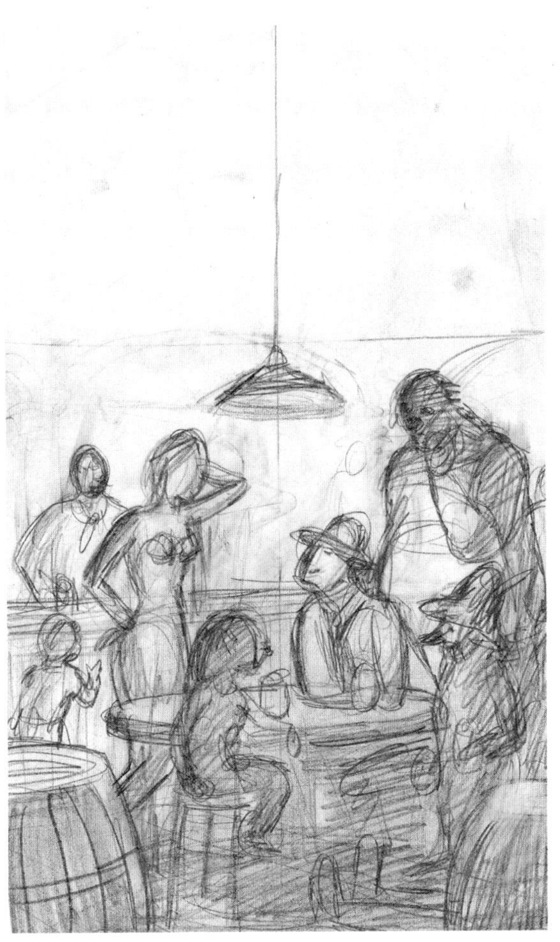

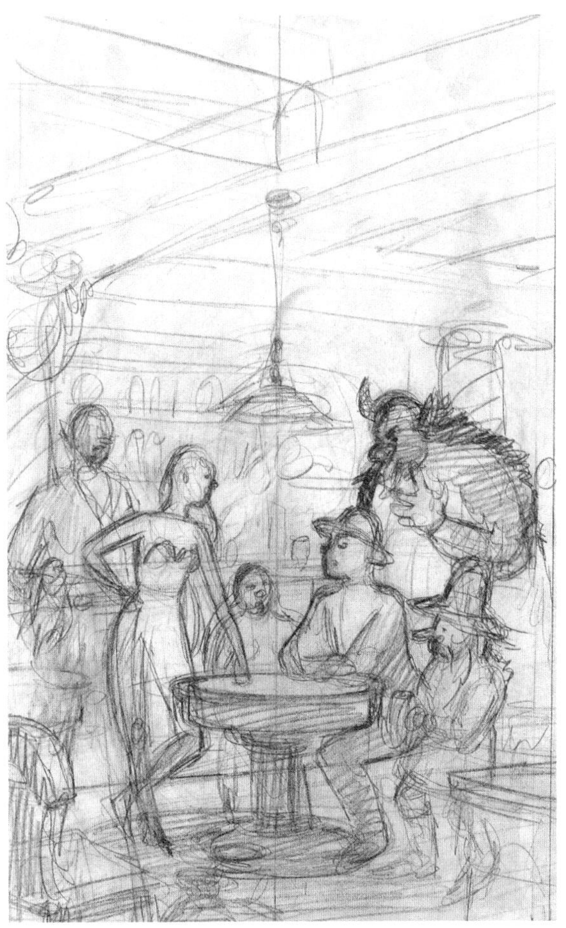

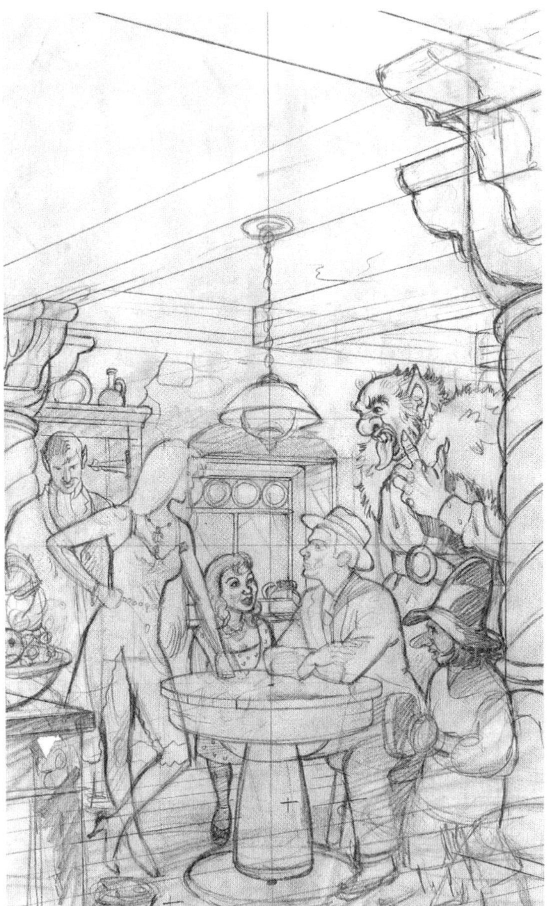

Development sketches for *Red Iron Nights*. Tim:
'I wanted the table in the centre so I arranged
everything around it.'

OPPOSITE PAGE **Bitter Gold Hearts**
Cover illustration for the novel by Glenn Cooke,
New American Library, 1987, acrylic on masonite.
Tim: 'Even though your models may be roughly the
same size, you sometimes have to alter their
proportions. The models used for the man and the
woman are actually husband and wife – and she is
by no means a dwarf! I like framing devices in
paintings; here the curve of the fireplace holds the
pictures together.'

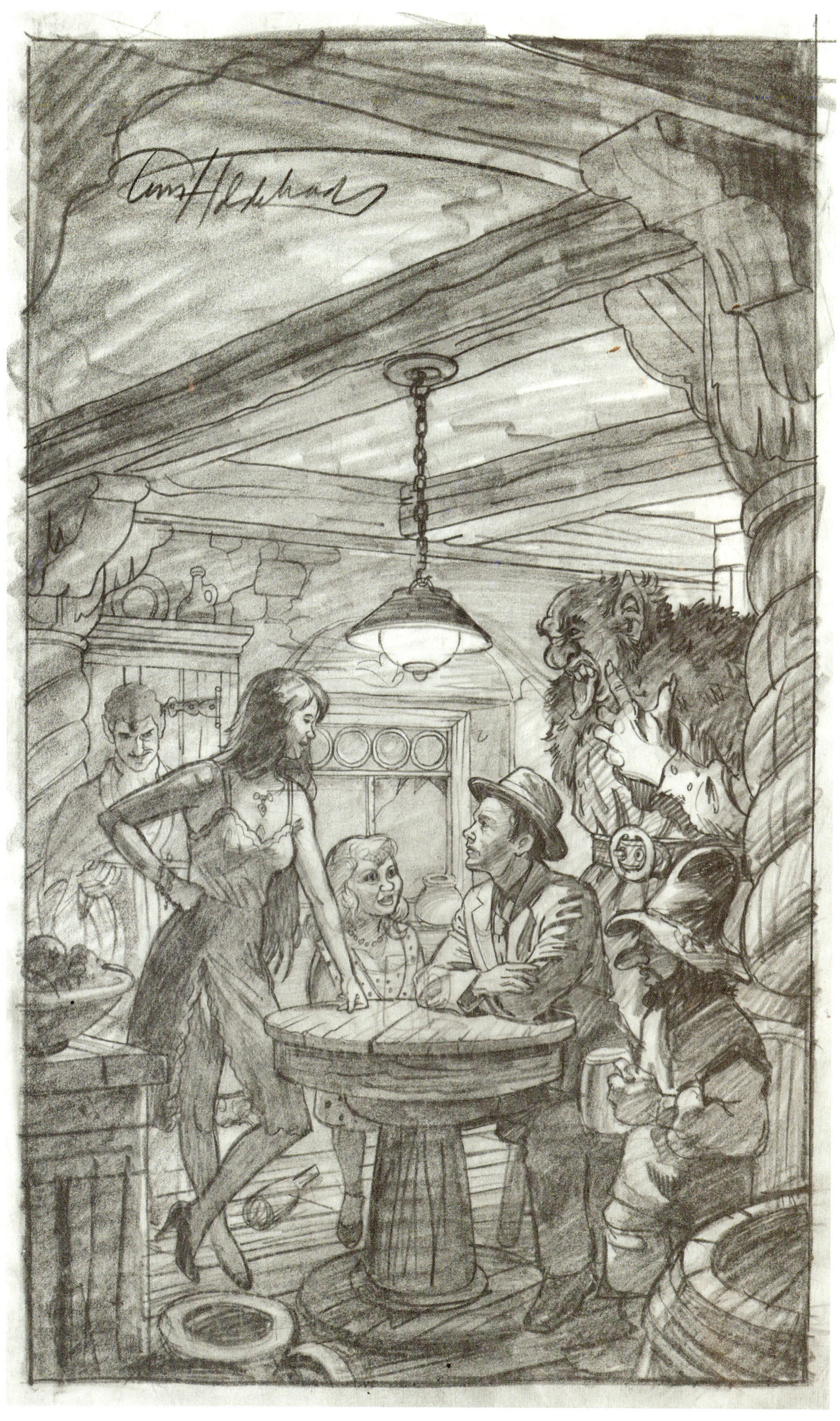

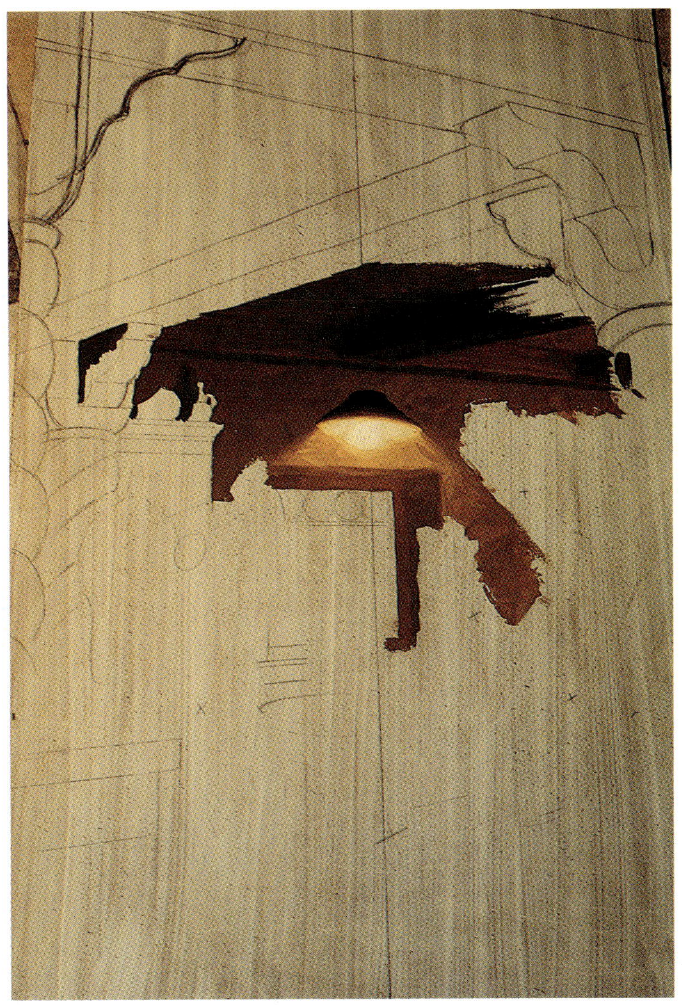

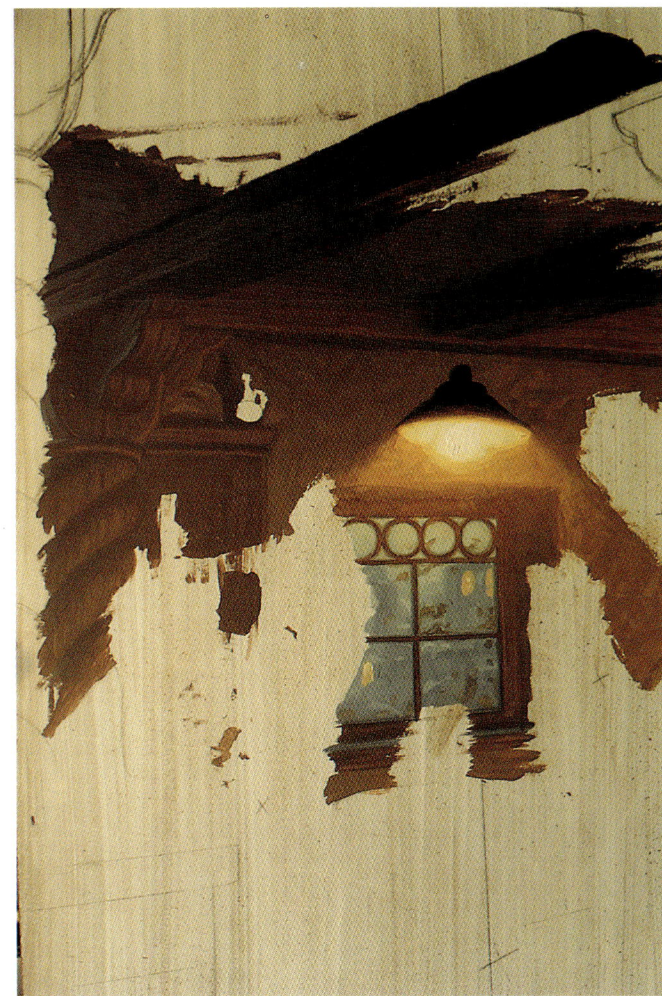

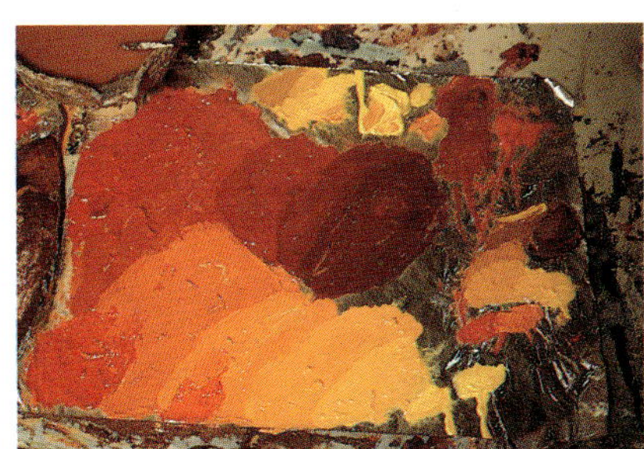

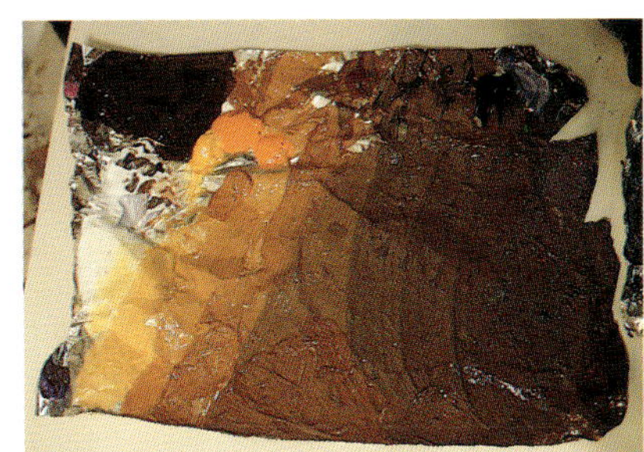

TOP LEFT Painting the backgrounds. Initially the gesso is applied to the masonite and sanded. Then just the background is pencilled in; TOP RIGHT Painting the midgrounds; BELOW LEFT The palette for skin tones. Tim: 'I mix eight values for the skin on aluminium foil'; BELOW RIGHT The palette for the background. 'The same is done for all the colours used. I keep the paint from drying by spraying it with water periodically.'

OPPOSITE PAGE Finished sketch for *Red Iron Nights*.

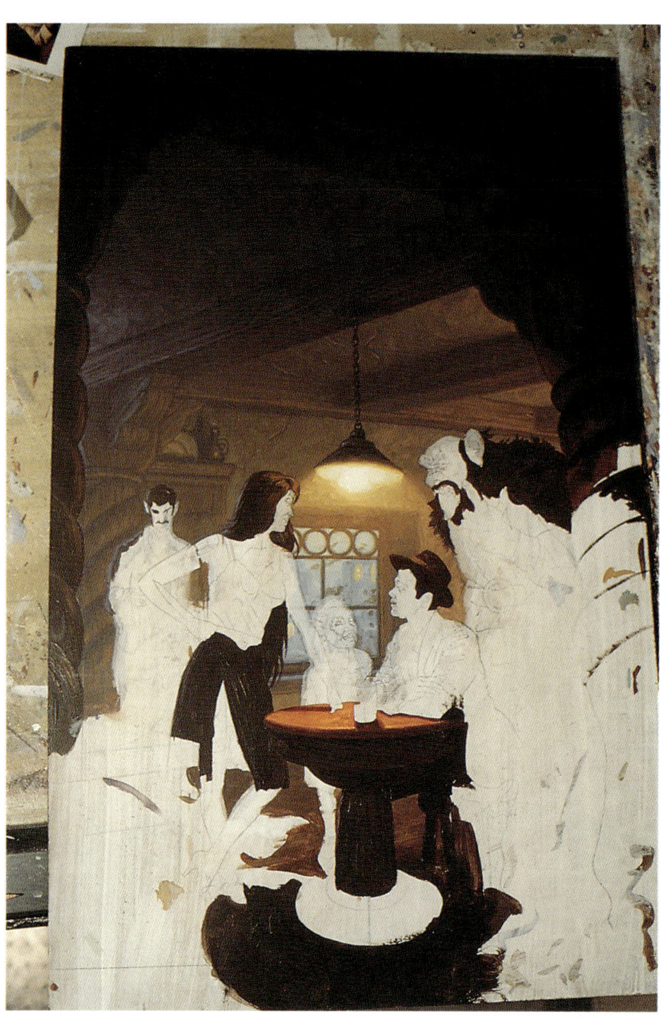 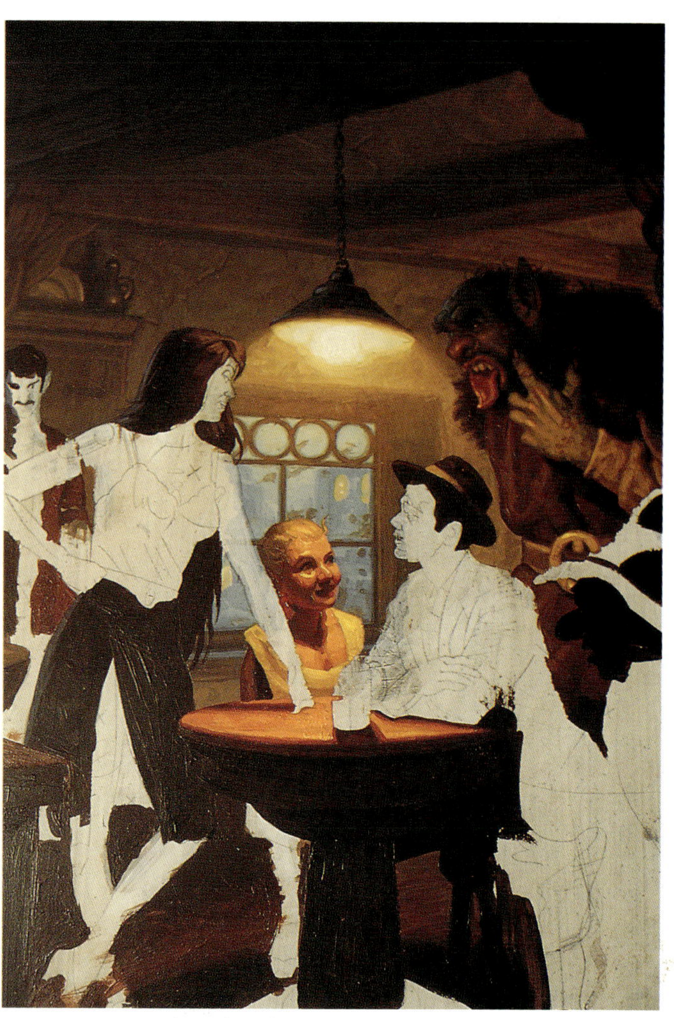

ABOVE LEFT Painting the foreground;
ABOVE RIGHT Painting the figures. Here
the troll is already finished.

RIGHT **Red Iron Nights**
The finished cover illustration for *Red Iron Nights*
by Glenn Cooke, 1991, acrylic on masonite. Tim:
'This picture is composed using two-point
perspective – the beams in the ceiling are angled
in two directions. Notice the blue light coming in
from the window.'

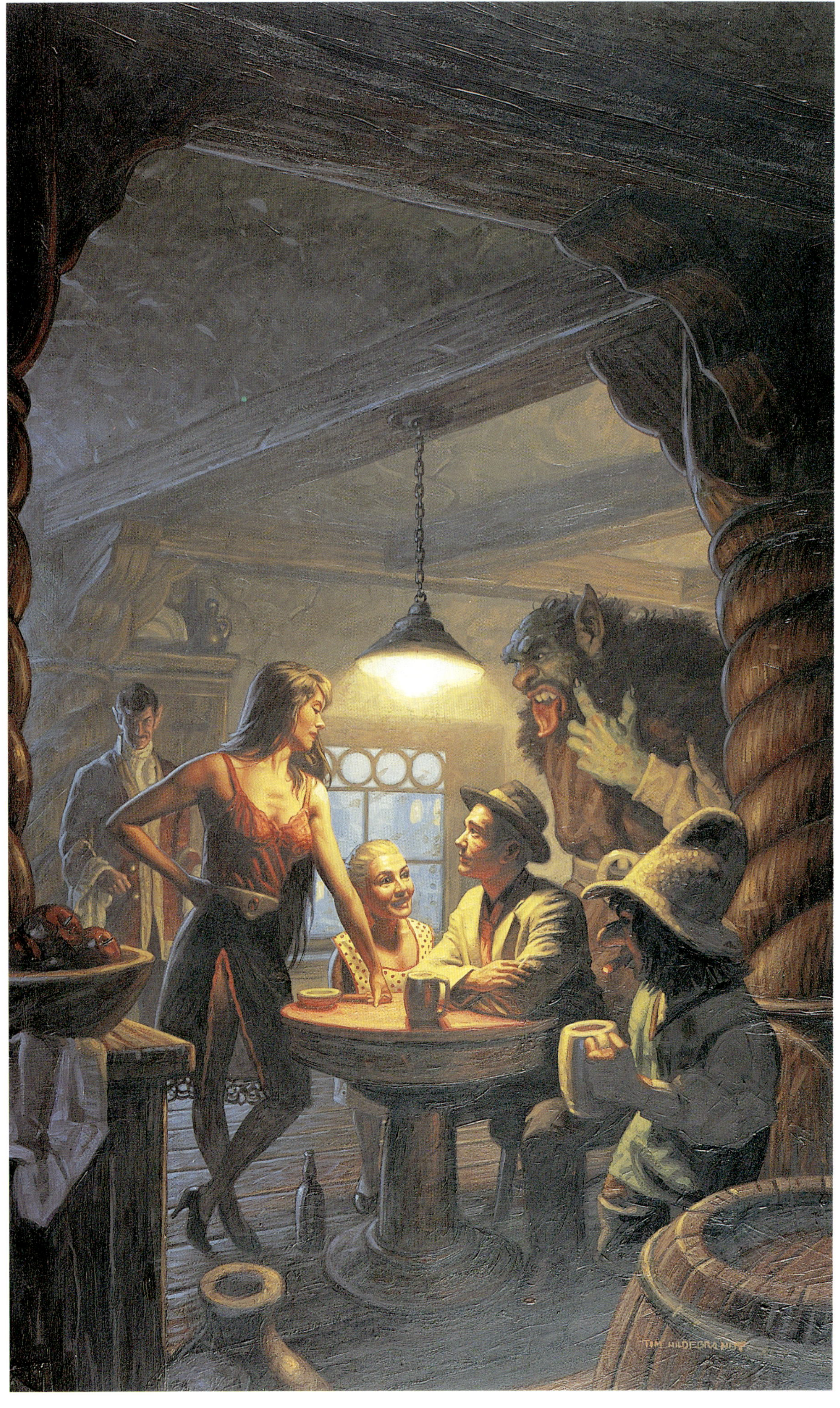

Homeward Bound
Finished pencil drawing from *The Unicorn Treasury*, Doubleday, 1987. Tim used as reference a plastic model of a pony lying down. He has over twenty different poses to chose from; BOTTOM Finished pencil drawing from the same book.

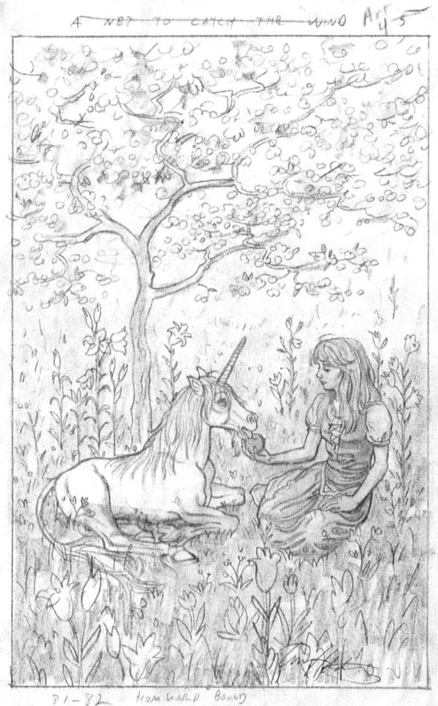

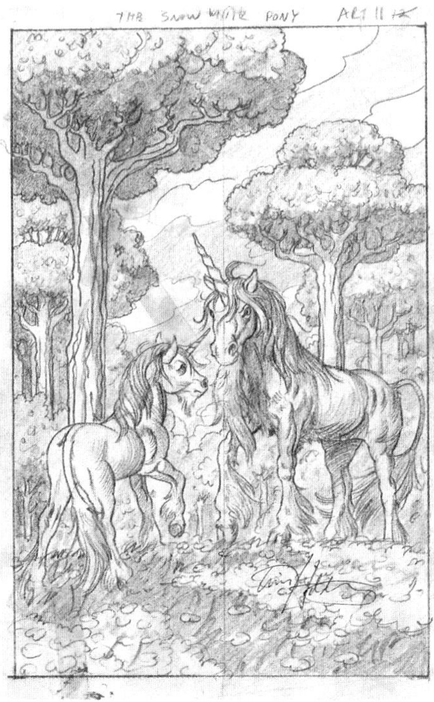

Section Three

Black & White

76

Black and white is probably the most versatile of all forms of illustration. It is the basis for anything you do in colour, and can be used as a tool to communicate ideas or concepts. It can be achieved through a variety of mediums: pencil, pen and ink, and even by painting. It is not unusual for any of these forms to be used as the final illustration itself.

At some point in our lives all of us have attempted to draw something. As a result, the thought of creating in black and white is not quite as alien as painting in colour. Almost everyone feels comfortable holding a pencil, while we tend to exhibit a certain awe or reverence toward an artist who wields a paintbrush. This leads to the notion that artists who work with colour are somehow superior to those who work in black and white. This is not true. While an artist who works exclusively in colour may be able to develop some techniques that are somewhat aesthetically pleasing, a superior artist will leave nothing to chance. This control involves a mastery over basic artistic principles that are learned from black and white.

It may surprise you to learn that creating realistic images through any of the black and white mediums described in this chapter require every bit as much effort as painting in colour. All of the steps toward creating a final colour composition are required to achieve realism in black and white, and are often even more important. The absence of colour demands that your compositions be more powerful, and characters more interesting, in order to make up the difference. Rendering the scene is always the last step in the process.

The process referred to is the formula that Tim uses for every illustration, regardless of the medium. It is based on a holistic approach to his art: every step in the creative process is an integral part of every other step. Every chapter in this book, and all of the topics discussed in each chapter, represent a part of the whole; the same process is followed, regardless of the medium.

Before you can even begin to create realistic images, you must master the basics. Some people have a tendency to want to rush things, especially when dealing with

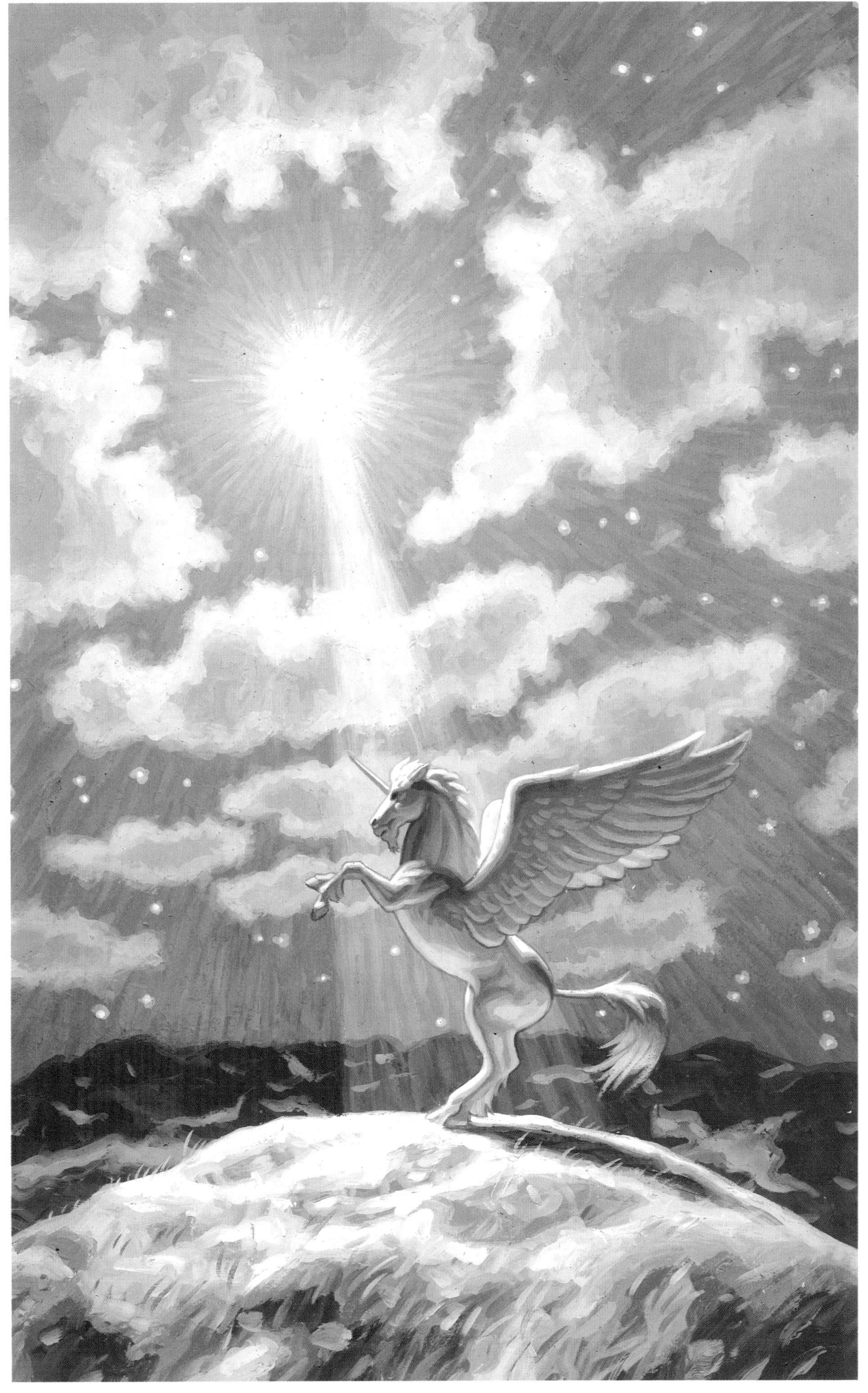

The Dwarf Village
Unpublished finished pencil drawing from
Urshurak, 1979. Tim: 'Several grades of
pencil were used here; 7H in the
distance to a black Prismacolor in the
foreground.'

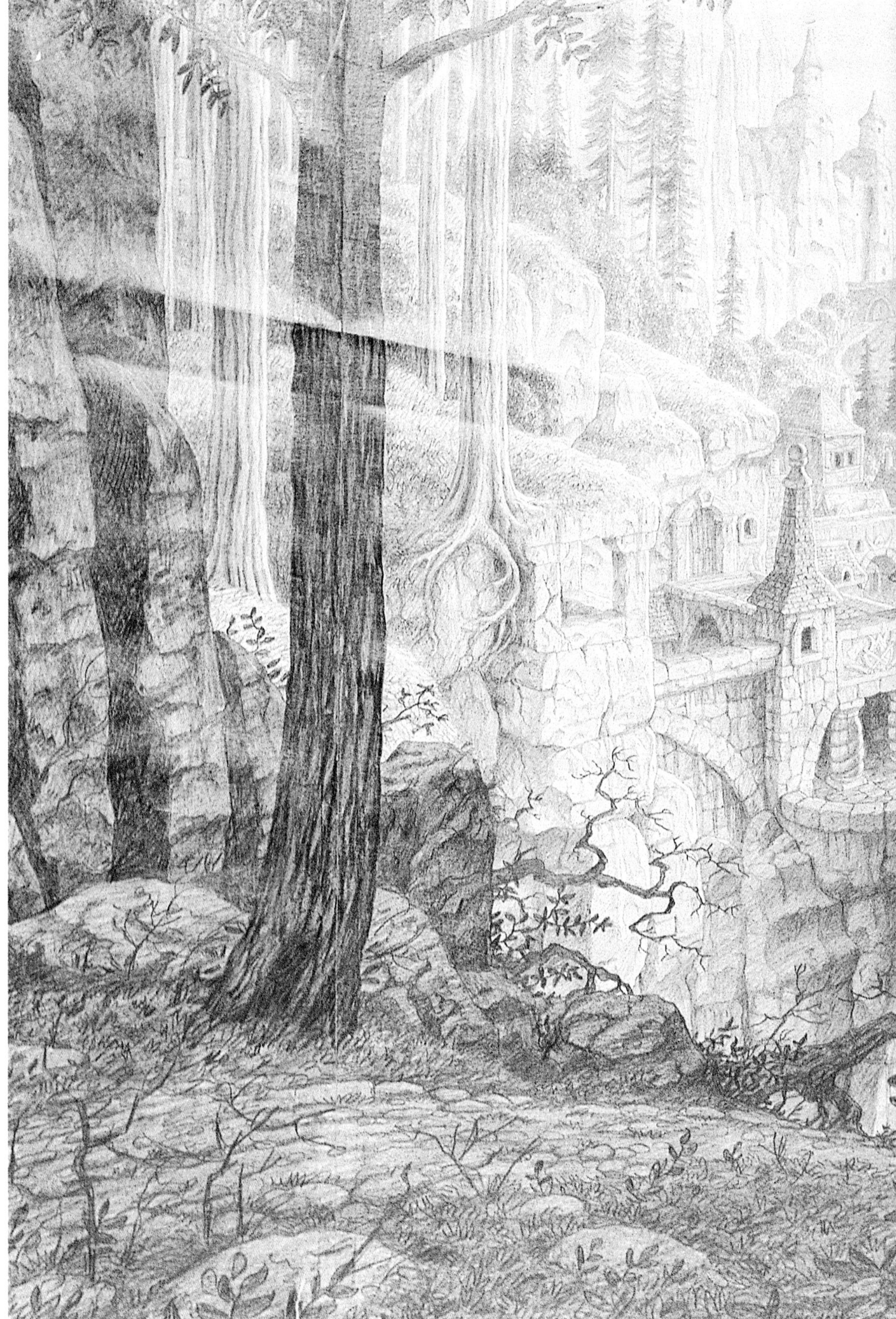

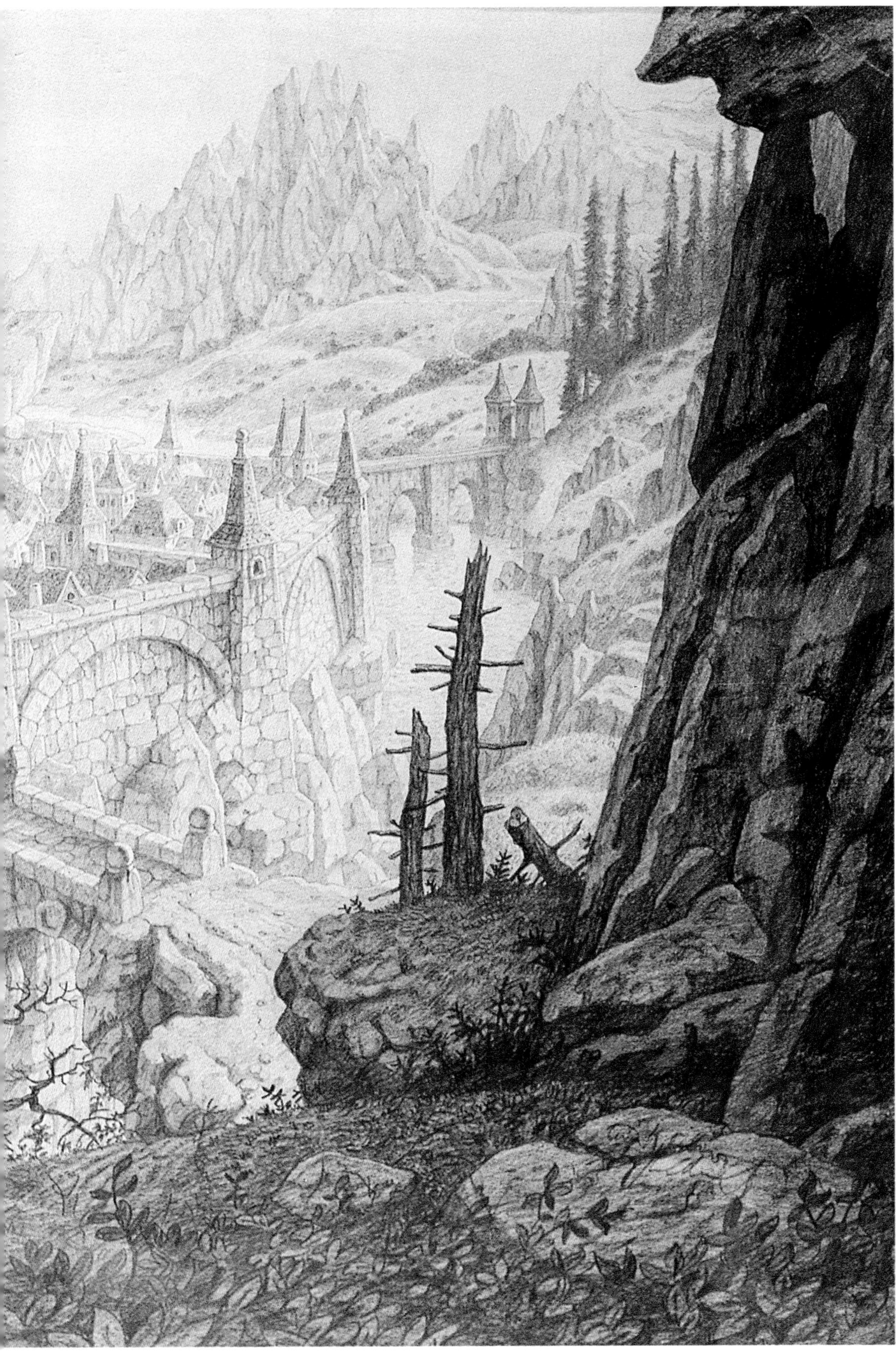

something as familiar as a pencil drawing. This is a mistake. It is understood that you must learn to crawl before you can walk. In art, then, you must learn basic skills before you can effectively synthesize realism.

For Tim, the most basic element involved in any illustration is the composition. Yet a strong composition implies that you have achieved a certain degree of development as an artist. You must first know your picture plane, and how it is divided. This in itself indicates a knowledge of your subject, where the centre of interest will be focused, and how the subject will be applied to the picture plane. It also means that you understand how the division of the picture plane will affect your point of view, which in turn demonstrates an understanding of how those divisions will affect perspective. At this point, you may begin to tackle the problems associated with perspective, which involves a knowledge of vanishing points and proportion. None of this even begins to approach the subjects of lighting, figure drawing (which in itself opens the doors to anatomy, costuming and photography), the placement of specific objects in the illustration, or any of the subtleties involved.

Yet as complicated as this may seem, it is important to realize that these are all elements that can be learned. You may have to begin with something as fundamental as shading spheres and cones, or drawing boxes in perspective, but when you have mastered these things, you move on. You learn these things first, not because they are the most interesting or fun things to do, but because they are the foundation for everything you might wish to do. It is only when you have developed a firm grasp on the basics that you can begin to incorporate them into a more satisfying, creative and realistic whole.

Learning to render realistic images is accomplished by observing for yourself how things are perceived, a strong desire to want to learn, and a lot of practise. Ultimately, you learn by doing. However, fantasy art often involves characters that are difficult to observe for yourself, and are usually not discussed in basic art texts. These guidelines for drawing fantasy figures may help you along.

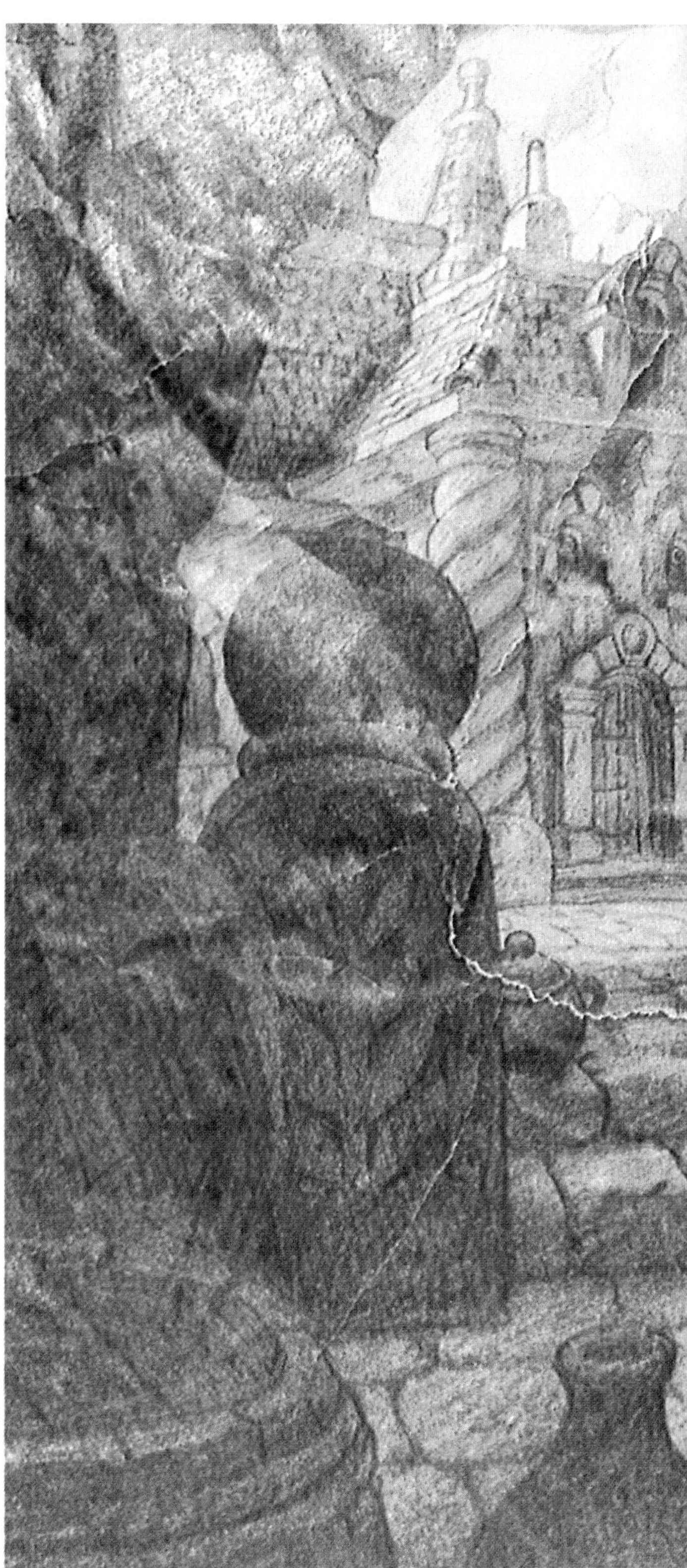

Unpublished finished pencil drawing from *Urshurak,* 1979. Note the *Pinocchio* influence.

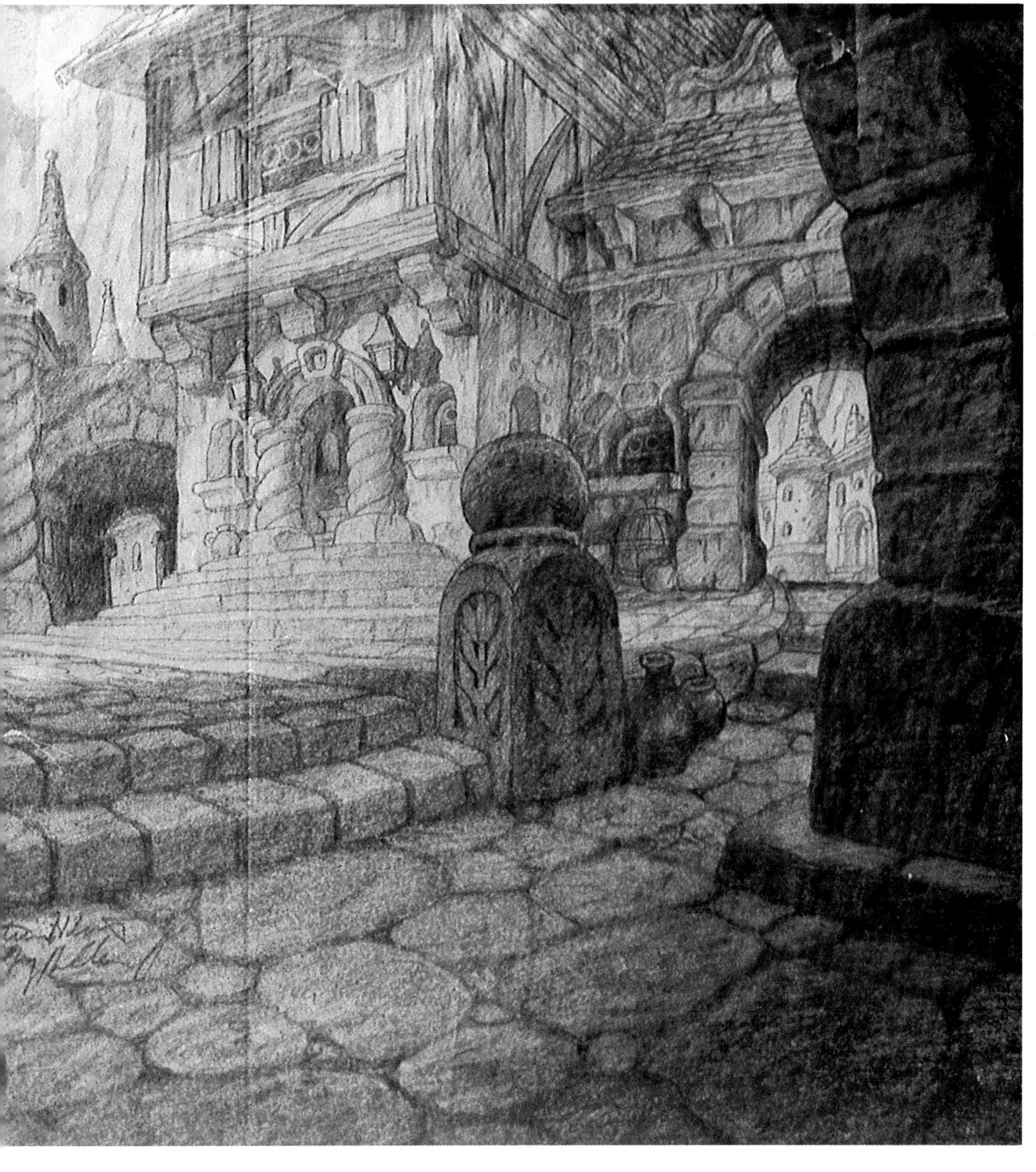

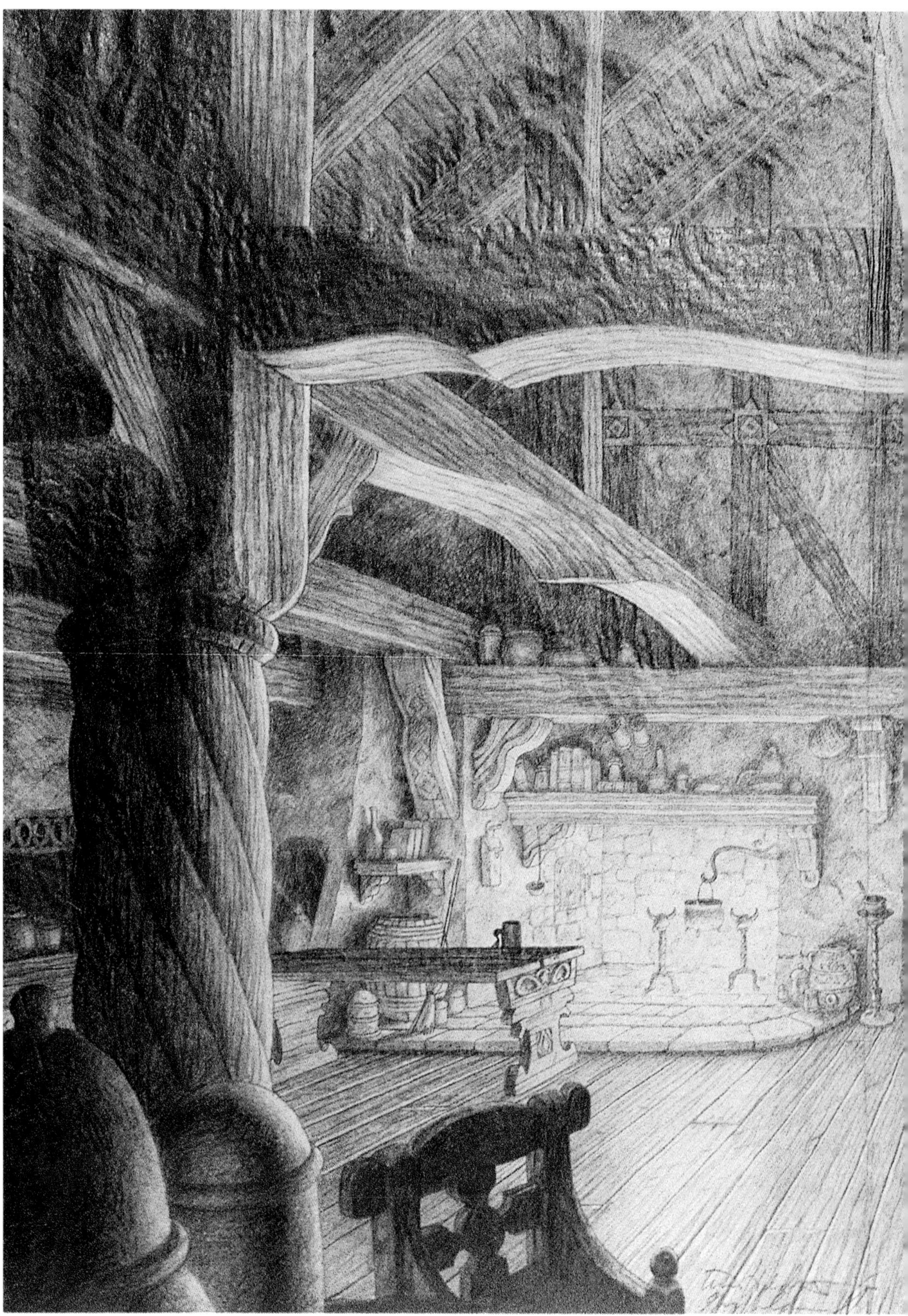

Interior View of Mowdra – Home of Elgan the Wizard
Unpublished finished pencil drawing from *Urshurak*, 1979. Tim: 'Before the writing of the novel *Urshurak* detailed drawings were made so that we would have some idea as to how and where the action should take place.'

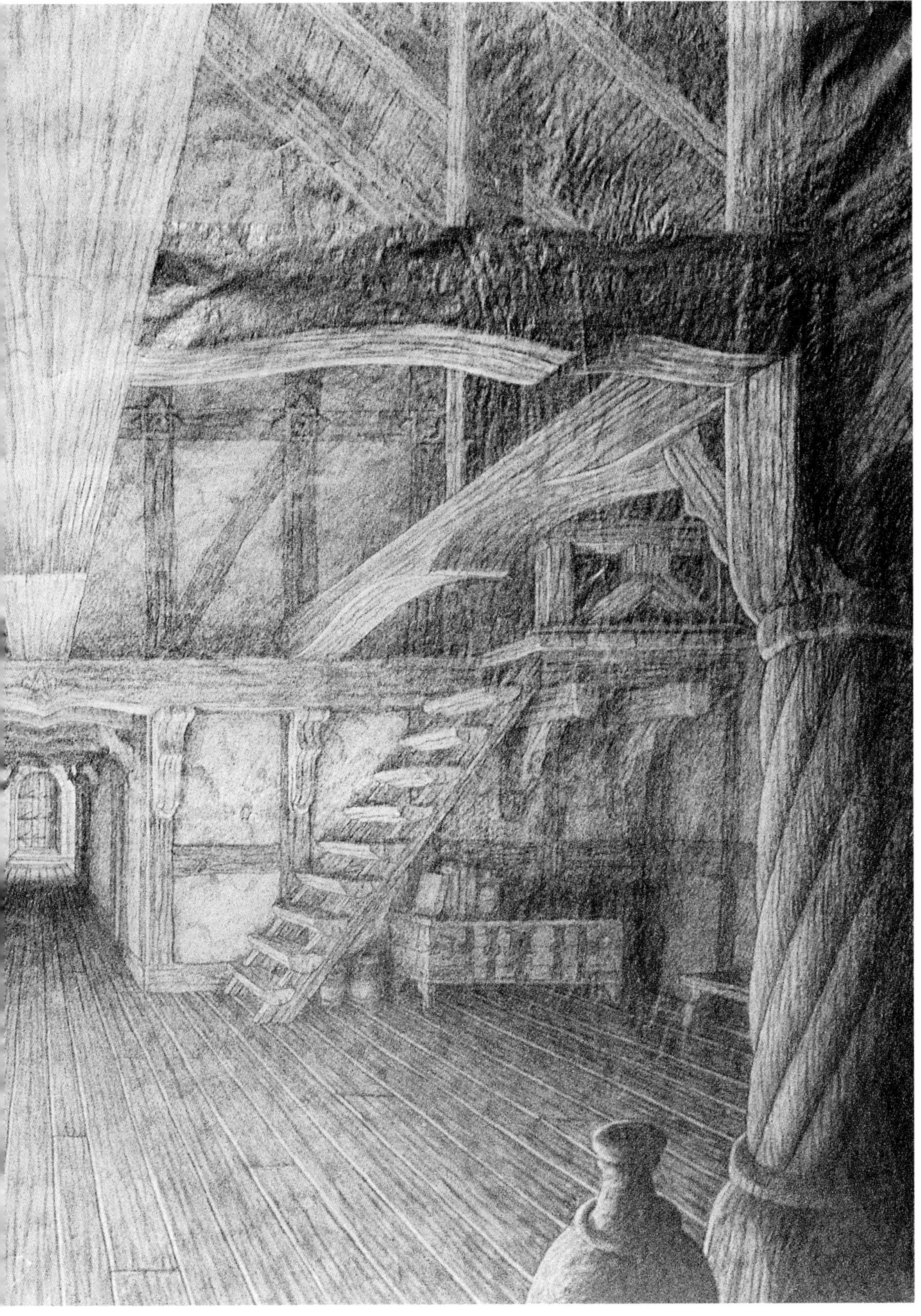

The ideal human figure is eight heads tall, which means that the head makes up one-eighth the height of the body. In reality, most of us are only seven and one-half heads tall. Drawing the figure slightly bigger gives it a larger than life quality that is often desirable in fantasy illustration. This figure is divided in half at the crotch. In our world, this division may vary, influencing how we appear and how we are perceived.

This ideal human figure is the basis for establishing the proportions of other fantasy figures. Dwarves and hobbits are usually four heads tall, though their heads are the same size as human heads. Their bodies are still divided at the crotch, which lies only two heads down on their bodies. Hobbits have a stockier build than most humans, and dwarves are wider still. Elves are somewhat shorter than humans, though proportionately, they are about the same. They also tend to be thinner than humans, and have rather delicate features. A giant is roughly ten heads tall, but once the proportions are established, the head is made smaller. Keep in mind that these are only general guidelines, and some variety should exist among the different characters in a scene.

Pencil drawing is the most fundamental medium found in the category of black and white, and one that all of us have experienced in some way. It is, as we have discovered, a tool for developing your composition, a means to communicate an idea or concept, and sometimes a medium for the final illustration itself. A pencil drawing may have other uses as well, depending on the intent of each individual artist.

A basic rule you should follow is to determine before you begin what your drawing will be used for. Your goals will automatically determine how the scene is rendered, and how much detail you should be concerned with. For example, a thumbnail sketch will establish your basic composition, a rough comp can be sent to an art director for approval, and a final comp can be the basis for future applications. At this point you may want to transfer the drawing to be painted, or position it for inking, or you may continue to render and refine the drawing to use as

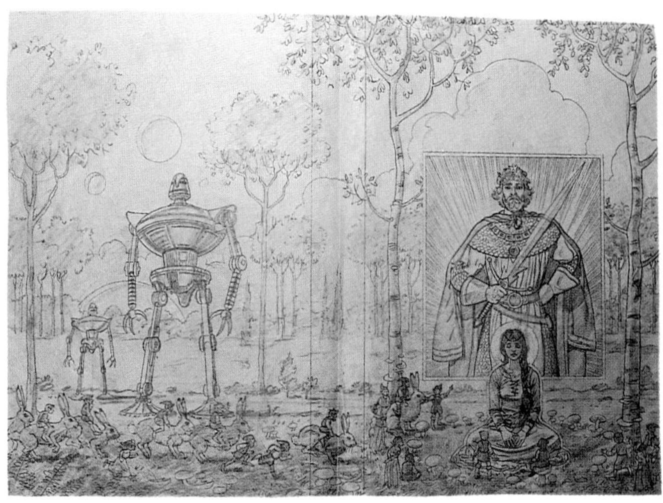

Unused cover sketch for *Fang the Gnome*. Tim: 'Sometimes, art directors aren't sure what they want. For this cover I ended up doing about twenty sketches. To see what the finished painting looked like turn back to page 51.'

RIGHT **The Home of Shandar the Sorcerer**
Finished pencil drawing from *Urshurak*, 1979.
Another example of two-point perspective.

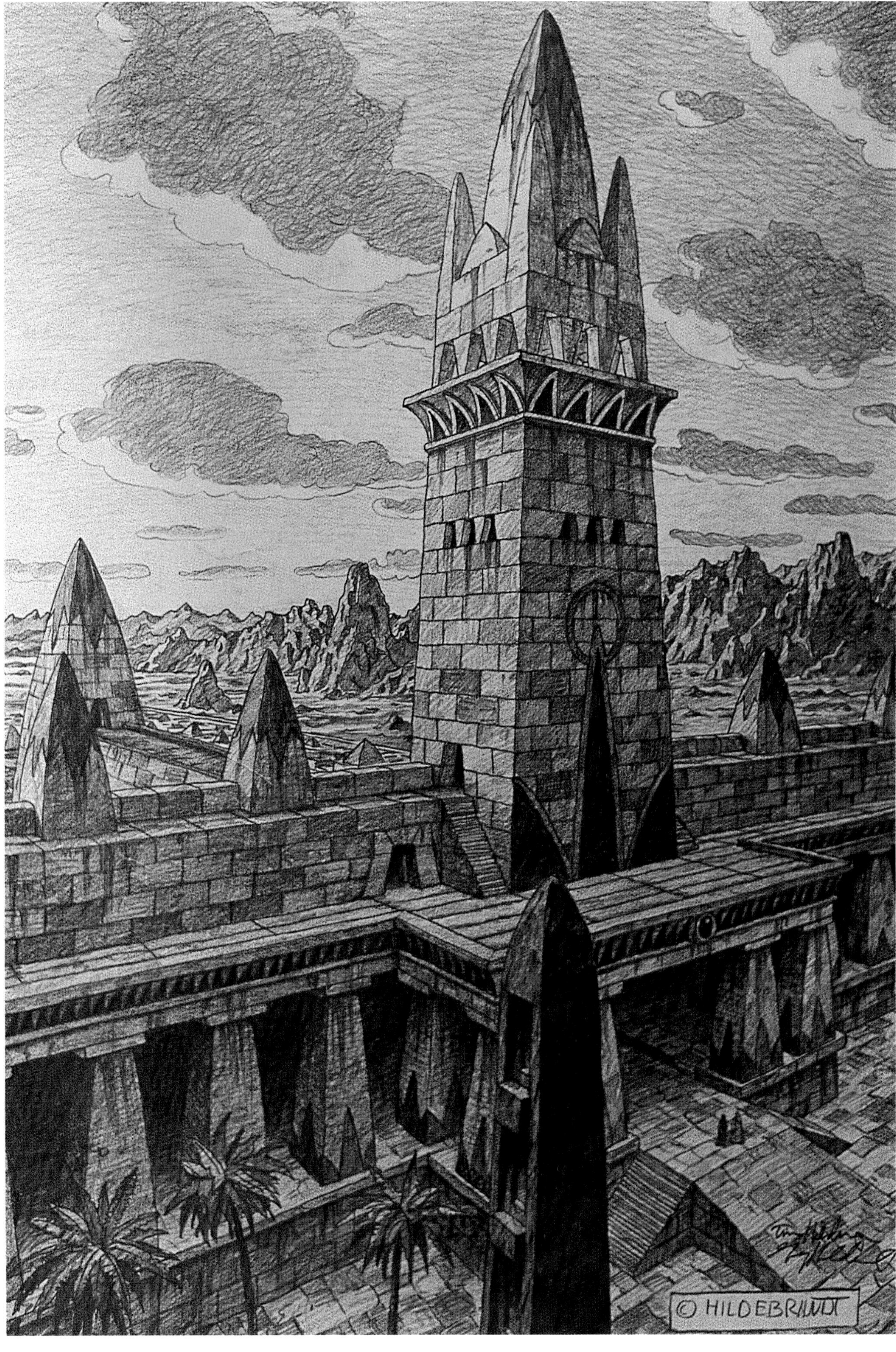
© HILDEBRANDT

Tal-Amon, City of the Azmurians
Finished pencil drawing from *Urshurak*, 1979. A formal composition using one-point perspective. The vanishing point is to be found at the top of the tower close to the horizon line.

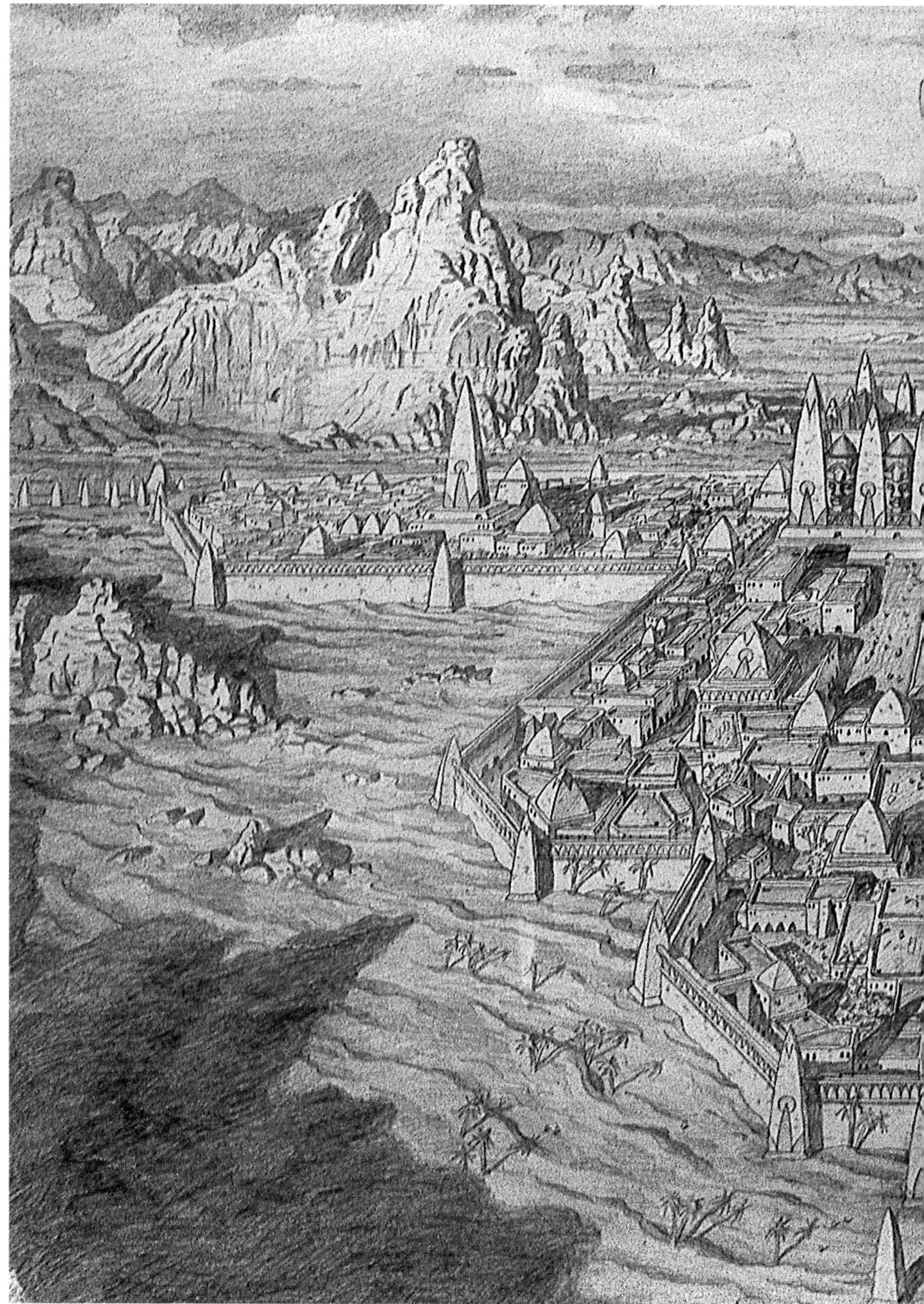

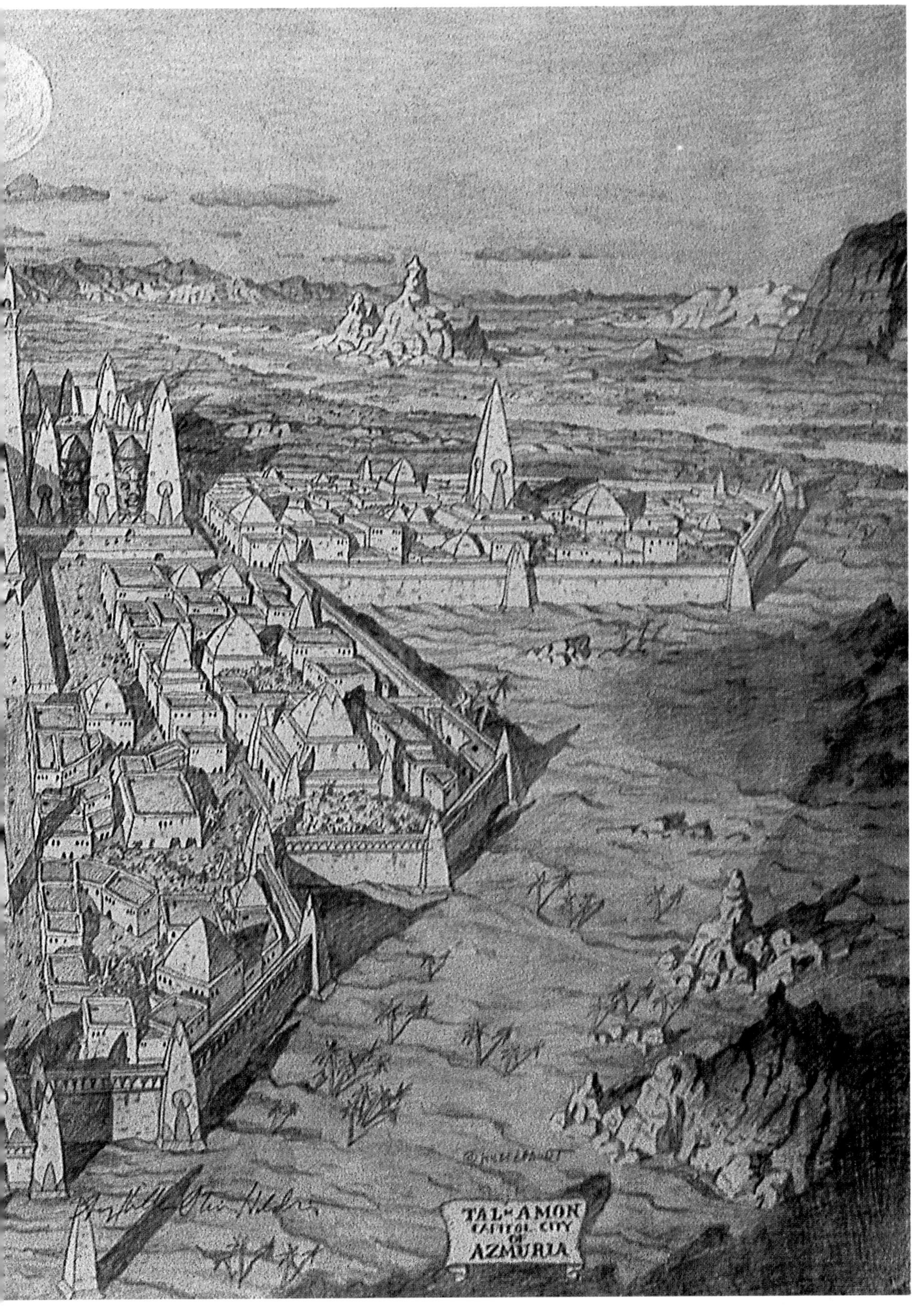
TAL-AMON
CAPITOL CITY
OF
AZMURIA

the final illustration.

One of the advantages of working with pencil is that it is accessible to nearly everyone. You don't need to make a huge investment in supplies in order to draw. A modest assortment of pencils, a selection of drawing paper, and a kneaded eraser are all you need to get started.

Tim uses graded art pencils for most of his drawings. Pencils are graded by the hardness of their lead, which gives them qualities that make them useful for different purposes. The pencils Tim uses range in hardness from 2B to 7H, and Prismacolor Black. The following will give you a quick reference to the different grades of leads, and their potential applications:

B: Pencils in this range have a soft, black lead that smears easily. These pencils produce a thicker line than others, and are useful for rendering foregrounds where the contrast is the greatest. They are sub-graded by number; the higher the number, the softer the lead.

F: Pencils in the F range are harder than the Bs and produce lines that are thinner, and lighter in value. They are more resistant to smearing than any of the Bs. They are useful for rendering objects in the midground where objects are further away and the contrast begins to diminish. Again, they are sub-graded by number.

H: These leads are the hardest of all, producing very light, fine lines that will barely smudge at all. Their values are the lightest, making them useful for rendering the most distant objects in a composition, or for filling in tiny details. The hardest lead that Tim typically uses is a 7H.

Prismacolor Black: This pencil produces an almost pure black line. It is often used to render extremely close objects in the foreground, or other area that requires the highest degree of contrast.

These descriptions only begin to hint at some of the possible applications for each type of pencil, and as you work with them you will probably develop others as well. For instance, drawing a very detailed object in the foreground

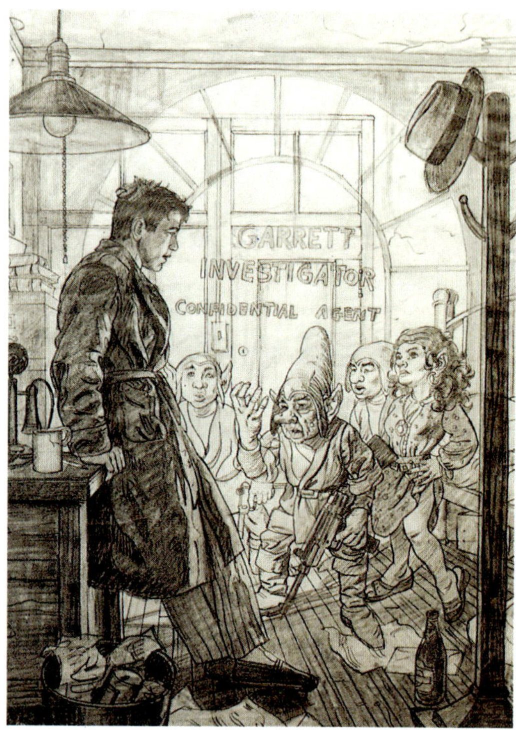

Sweet Silver Blues
Cover sketch for the book by Glenn Cooke, New American Library, 1986. Tim: 'As normal-sized people posed for the dwarves I had to shrink them down to a four-heads height.'

RIGHT **Hugh Oxford's Departure from Vandor**
Finished pencil drawing from *Urshurak*, 1979. Tim: 'This is the first picture in the story. I wanted the figure running from left to right to encourage the reader to turn the page.'

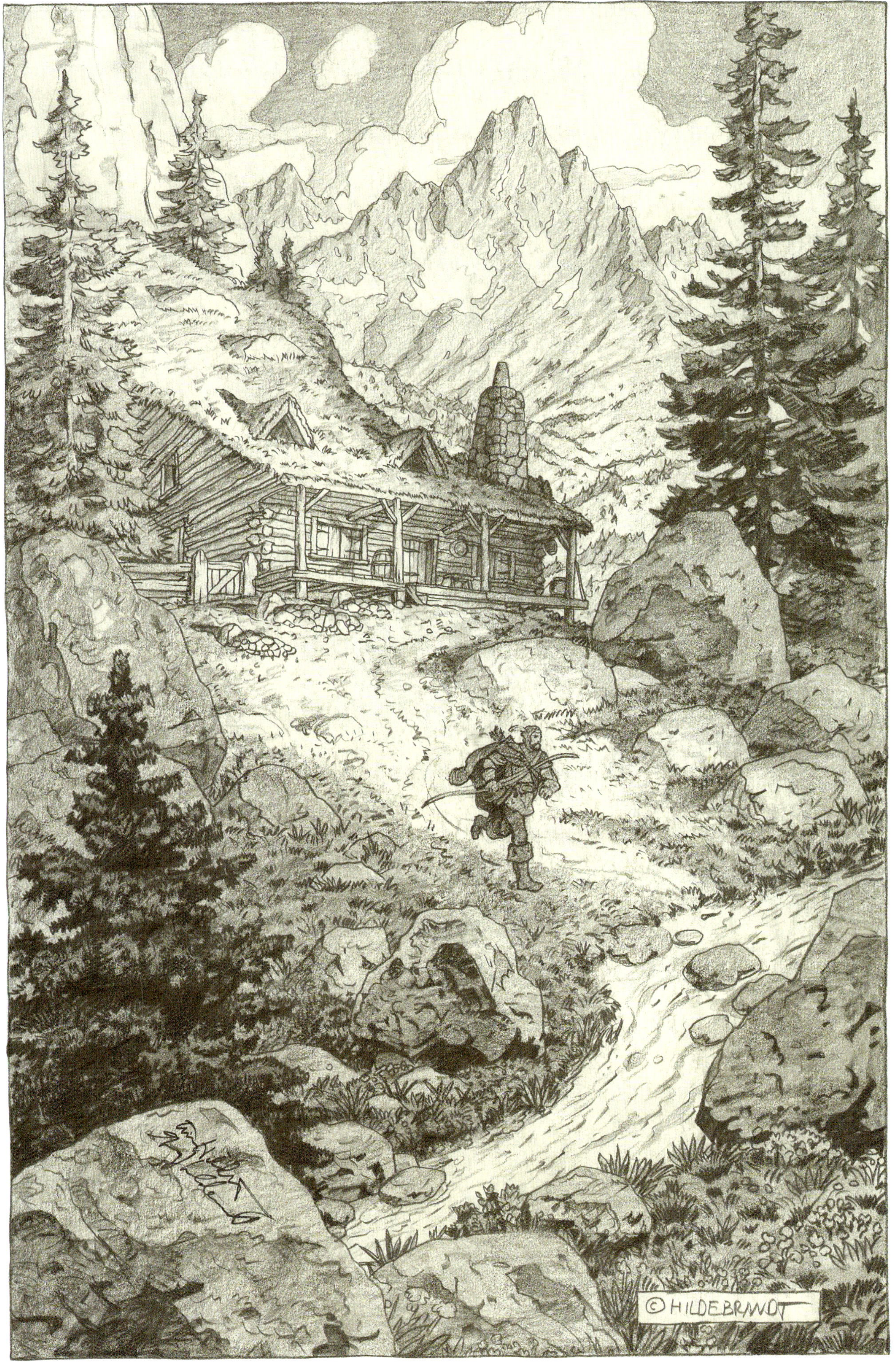
© HILDEBRANDT

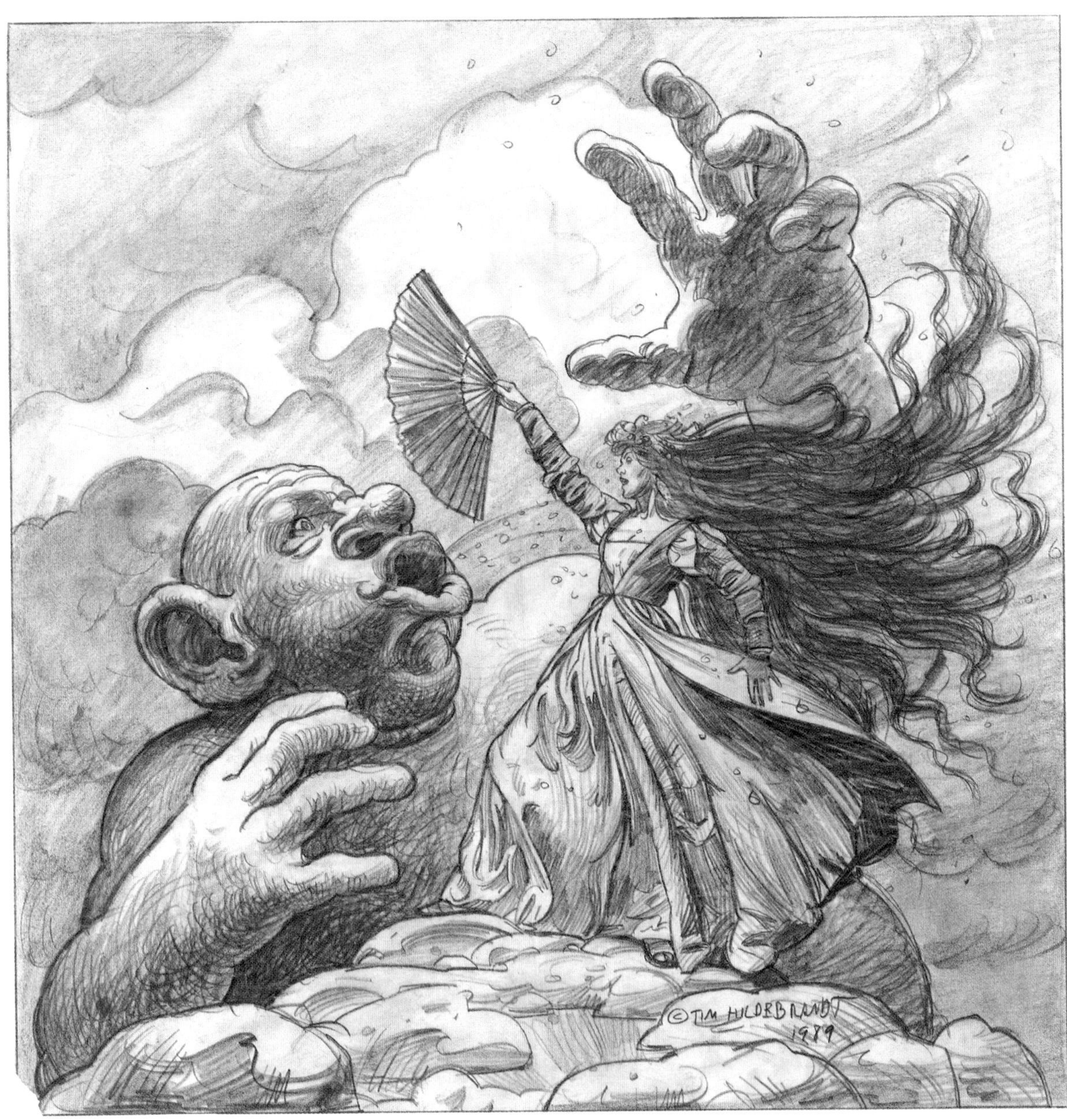

Xanth
Sketch for a calendar by Piers Anthony, 1989.
Tim: 'In posing the model I had a strong fan
blowing her clothes back. I then took a
photograph using a fast shutter speed to capture
the dramatic pose.'

RIGHT **The Worm Oroborus**
Finished cover sketch, 1990. Tim: 'I have many
bird books in my library. Luckily, I found a good
picture of a hawk landing. Fortunately it was lit the
way I wanted.'

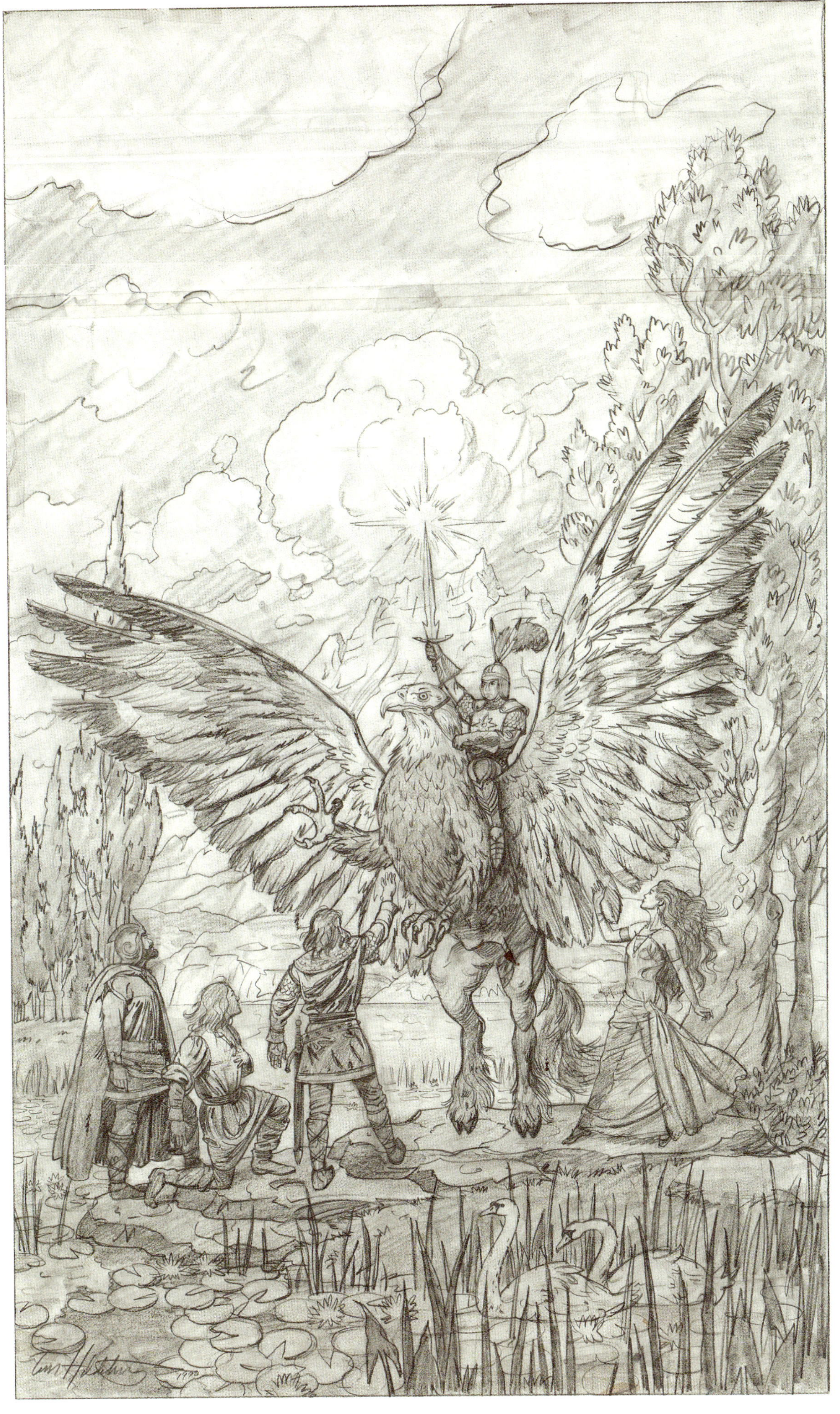

might be accomplished by first rendering the mass of the object with a softer lead, then filling in the detail with increasingly harder leads.

The realism you are able to capture when rendering objects in pencil depends entirely on your understanding of the basics. Despite the different grades and possible uses of pencil leads, they give you essentially only two tools: line and shade. Lines are used to define an object, and shadows are created by filling in the lines, smudging the lines with your finger, or both. Given these limitations, Tim cryptically notes that when rendering images 'everything is the same, but different'. The translation is that when rendering objects, the technique used for everything is identical: identifying the mass, detailing, smudging and erasing. It is how you apply those techniques that define what the object really is.

In addition to pencils, the artist needs a drawing surface. The paper can be any good, smooth drawing paper. Tim rarely uses textured papers, unless he is trying to achieve a certain effect. The paper he chooses is determined by what the drawing is to be used for.

For thumbnail sketches, Tim works on any paper that is available at the moment. Since the chief value of a thumbnail sketch is in capturing basic shapes, lighting and direction of the composition, he usually gives little thought to what paper is being used. He has often worked out thumbnails while away from his studio on paper scraps, the backs of envelopes, and even paper napkins, when nothing else was available.

Most of the rough comps developed by Tim are the basis for a painting, so once again the choice of paper is not really critical. He does have certain preferences that work within his system, and most rough comps, clean-up drawings and final comps are drawn on a large pad of artist's tracing paper. The brand is unimportant, so long as the paper is strong and smooth. For drawings that will serve as the final illustration, any smooth, high quality drawing paper will work.

Tim's first concerns are to establish the picture plane, and to find the exact centre of that shape. His thumbnail

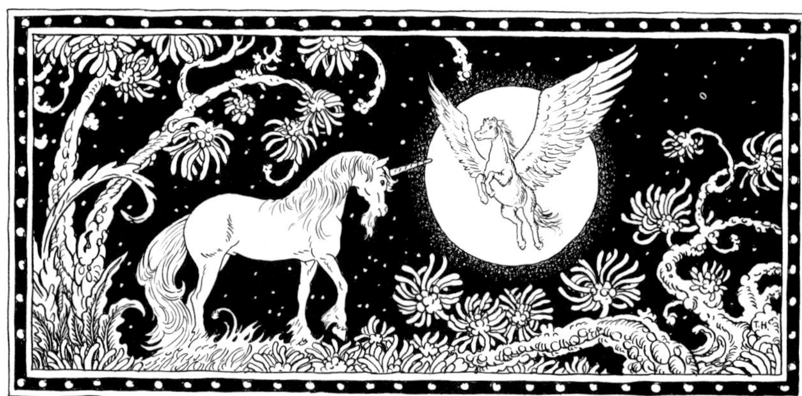

TOP **Valley of the Unicorn**
Pen and ink drawing from *The Fantasy Cookbook* by Rita and Tim Hildebrandt, published by Bobbs-Merrill, 1983.

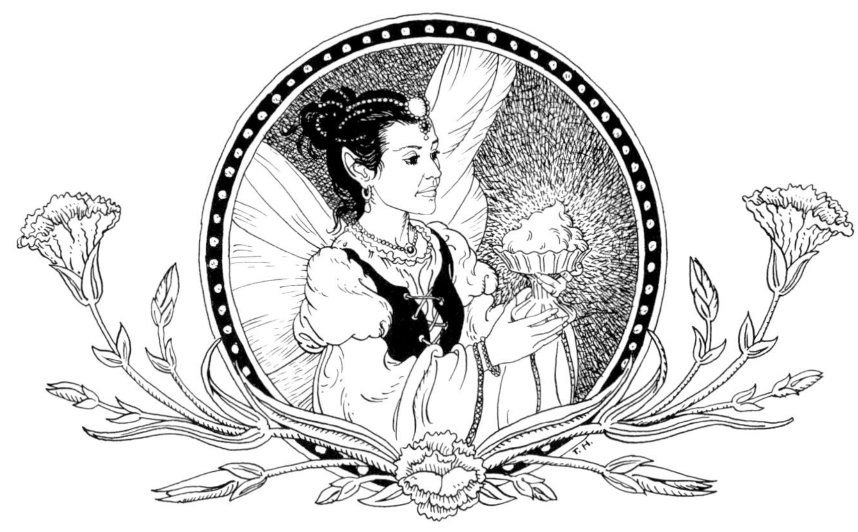

BELOW **The Fairies**
Pen and ink drawing from *The Fantasy Cookbook*, 1983.

RIGHT **The Amazons**
Pen and ink drawing from *The Fantasy Cookbook*, 1983.

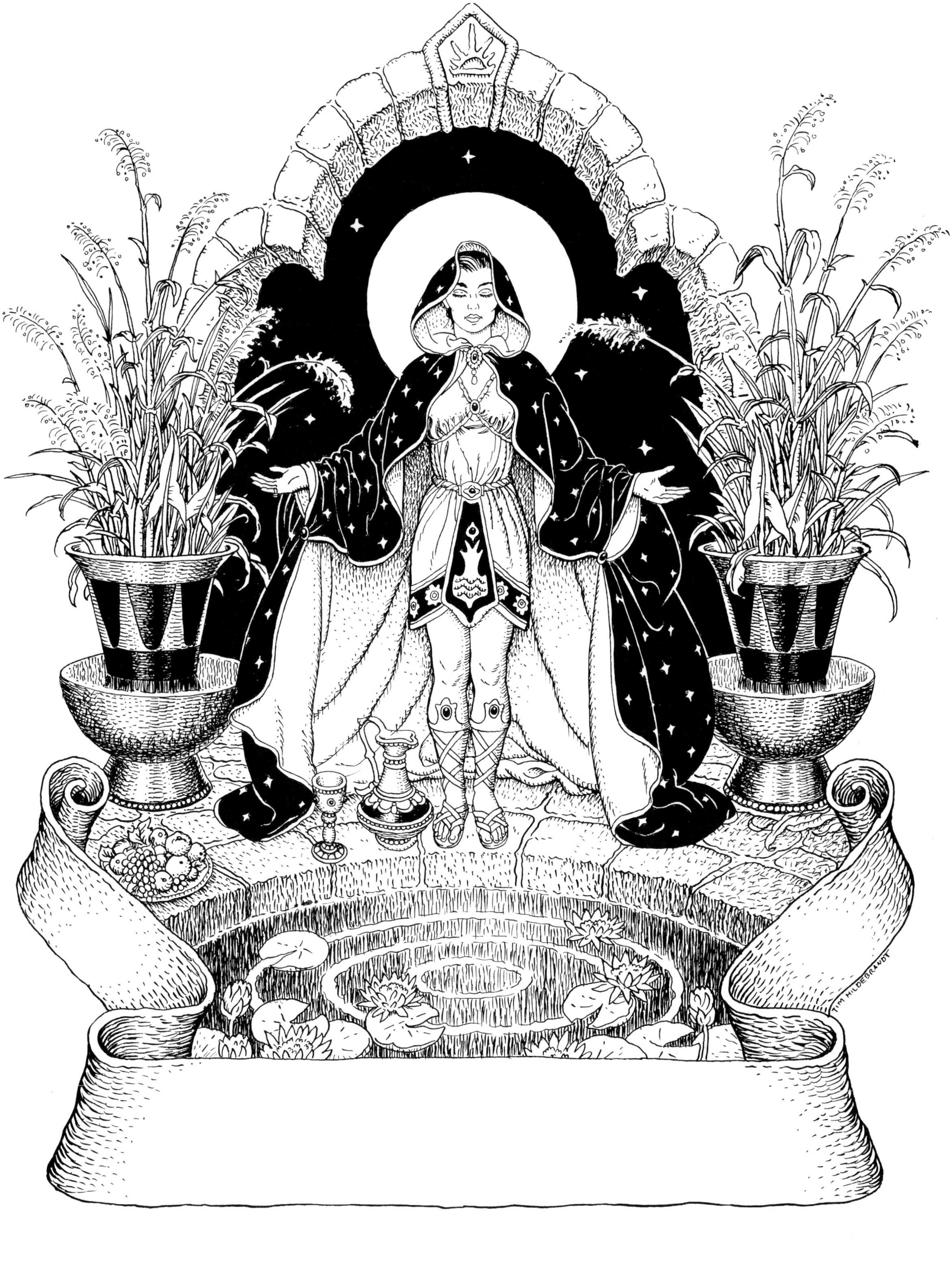

sketch then serves as a guide for roughing in the main elements of his composition. At this point, he is still concerned mostly with shapes and lighting, although he does begin to work on some details of the major objects.

Tim then collects all of the required reference material, and places a clean sheet of tracing paper over the rough comp. Nothing is actually traced, however. The rough comp, together with the reference material, serve only as guides to where objects are placed in the composition. Images are rendered in more detail, and changes are made if necessary. This process of 'cleaning-up' the drawing may be done several different times before Tim achieves a satisfactory final comp.

When working with pencil, mistakes are corrected by simply erasing them. Tim uses a kneaded eraser, which is soft and pliable, and lifts lead from the page without leaving bothersome eraser shavings. These shavings can be more than a nuisance, as they might cause unwanted smudging when you brush them away. Kneaded erasers can also be shaped to fill a variety of special needs. For example, you could twist the tip of a kneaded eraser to a point, then lift a tiny dot of lead from the page. This dot might serve as a final highlight for a character's eye or a star in a night scene.

The applications of a kneaded eraser are limitless. You can use it to lightly lift lead from around the moon during a night scene, creating a gradual blend of values there, and to soften the edges of clouds in the sky. To render hair, you might first draw a grey mass, then stroke the kneaded eraser in the direction that the hair would flow. You would then pencil a few strokes over those highlights in the same direction to finish. Grass can be created in the same way. The number of possible uses is only limited by the imagination of the artist.

Pen and ink is another medium that can be used to produce a black and white illustration. It is also very demanding, and requires as much effort to develop a good technique as painting. Pen and ink is an exercise in bringing order from chaos. However, the absolute quality of stark black on white makes it well worth the effort.

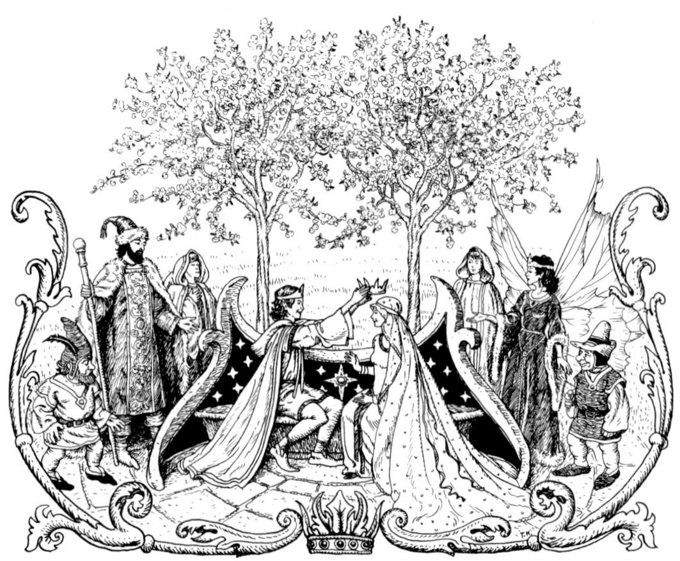

Crowning a new Elf Princess
Pen and ink drawing from *The Fantasy Cookbook*,
1983.

RIGHT, ABOVE **Amazon Tournament**
Pen and ink drawing from *The Fantasy Cookbook*,
1983

RIGHT, BELOW **Amazon Musicians at the Oasis**
Pen and ink drawing from *The Fantasy Cookbook*,
1983.

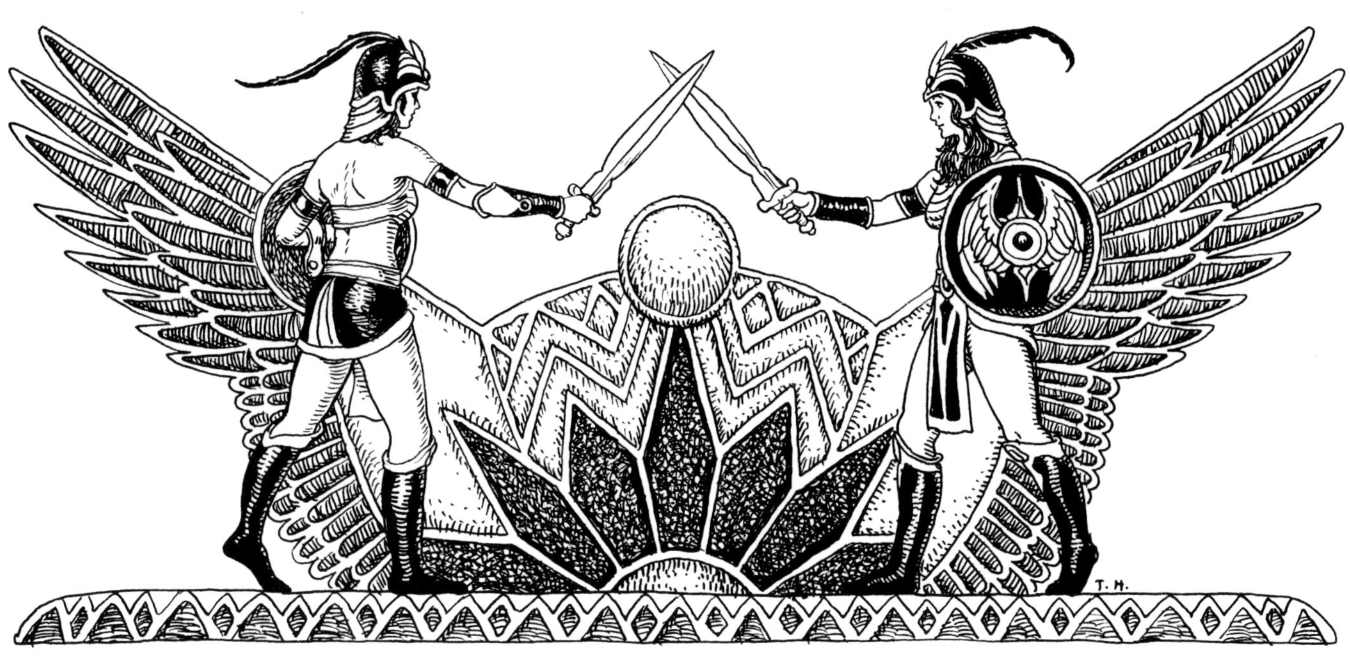

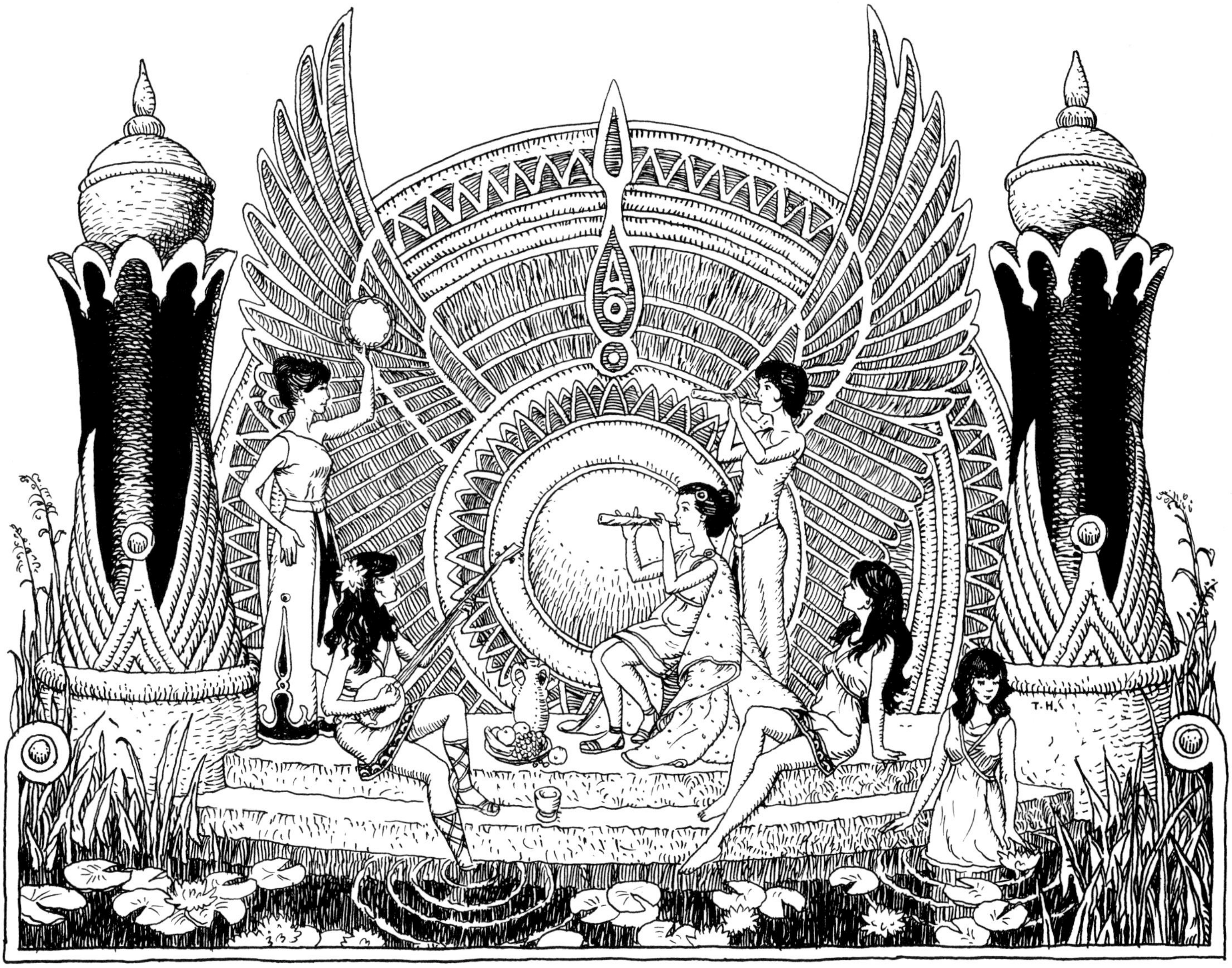

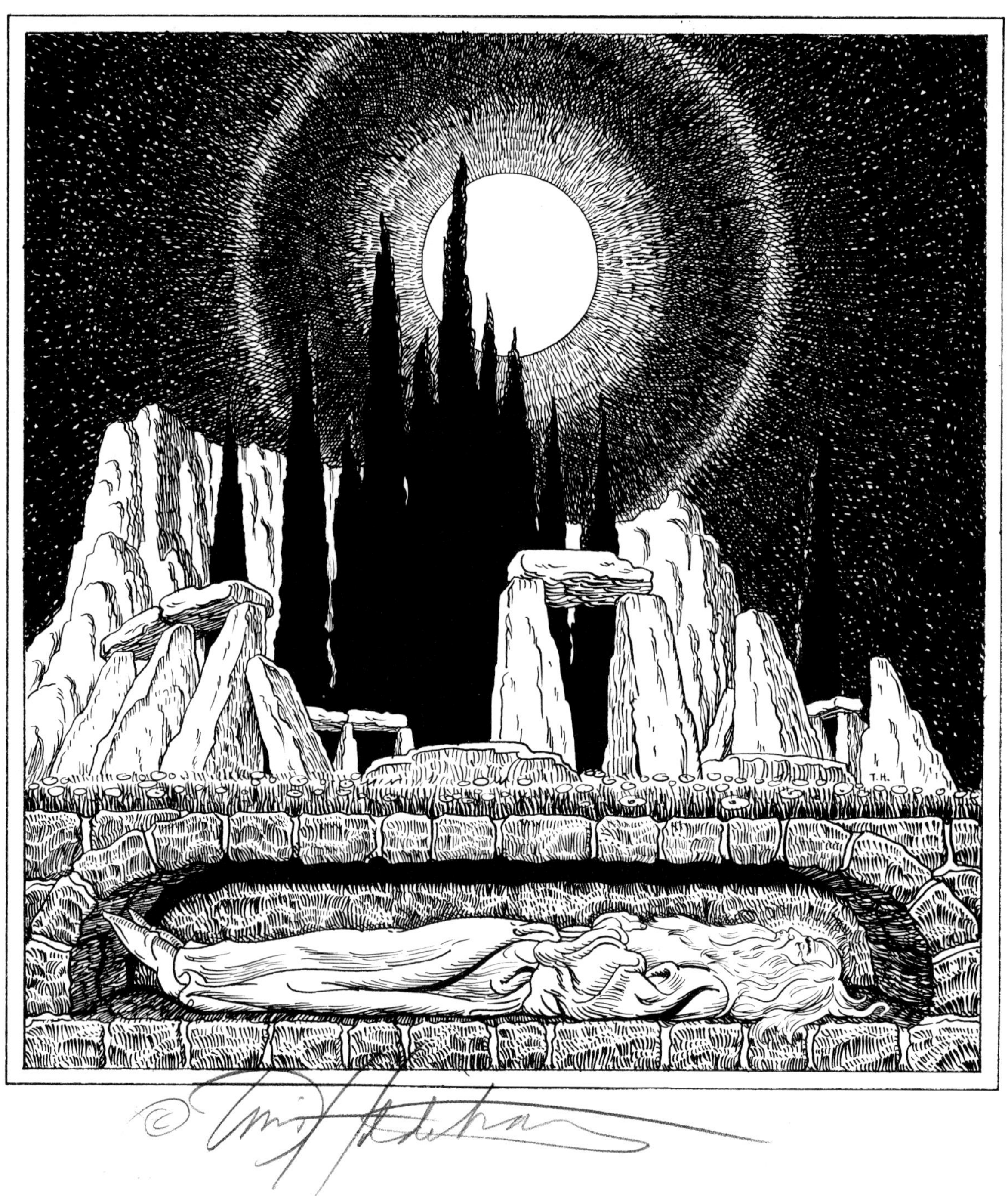

The Great One Sleeps
Pen and ink drawing from *Merlin and the Dragons
of Atlantis* by Rita and Tim Hildebrandt, 1983.

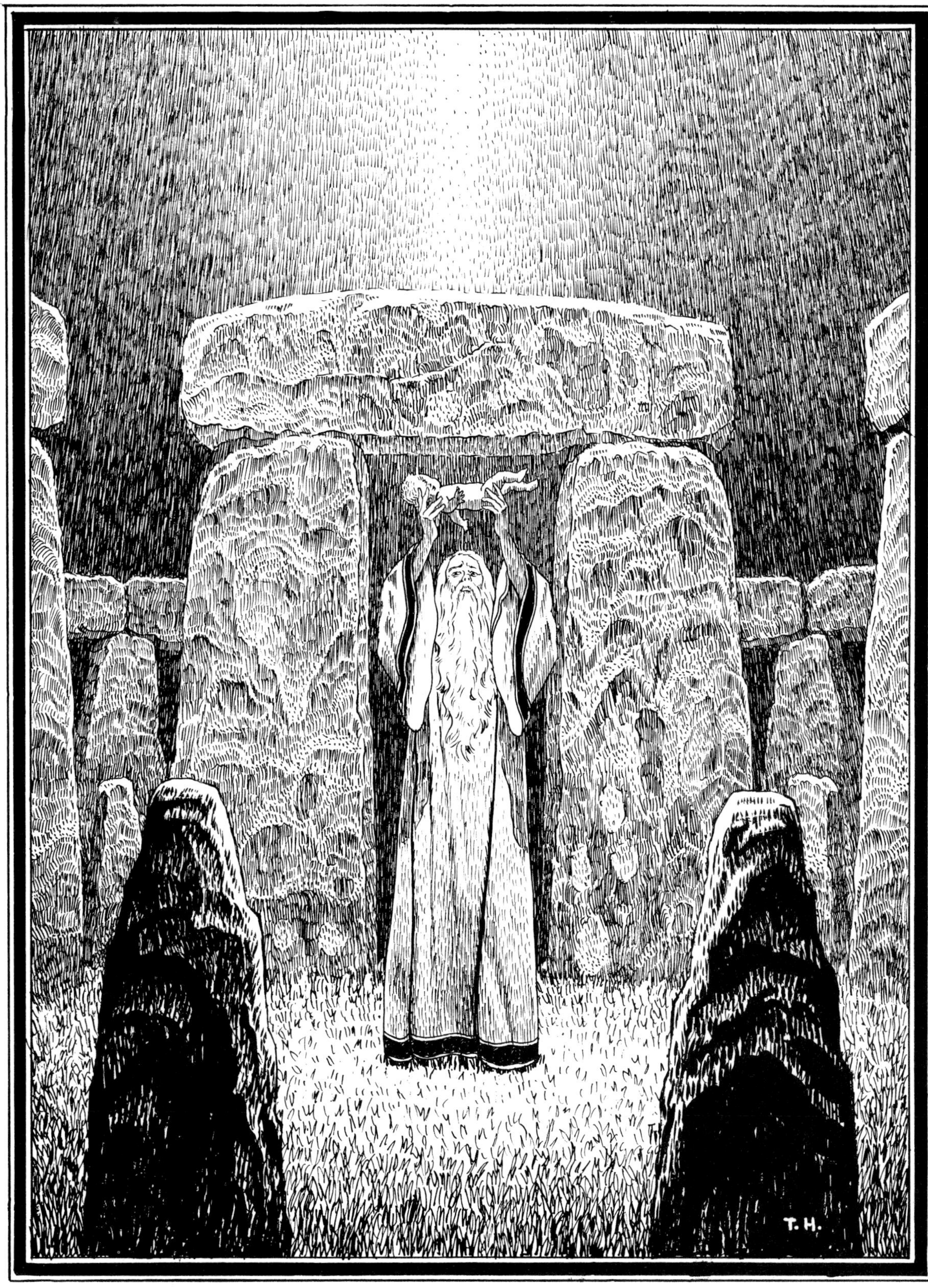

Rebirth
Pen and ink drawing from *Merlin and the Dragons of Atlantis*, 1983.

All of the principles involved in working with other mediums apply evenly here. Composition, shapes, highlights and shadow are all involved, but applied in a simpler way. Tim usually uses only one light source in a pen and ink design, and the drawings themselves tend to be simpler. Subtleties are lost in pen and ink due to its absolute nature. To compensate, pen and ink renderings usually take on a more graphic, designed or decorative look.

The indelible nature of ink on paper leaves no margin for error. In order to avoid mistakes, Tim first renders a very fine pencil drawing to serve as a guide. Instead of transferring the drawing to the inking surface, Tim places the drawing on a light box, and covers it with a sheet of 1-ply Strathmore illustration paper. The design is then rendered in ink, either by pen, brush or a combination of both.

As a rule, Tim usually fills in any large, black areas first. This is done with a brush. The detail is then applied with any number of cross hatching or dot techniques.

Cross hatching is simply a series of overlapping pen and ink lines that are used to create shadows or texture. There are as many cross hatching techniques as there are artists, so it is best if you develop you own. Dots are sometimes used in place of lines; shadow and texture is determined by the closeness of the dots. The technique is often referred to as stippling. Whether you cross hatch or stipple, remember that it is the application of technique that produces realism, not the technique itself.

Tim uses either a crow quill pen or a round, pointed brush to apply the ink, although he finds the pen much easier to control. The advantage of using a brush lies in the freedom to manipulate the thickness of the line. This is controlled by increasing or decreasing the pressure exerted on the brush.

Pen and ink places enormous demands on the artist, yet it is one of the most dramatic of the black and white mediums. If you are just learning don't expect instant success. Like anything else it can be learned through much practise.

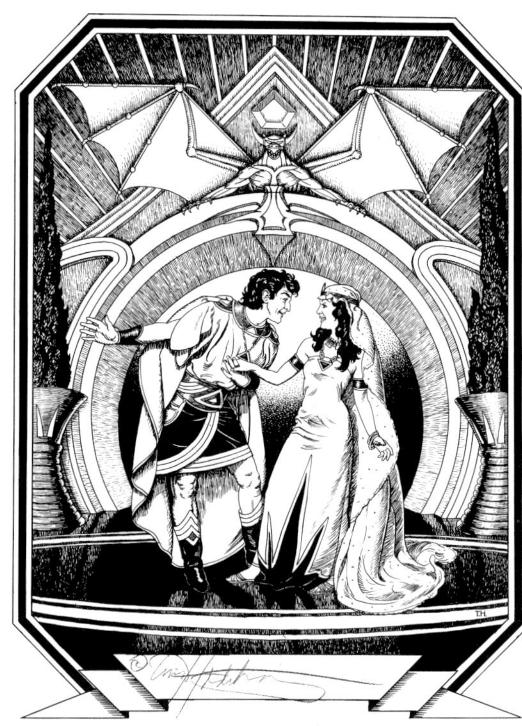

Merlin and MaReenie
Pen and ink drawing from *Merlin and the Dragons of Atlantis*, 1983.

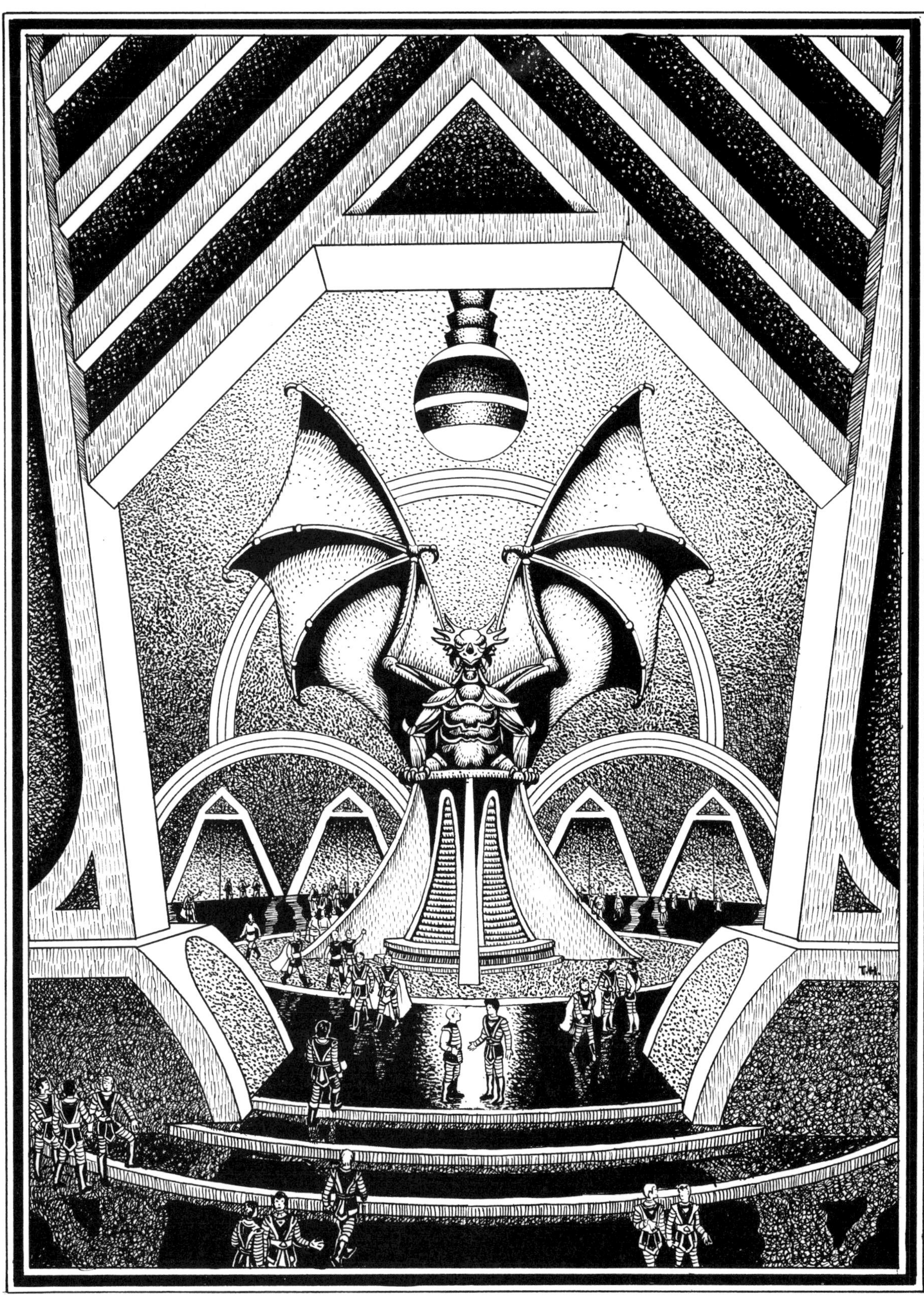

Alta
Pen and ink drawing from *Merlin and the Dragons of Atlantis*, 1983.

Occasionally, Tim might be presented with a somewhat unusual request: an art director needs a painting for an illustration, ultimately to be reproduced in black and white. Rather than go through the effort involved in rendering a colour painting, Tim finds it much easier to render the painting in black and white. He follows the same step-by-step process used for every other medium. First, a scene is selected, or an idea thought out. A thumbnail sketch is made, taking into consideration the picture plane, lighting scheme and object placement. A rough comp is then rendered and resource materials are gathered. A clean-up drawing is made, which ultimately leads to a final composition. At this point the picture may be fully rendered in pencil or pen and ink, or transferred to another surface to be painted.

It would be pointless to try to discuss specific painting techniques here since the techniques for all painting are described fully in the following chapter. Instead, there are certain characteristics unique to black and white that deserve special attention.

To begin with, black and white painting deals only with light and dark values. As with other black and white mediums, this means that your composition and characters must be powerful enough to command the scene in the total absence of colour. You only need a single palette, with values that range from the lightest light to the darkest dark. The opposite is true of pure white; most objects in a scene are shaded to some degree, and pure white is generally reserved for only the brightest highlights. A possible exception to this rule is when the scene calls for an object to appear as though it is glowing. These objects must always appear brighter than everything else in the scene in order to appear realistic. Lighter values are always painted over darker values, gradually bringing the highlights of an object out from the shadows.

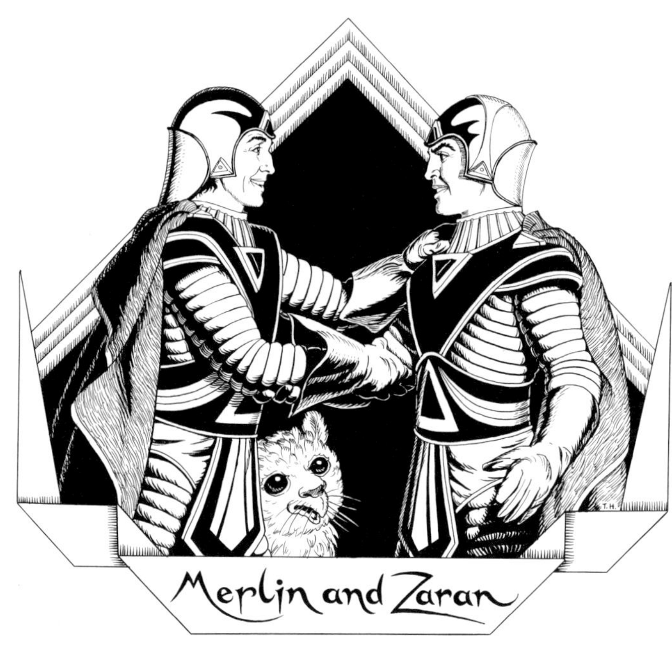

Merlin and Zaran
Pen and ink drawing from *Merlin and the Dragons of Atlantis*, 1983.

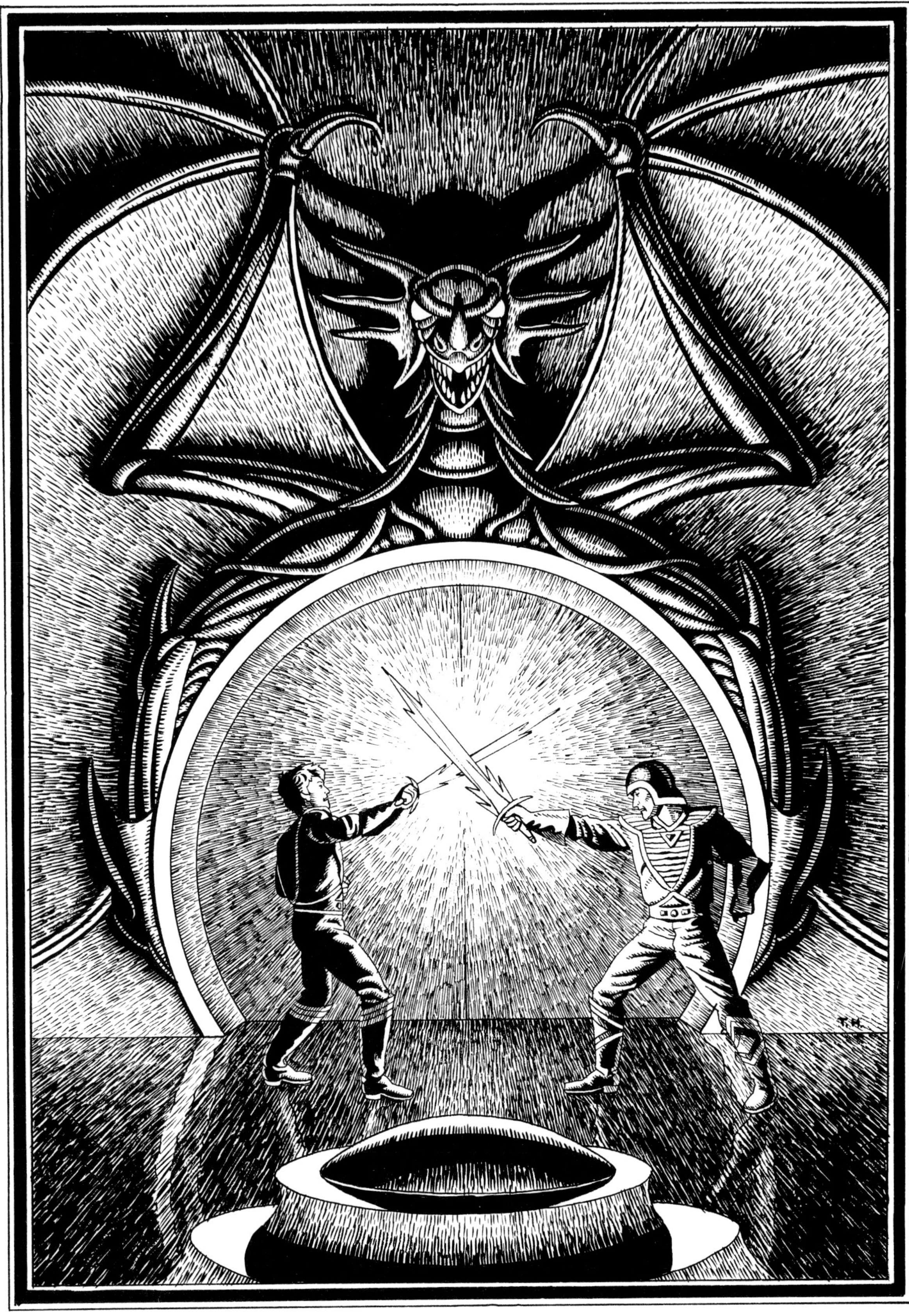

Merlin and Zaran Duel
Pen and ink drawing from *Merlin and the Dragons
of Atlantis*, 1983.

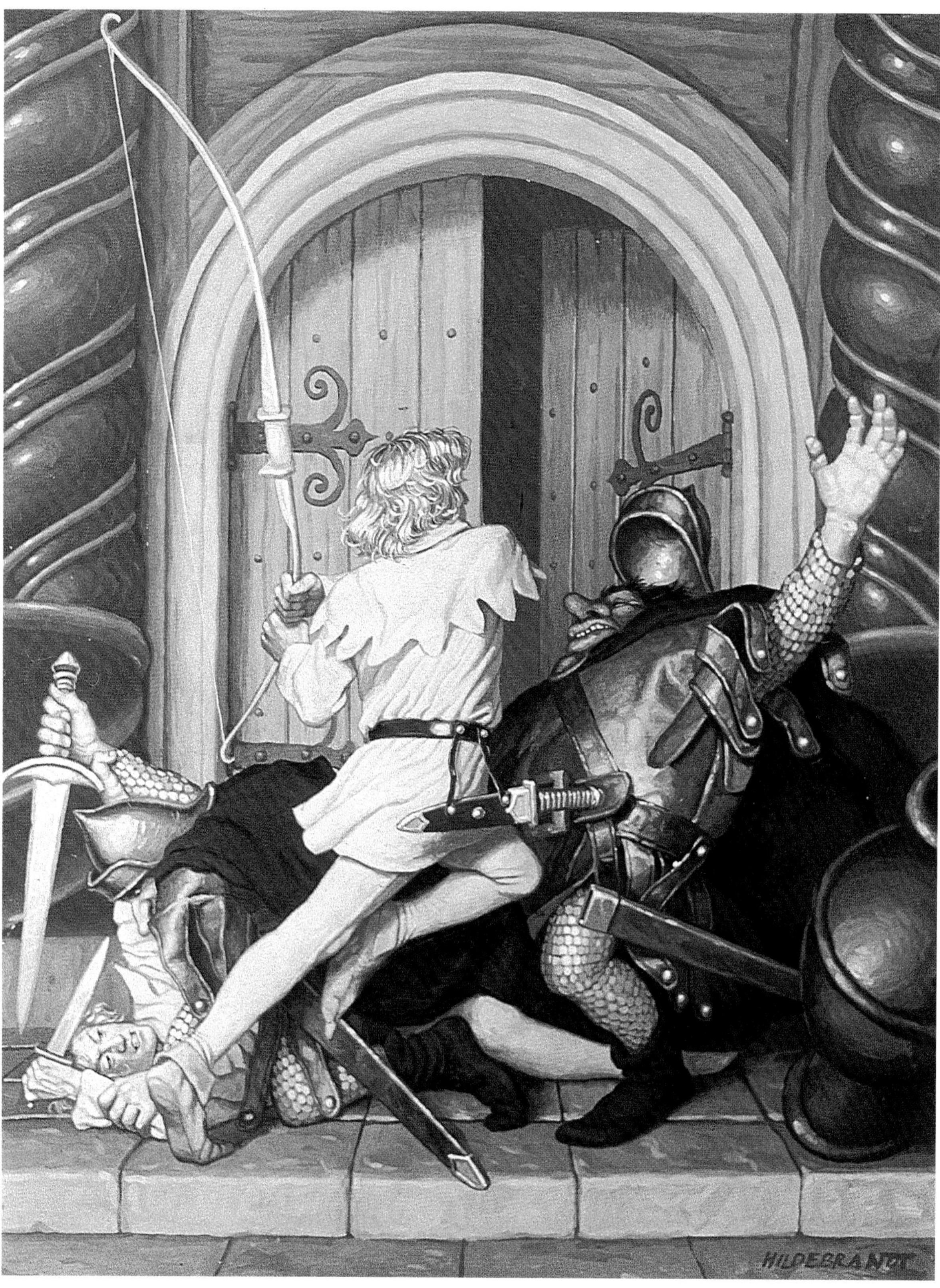

Black and white painting from *The Sword of Shannara*, Ballantine Books, 1977, acrylic on masonite.

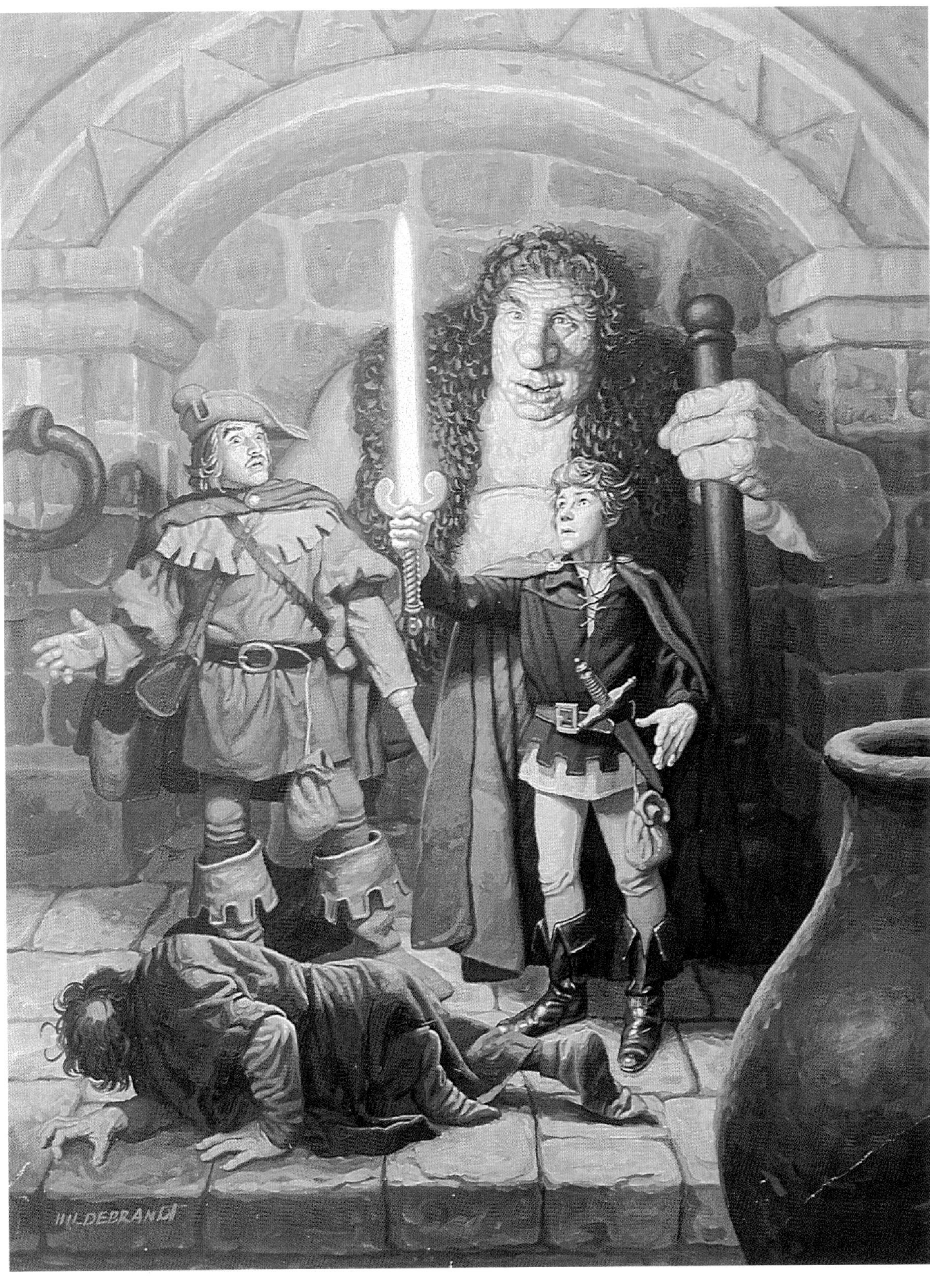

Black and white painting from *The Sword of Shannara*, Ballantine Books, 1977, acrylic on masonite.

Black and white as a whole is a creative outlet often overlooked by beginning artists who don't really understand its value. They might see colour as the only true creative form. However, the usefulness and versatility of black and white is only overshadowed by the stark drama it can create, which makes it a medium worth discovering.

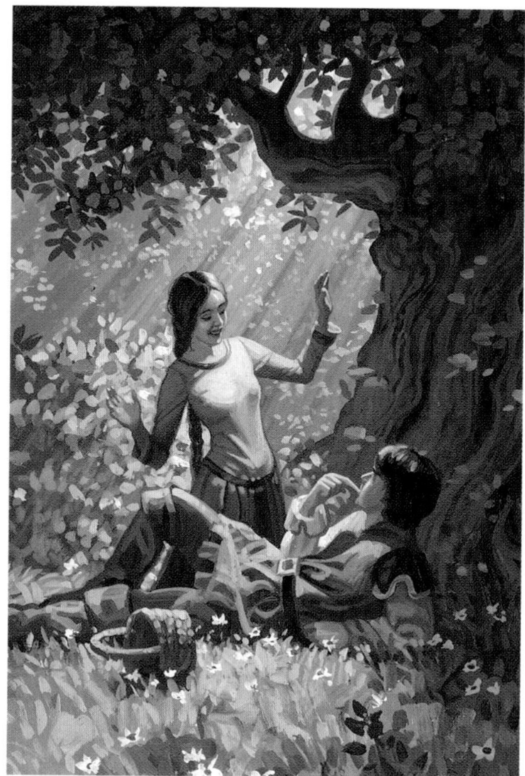

Two black and white paintings from *The Unicorn Treasury*, Doubleday, 1987, both acrylic on masonite.

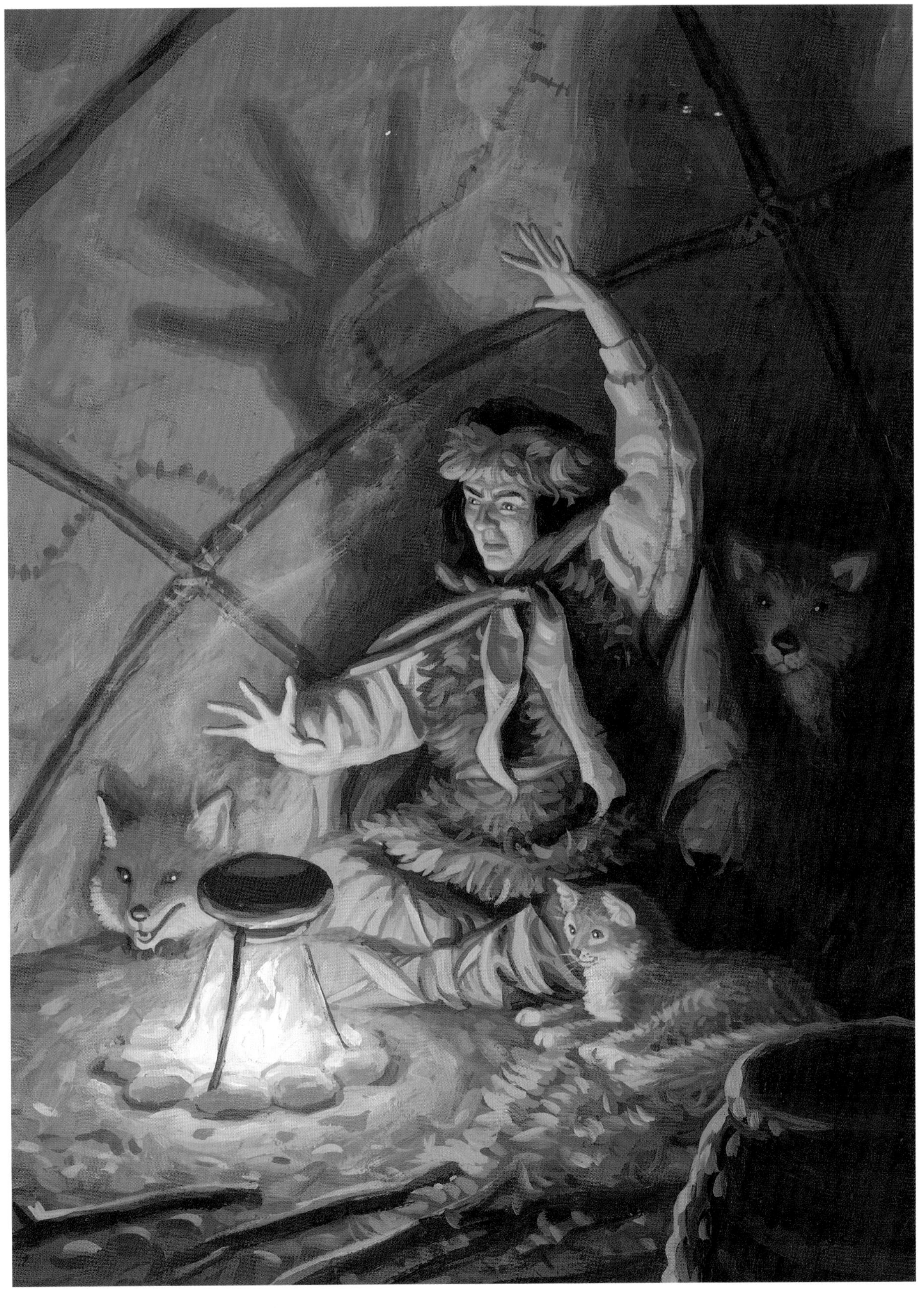

Painting & Colour

Without a doubt, it is the illusion of life that Tim Hildebrandt is able to capture in a composition that makes his paintings so remarkable. Yet it is only an illusion produced by a specific process involved in every medium he works in. Perhaps the most important implication of this is that with practise anyone can learn to utilize these techniques. The only 'gift' involved is the intense desire and dedication it takes to motivate you when you feel like giving up.

Rendering a painting in colour is only an extension of the processes that have been described elsewhere in this book. From this point on everything is just as systematic as before, with nothing left to chance. However, you should keep in mind that the specific methods discussed in this chapter are secondary to the painting as a whole. Technique should never become an end in itself.

There are several fundamental principles involving nature and perception that Tim observes when painting any composition. These rules are the foundation for rendering any object in colour and, to some extent, black and white. If you are hoping to achieve realism in your own paintings it is crucial you apply these rules evenly throughout your composition.

In nature, *objects in the distance have less contrasting values than objects in the foreground.* This is largely due to the fact that we are looking through many more layers of atmosphere than we do when we observe objects that are close to us. As a result, the objects appear to be more monochromatic with little contrast.

In part, this effect is simulated by painting the most distant objects in a composition first. In an outdoor scene this is usually the sky. The next most distant objects are then rendered, which in this case could be the clouds. Everything in the midground is then painted, followed by the foreground. Except for distant characters in the background, figures are always painted last. Every object on every level is rendered completely before Tim moves on to the next.

To complete this effect, Tim must render distant objects with values that are less contrasting than objects

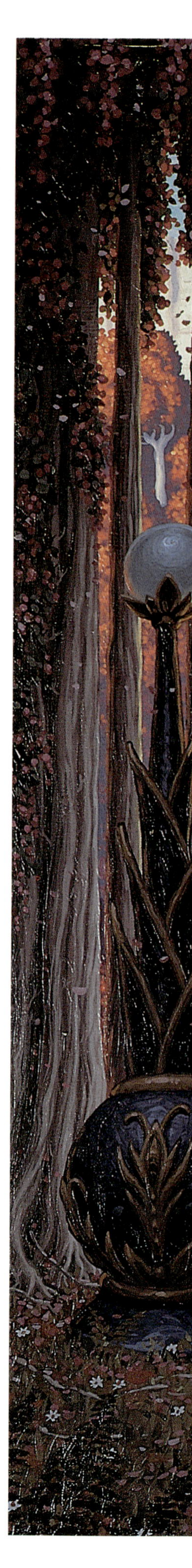

Elven Council
Illustration from the *Realms of Wonder* calendar, TSR, 1983, acrylic on masonite. Tim: 'In the distance there is a warm light – the shadows are therefore cool. The foreground is in shadow so the highlights are cool and the shadows, lit from the blue sky, are warm.'

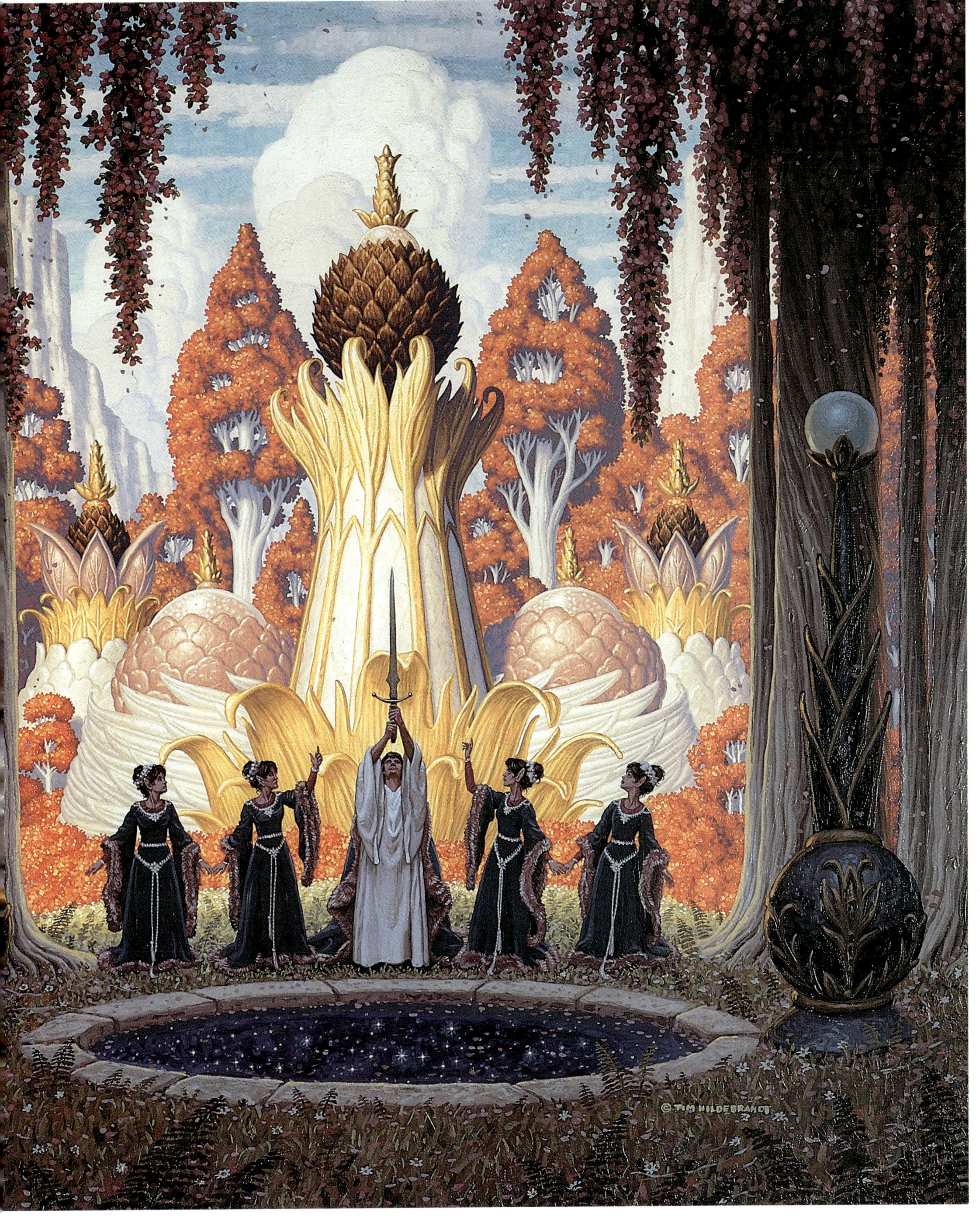

in the foreground. Distant objects in a scene would appear to be more blue. Notice that this is a gradual effect; only objects in the extreme foreground are seen with perfect clarity.

Another major rule of painting in colour greatly affects the actual colours you will use to render a scene. This rule states that *the light source always determines how a colour will appear in any scene.* For example, in a night scene in which a flaming torch is used for a primary source of light a white dress would not be rendered in white. Instead, it would take on the orange and yellow tones of the fire. A red cloak under moonlight would be rendered more purple than red due to the addition of blue light from the moon. Yet, in context with the painting as a whole, the white dress actually appears to be white and the red cloak appears to be red.

Determining how the light source affects all of the colours in the scene is not a random process. You must first determine what the source of light is. Next, you must decide how the colour white would appear *under those lighting conditions.* White is a neutral colour and is useful for comparison. Once the 'correct' colour for white is established, the same tones that were added to white to correct it are added to all the other colours in the scene. In the bluish light of the moon, green would be rendered bluegreen, yellow would take on a greenish tone and so on. Yet in relation to all of the other elements of the painting these colours will appear correct.

In addition to correcting the colours of a scene you must also be concerned with value. A value is the relative lightness or darkness of a given colour. Values are established by taking the absolute colour of an object to its highest highlight and its darkest dark. At the same time, you're still concerned with the correctness of the colour under the given lighting situation. Take, for example, the white dress being lit by the torch. You might start with a middle value of raw sienna and white as the absolute value of white under those conditions. The next higher value would be cadmium yellow medium, and proceed to a final highlight of cadmium yellow light.

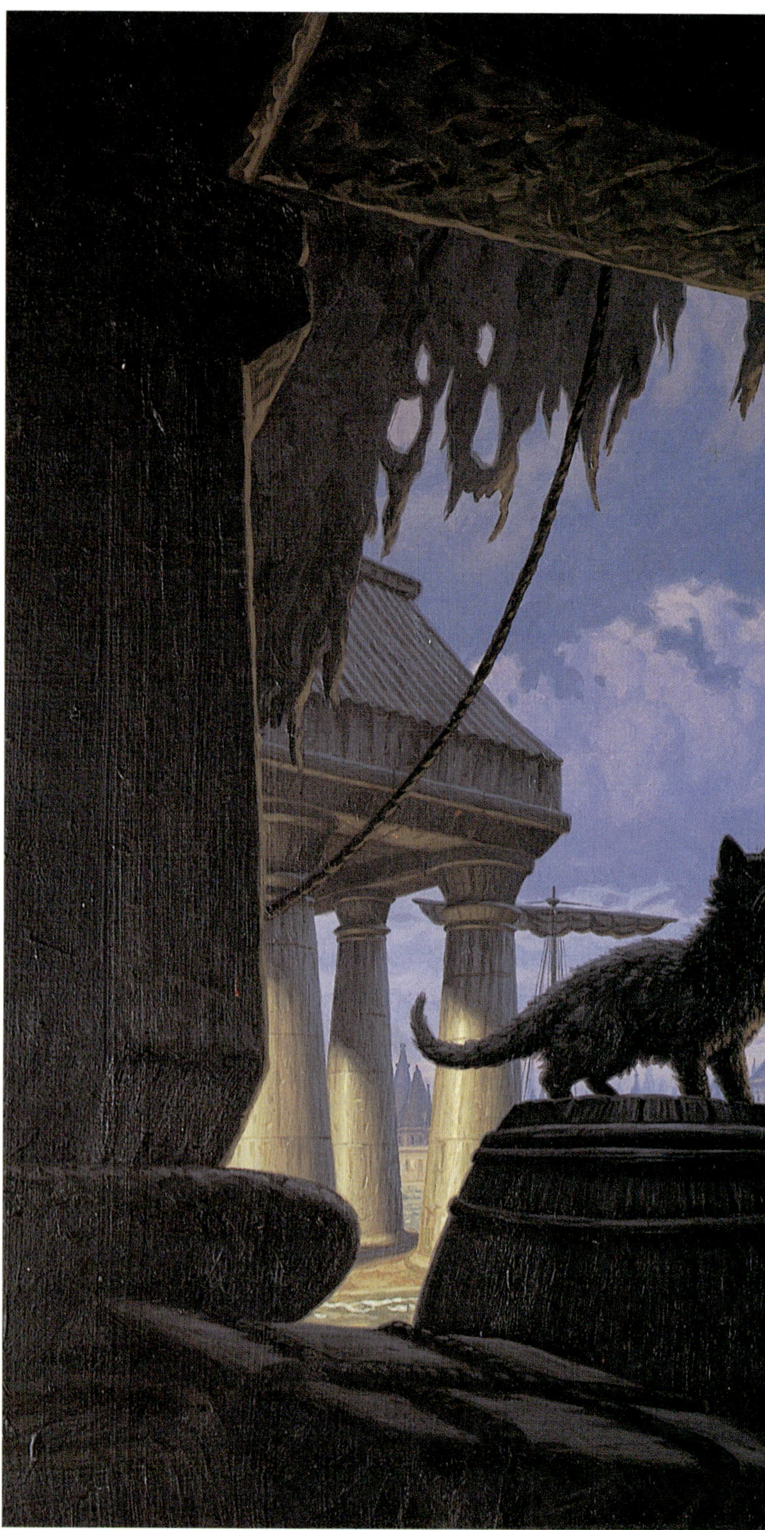

Illustration from the *Merovingen Nights* series, DAW Books, 1987. Tim: 'The buildings in the distance have less contrast than the foreground and the shadows are blue. The closer objects are stronger in contrast and contain less blue in the shadows.'

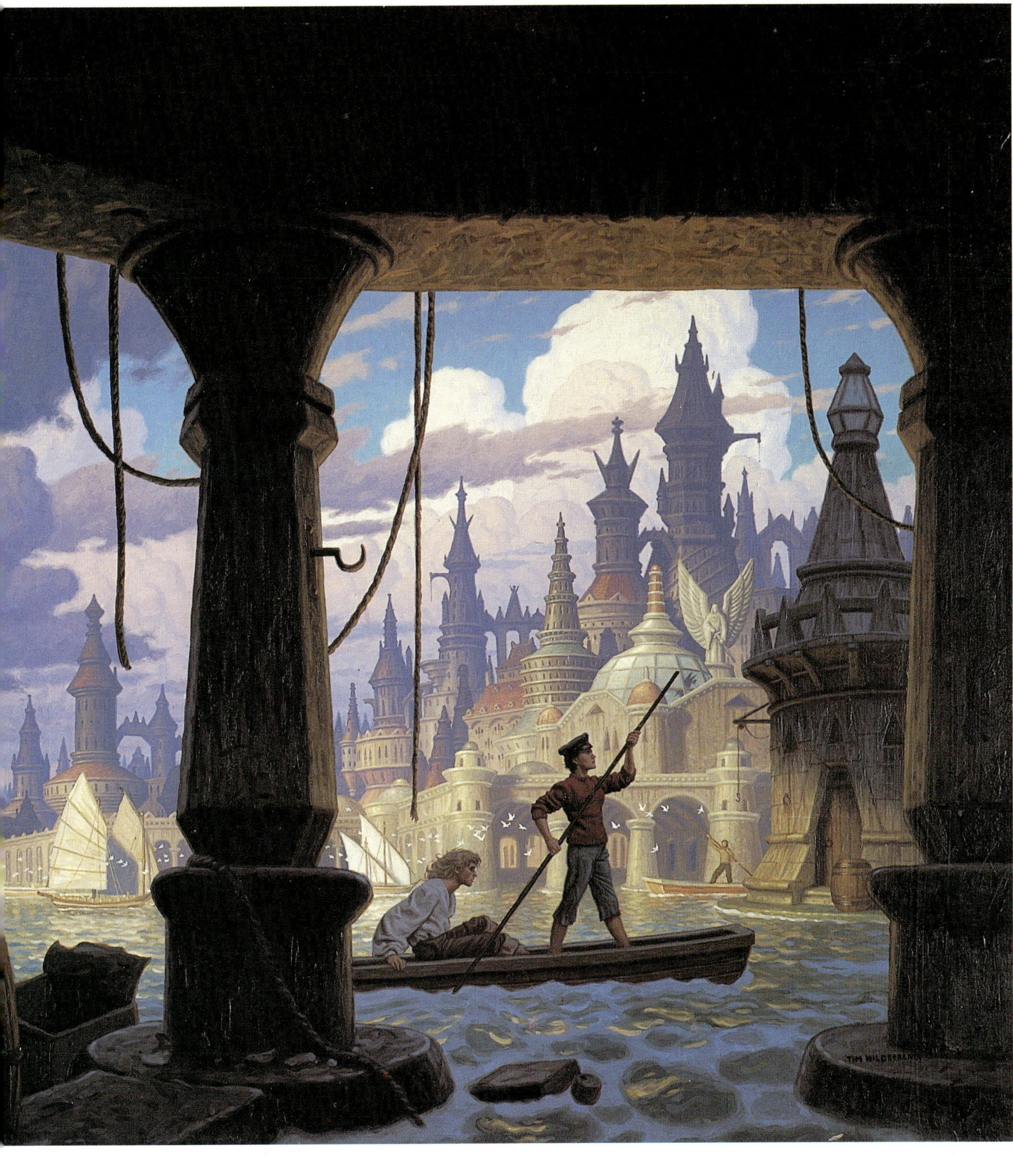

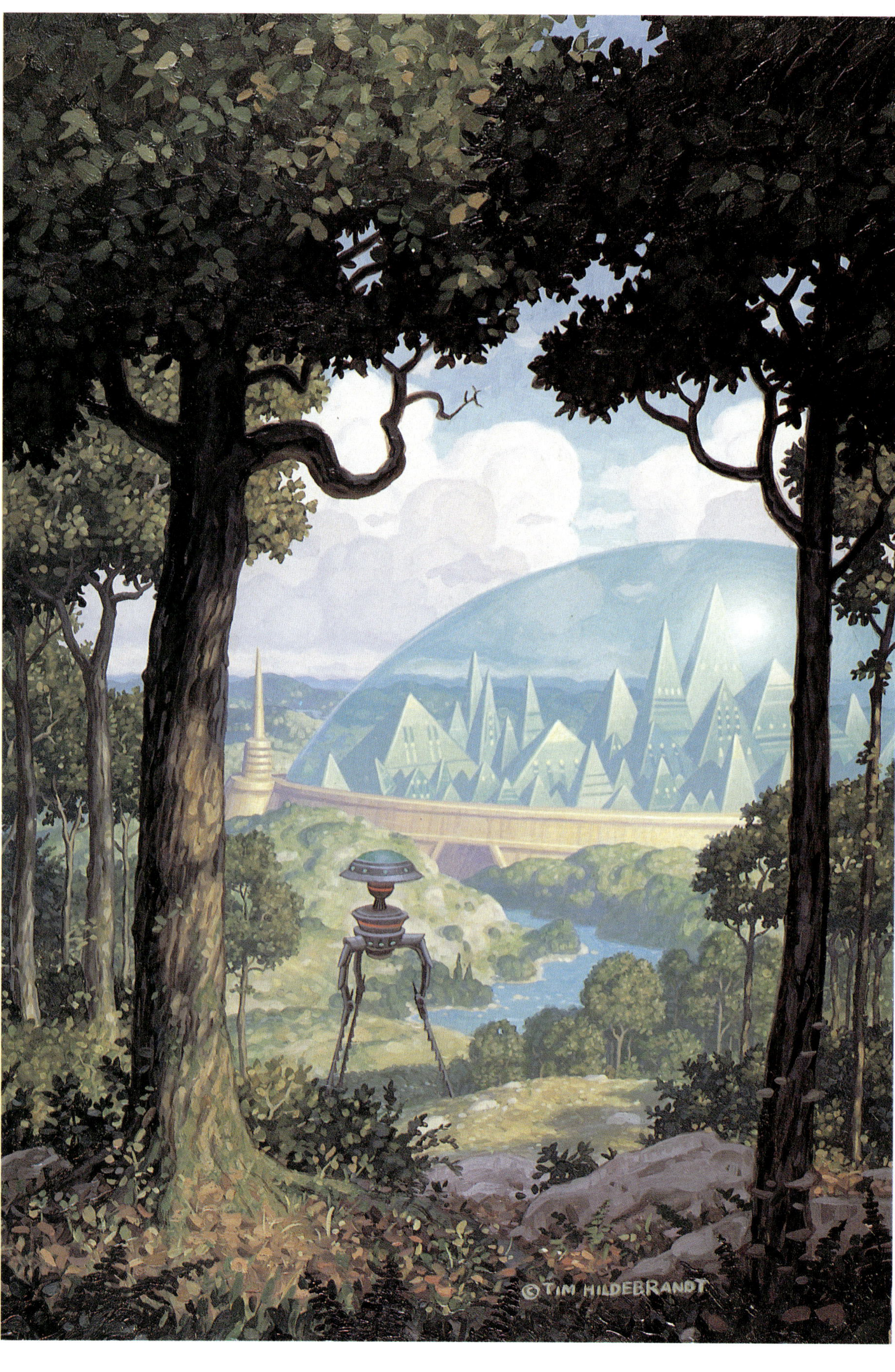
© TIM HILDEBRANDT

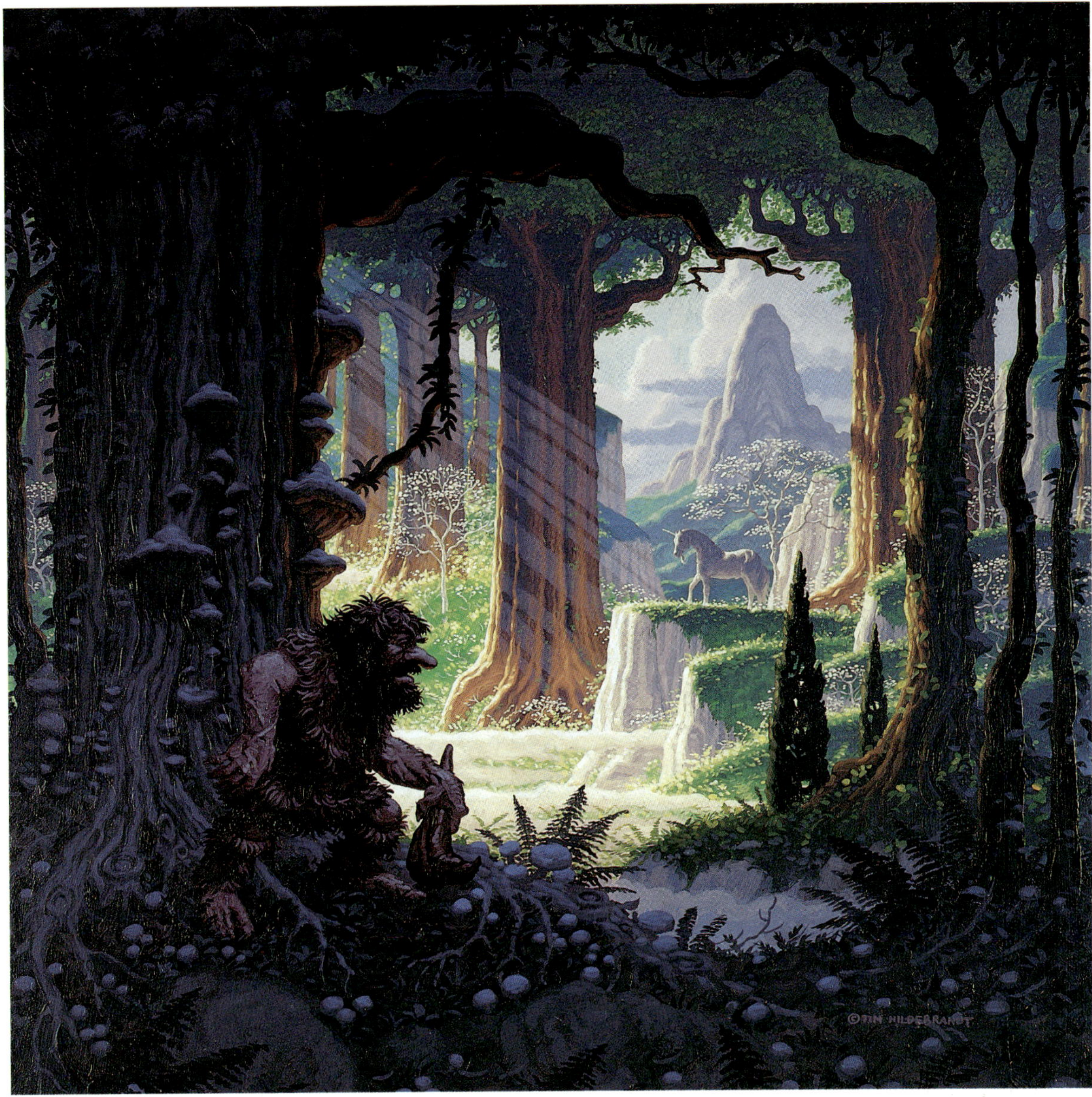

Forest of the Unicorn
Illustration from the *Realms of Wonder* calendar,
TSR, 1982, acrylic on masonite.

LEFT **The Tripods**
Book cover, acrylic on masonite. Tim: 'I always
plan for a painting to be created in separate
stages. In this case the first stage was the sky
and clouds; the second the mountains; the third
the domed city, the land and the river; the fourth
was the tripod and trees close to it; the fifth stage
was the foreground. As each level "advances"
towards you there is an increasing intensity of
colour.'

Shadows would digress in value to orange, then perhaps burnt sienna. Although the colour white is not used to render this example, when placed in the painting the dress would appear to be white.

This technique is used for rendering every object in the painting: a middle value is established under the specified lighting conditions and taken to its highest highlight and darkest dark. In addition, there is another characteristic of values that you should be aware of: *if the light source is warm, the shadows will be cool. If the light source is cool, the shadows will be warm.* The sun is a good example of a warm light source, while the moon would be an example of a cool light. An overcast day would also be treated as a cool light, since the light would be emitted from the clouds.

If all of this sounds confusing, don't worry. Every colour illustration in this book utilizes these principles, so there will be plenty of examples to look at. An understanding of what warm and cool colours are will also help, and will be described in a moment. For now, the important thing to remember is this: warm light, cool shadows, cool light, warm shadows.

In painting, warm indicates any colours that involve reds, yellows or browns. Cool colours indicate blues or greens. To apply this to the above rule you would first determine your light source. For example, your scene might be primarily lit from above by the moon. This is a cool light, so you would introduce a warm colour into the shadows. This doesn't mean the shadows themselves would be red, yellow or brown; rather, one of these colours should be introduced to your darker values to warm them up.

These rules are very much a part of the formula that Tim follows every time he renders a colour composition. They are applied to every object in every scene, leading once again to the somewhat Zennish statement, 'everything is the same, but different'. Once these problems have been solved, the most difficult part of painting is over. It is then a matter of mixing your colours and applying them to the painting surface.

To begin, there are three items you must have

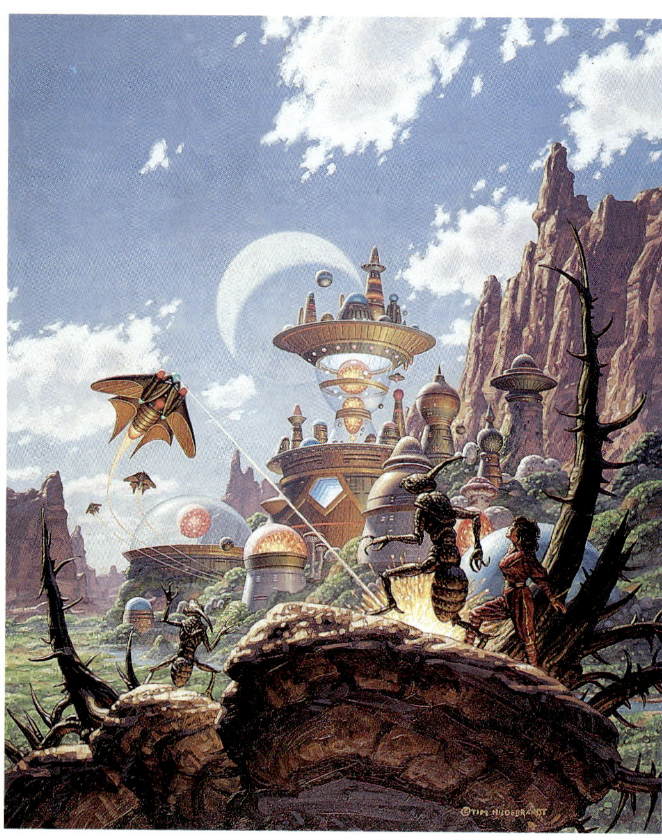

Amazing Stories
Cover illustration, April 1991, TSR, acrylic on masonite. Tim: 'The colours I used to paint the sky were Thalo blue, cerulean blue, burnt sienna (very, very little) and white. To achieve a darkening in the sky towards the top of the picture I added cerulean blue and cobalt blue. If I had wanted it really dark I could have added ultramarine.'

RIGHT Book cover, New American Library, 1987, acrylic on masonite. Tim: 'The colours used for clouds are mixed in this order: first white and a touch of cadmium yellow medium; then white with a little raw sienna; thirdly, just a hint of purple; and, lastly, cobalt blue. Notice again that the far distance contains less contrast and the shadows are cool. The yellow grass is lighting the white dress a yellowish colour. The skin and all other objects and figures are lit with this warm cast. But of course the brightest light is coming from the sun above and is a much whiter light.'

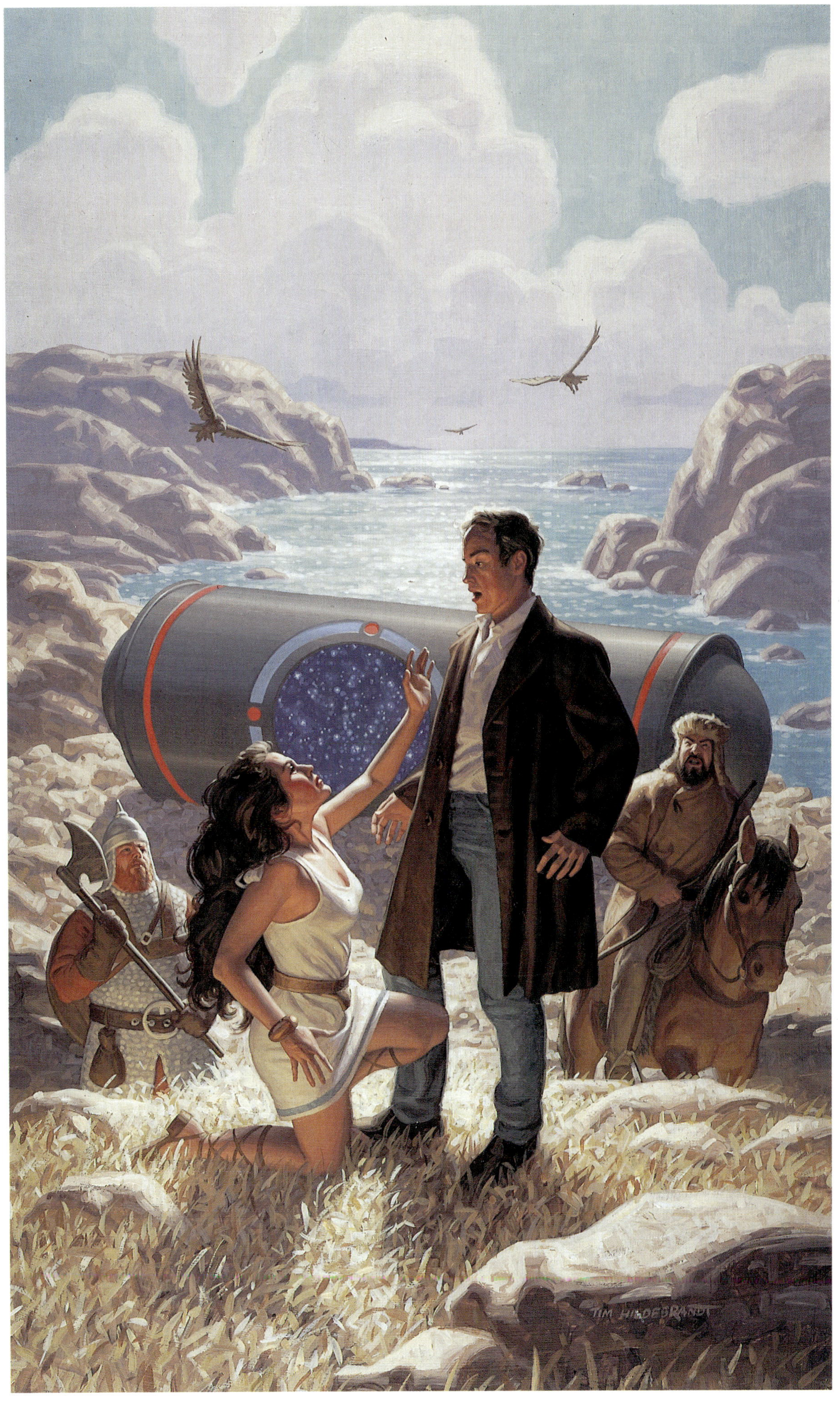

The Dragon's Keep
Centrefold from the *Realms of Wonder*
calendar, 1983, acrylic on masonite.

OPPOSITE PAGE **The Gold Dragon**
Illustration for *The Dragonriders of
Pern* calendar, 1984, acrylic on
masonite. Tim: 'I used a stuffed
iguana for the head of this dragon.
The colour scheme is basic. – it's
actually the three primary colours:
red, yellow and blue.'

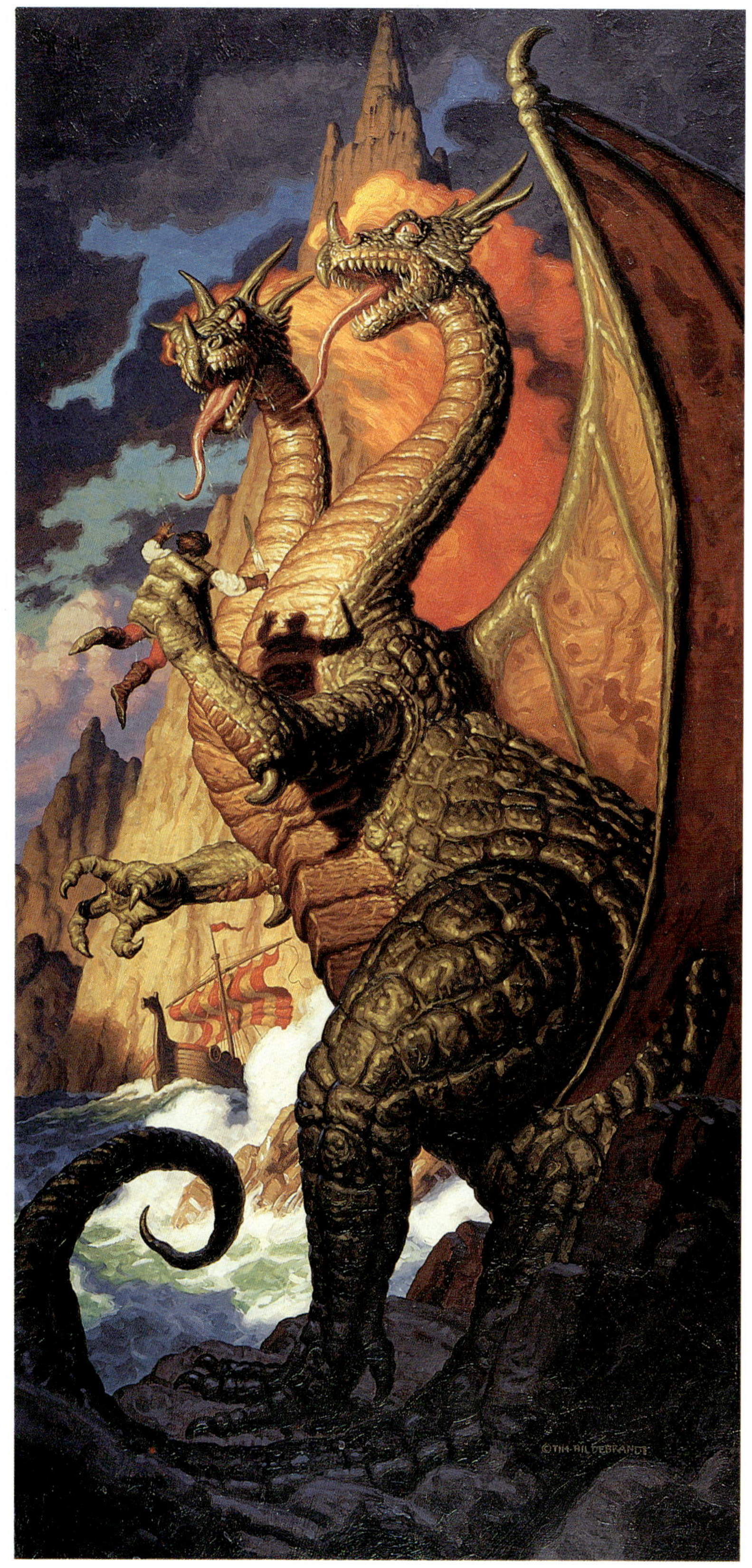

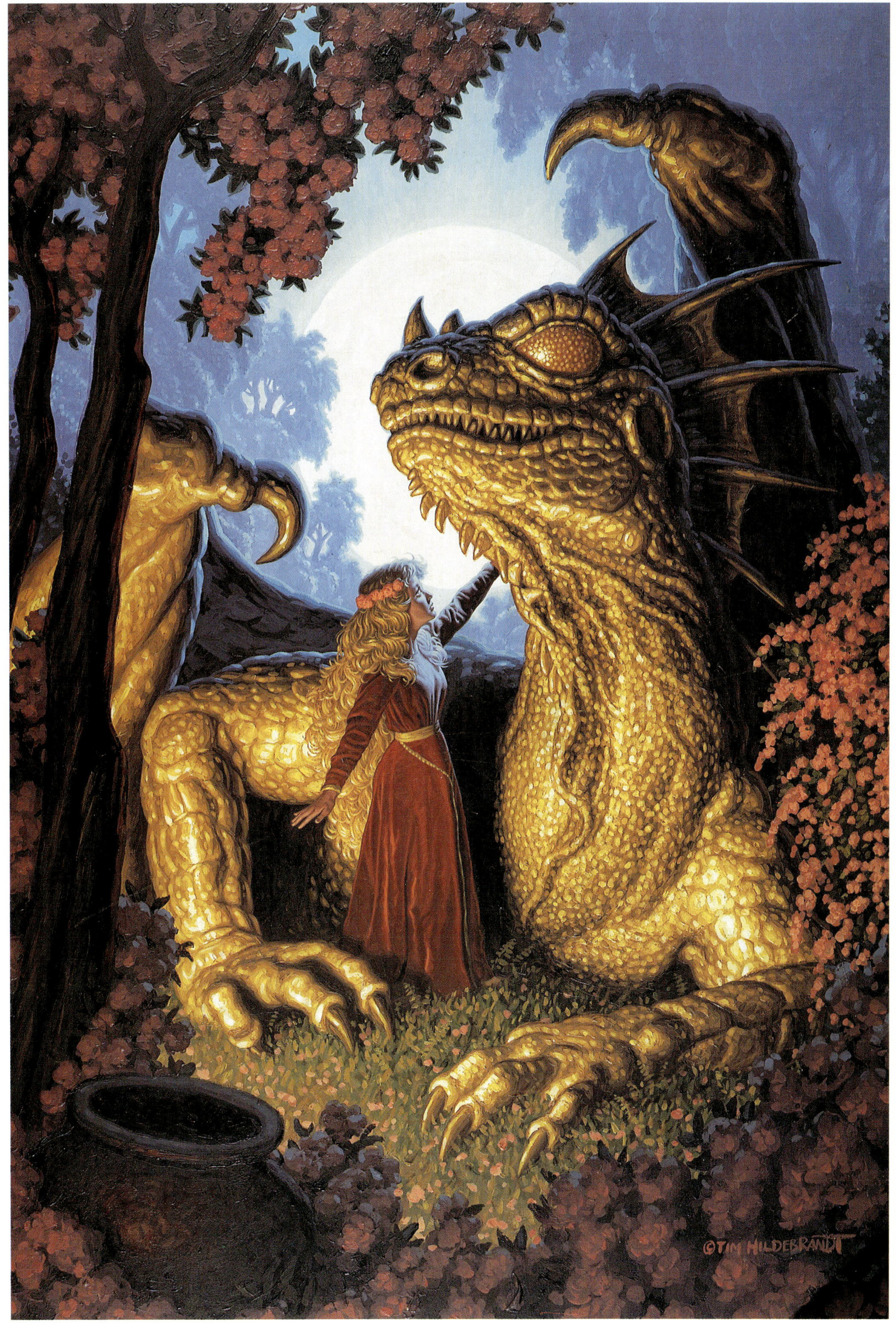

prepared. You must have a final composition rendered in pencil. You need a painting surface, and you also need something to facilitate the transfer of the drawing. As we have already discussed the drawing in previous chapters we will concern ourselves here with the painting surface and the means of transfer.

Tim works almost exclusively with acrylic painted on masonite. Masonite is a thin, pressed board that is very durable and very smooth. Compared to the costs of canvas, it is also very inexpensive. It does, however, require some preparation. The board must first be cut in the shape of the picture plane, and the rough edges sanded smooth. One or two coats of gesso are then applied to the surface and allowed to dry. Once dry, the gesso side of the board is sanded with fine sandpaper until a smooth, eggshell-type finish is achieved. It is then ready to be used.

In order to transfer the drawing, you need a medium. Graphite paper is commonly used, but is seldom sold in large enough sheets to transfer a whole drawing at a time. To solve this problem, Tim makes his own. He uses a regular sheet of tracing paper, coats it with lead from a soft pencil and wets the paper with regular rubbing alcohol. When it is dry, it is ready to be used.

To transfer the drawing, Tim places the leaded side of the graphite paper toward the gesso side of the board and the drawing over the graphite paper. From there, it is a simple matter of tracing over the lines of the drawing with a pencil until the entire drawing is transferred.

Tim paints almost exclusively with Grumbacher and Liquitex acrylic colours, and has established a basic palette that is adapted to paint any scene. His paints could be classified under the primary colours since they encompass several shades or red, yellow and blue. However, Tim prefers to think of them in terms of cool, warm or earth tones. His cool colours include Thalo green, cerulean blue, Thalo blue, Grumbacher purple, cobalt blue, ultramarine blue and permanent green light. The warm colours consist of titanium white, cadmium yellow light (medium), cadmium orange, yellow ochre (light), cadmium red (light), and cadmium red (medium). His earth

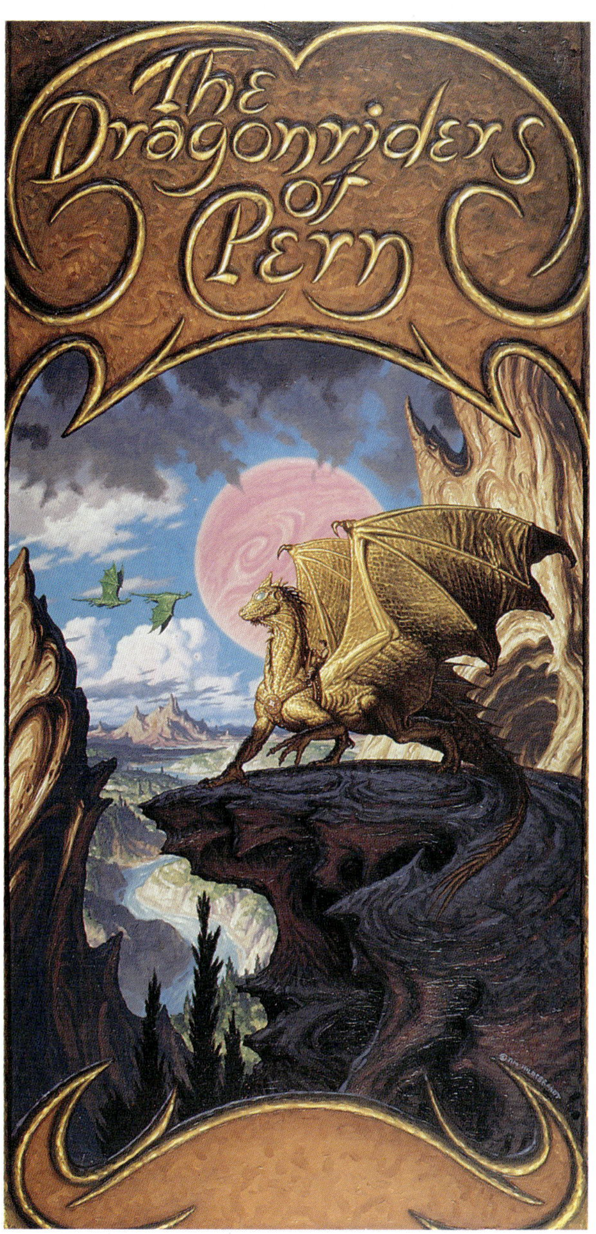

Cover from *The Dragonriders of Pern* calendar, 1984, acrylic on masonite.

RIGHT **The Mutant Warrior**
Limited edition print, acrylic on masonite.

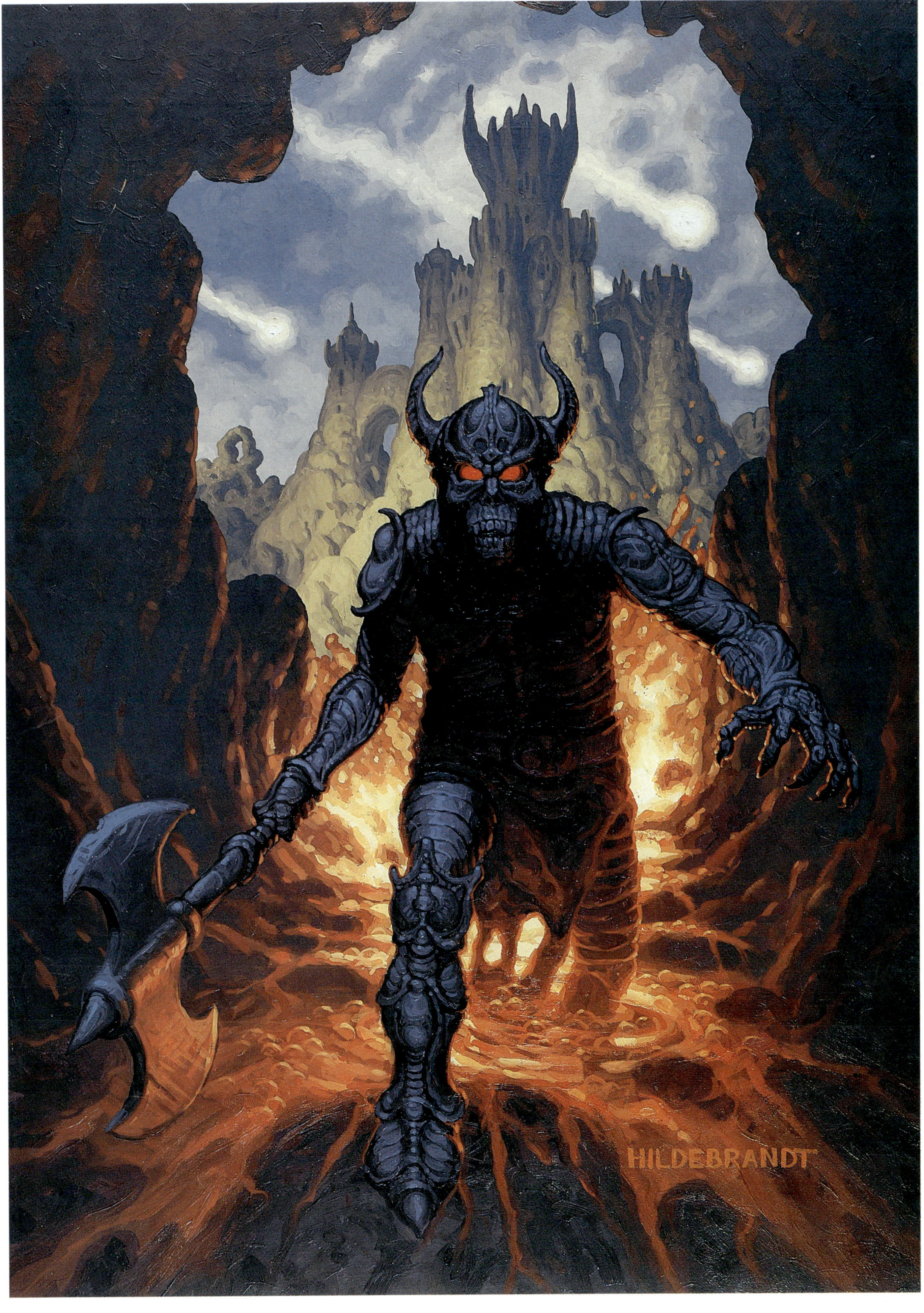
HILDEBRANDT

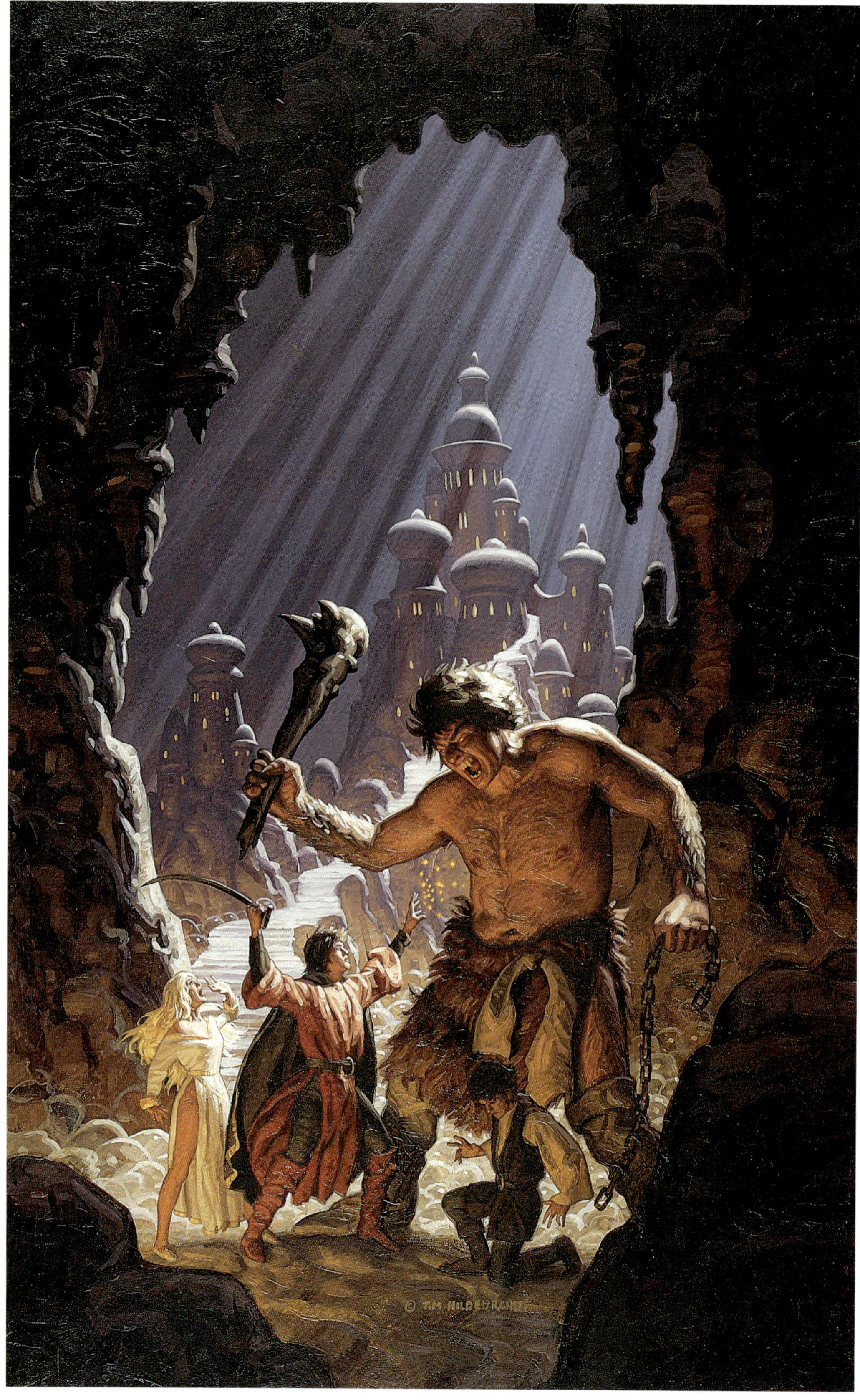

After the Spell Wars: Book One: Ogre Castle
Cover for the book by F. J. Hale, Pageant Books,
1988, acrylic on masonite.

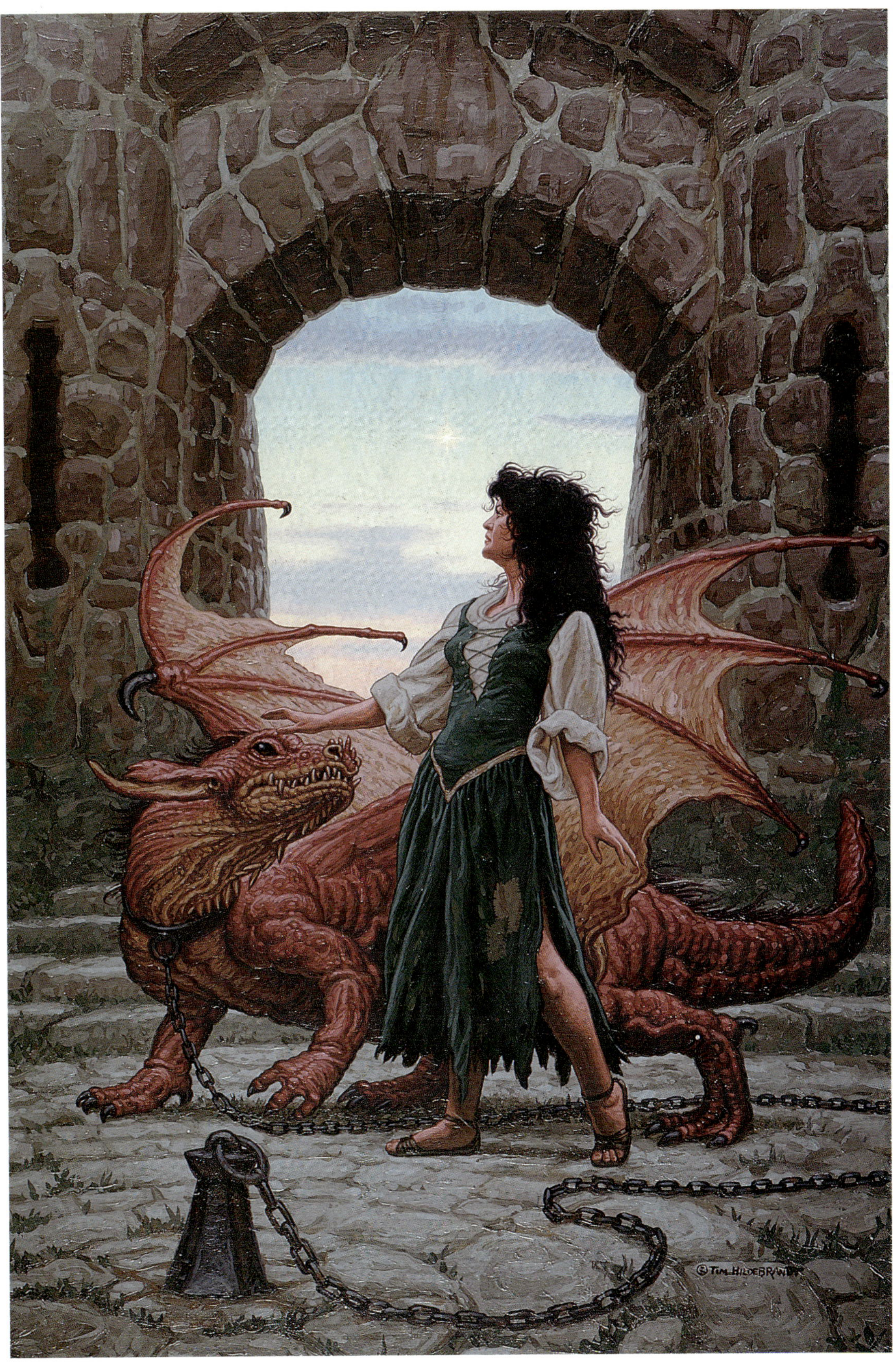

Illustration from *The Dragonriders of Pern* calendar, 1985, acrylic on masonite. Tim: 'This scene is lit by a blue light coming from the sky directly above. The lightest skin colour is purple and white, the middle value is purple, red oxide and white, and the darkest value is burnt sienna.'

120   tones are made up of burnt sienna, raw sienna, burnt umber, raw umber and Portrayt. In addition to these there are some colours that lend themselves to certain applications, and are included for their usefulness: Payne's grey, Turner's yellow and alizarin crimson.

Tim uses very fine Windsor & Newton brushes for most of his work, typically in the 000 range. He prefers the smaller brushes because they allow him a great deal of control over even the finest details. To block in larger elements of a composition, such as a sky, he switches to a much larger brush.

One other tool that must be considered before Tim can begin is the source of light that illuminates his workspace. Regular incandescent lighting would cast a yellowish hue across the work surface, which would in turn cause him to leave most of the yellow out of the painting. Kelvin lighting casts a bluish light, which would cause him to leave out most of the blues. In order to compensate for this effect, Tim uses a combination of the two lights. This balances the colours and provides a pure, white light.

Tim's next concern is to establish a palette for the most distant object in the composition. The palette itself is simply a square sheet of aluminium foil. Using the rules concerning colour and perception he then establishes a middle value (or the absolute colour) for the object, then takes it to its highest highlight and its darkest dark. On any given palette, there is usually a range of at least six graduating values. Using the rule of 'warm light, cool shadow; cool light, warm shadow', warm or cool colours are introduced to the darker values. The paints are mixed to a consistency that is thick enough to cover the space being painted, but thin enough to flow smoothly. Acrylic paint has a tendency to dry quickly, so Tim frequently mists the colours on the palette with clean water from a spray bottle.

Typically, the most distant image in an outdoor scene is the sky. Tim's first palette, then, would be established by what type of sky he wants to portray. It could be a morning sky or mid-day; a night sky; clear or cloudy, or stormy and threatening. These decisions are made when

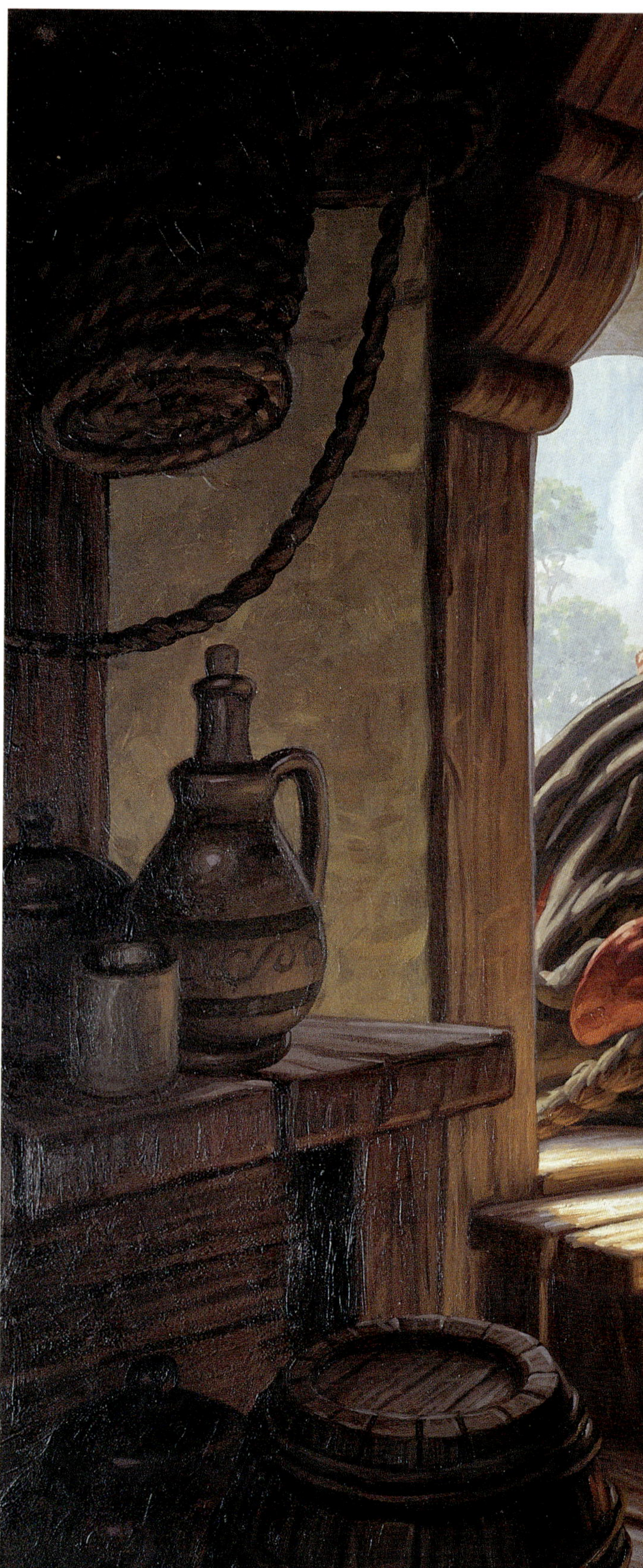

Rapunzel
From the *Xanth* calendar, Piers Anthony, 1988, acrylic on masonite.

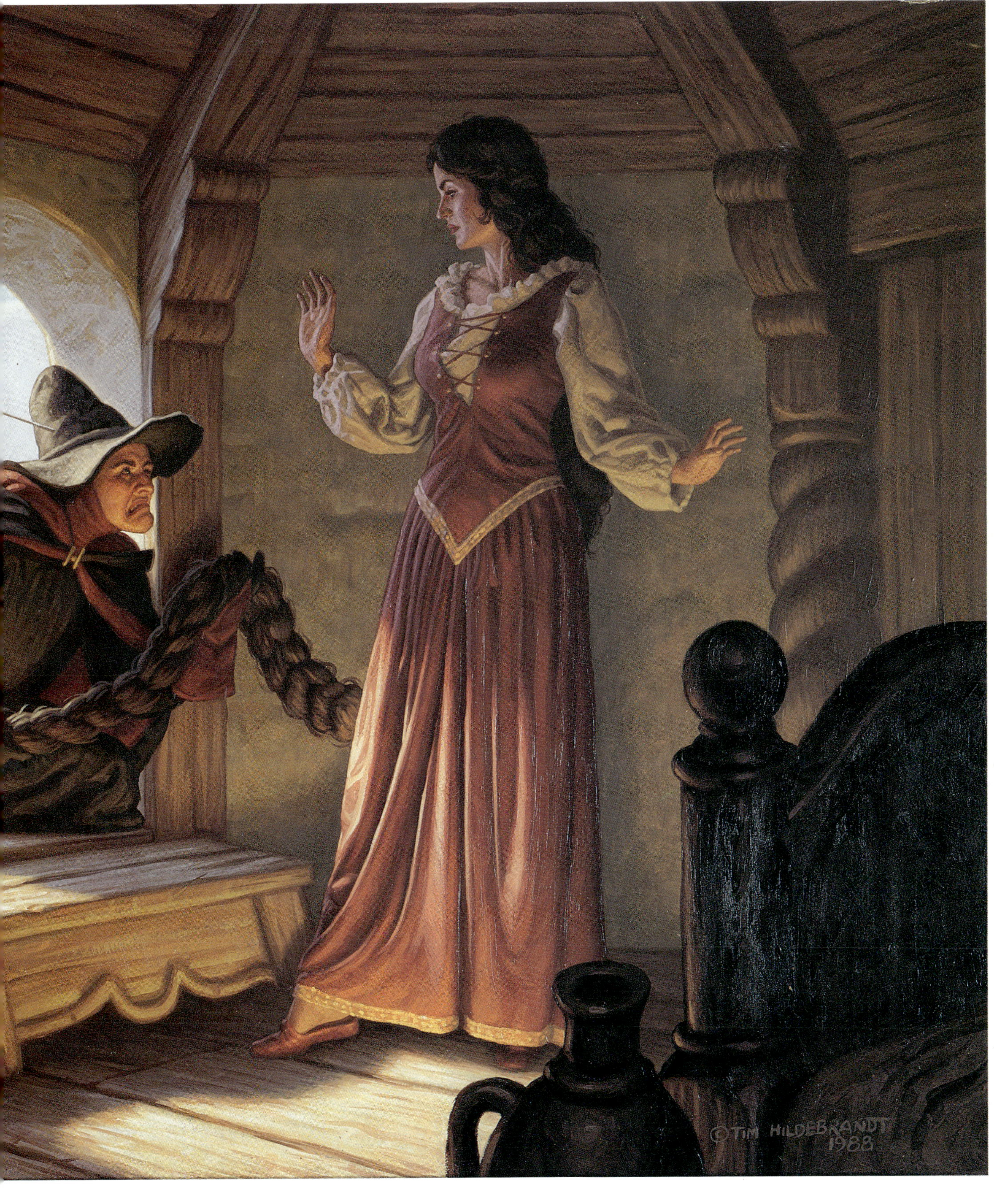

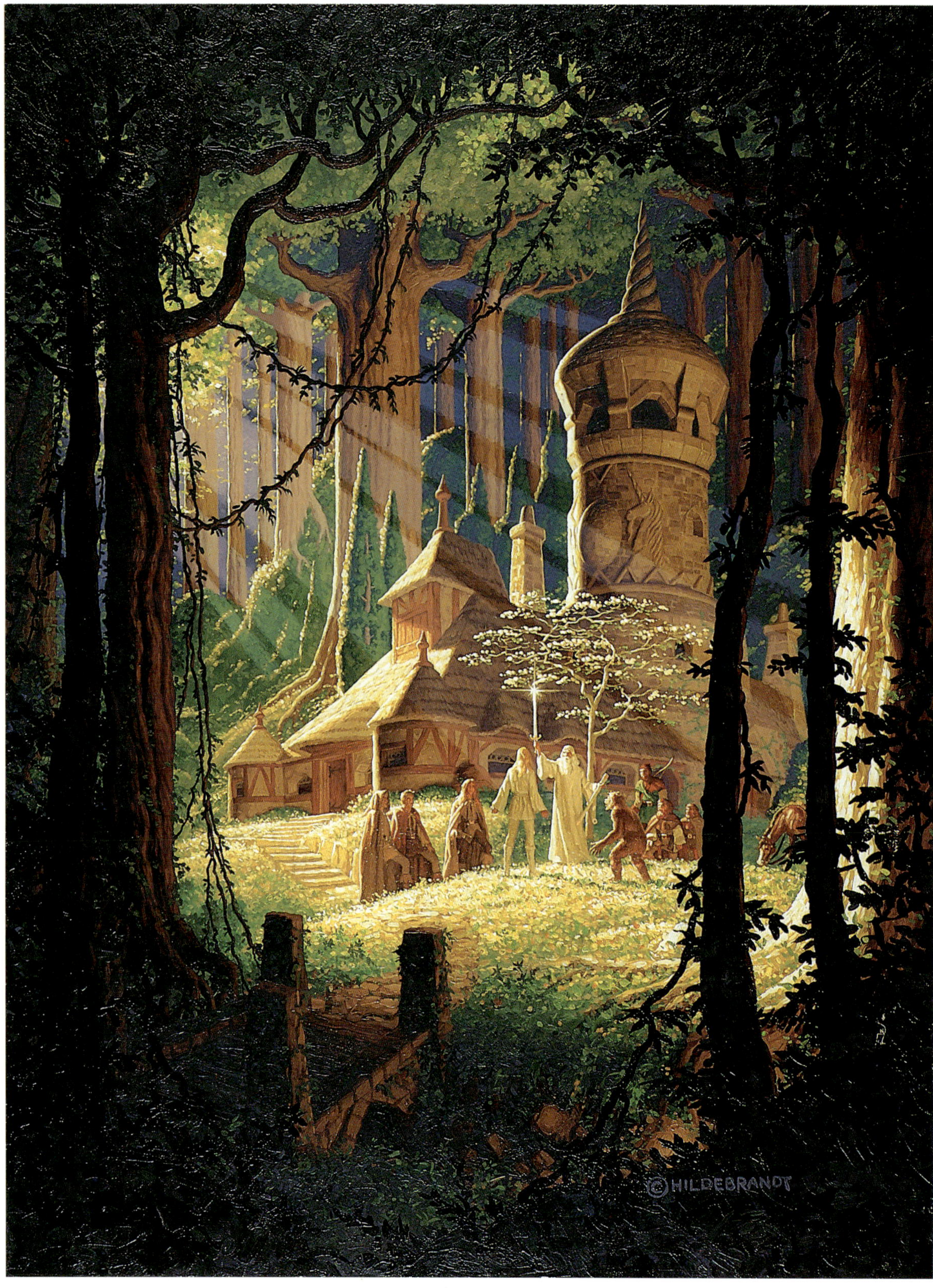

Mowdra
From *Urshurak*, 1979, acrylic on masonite.

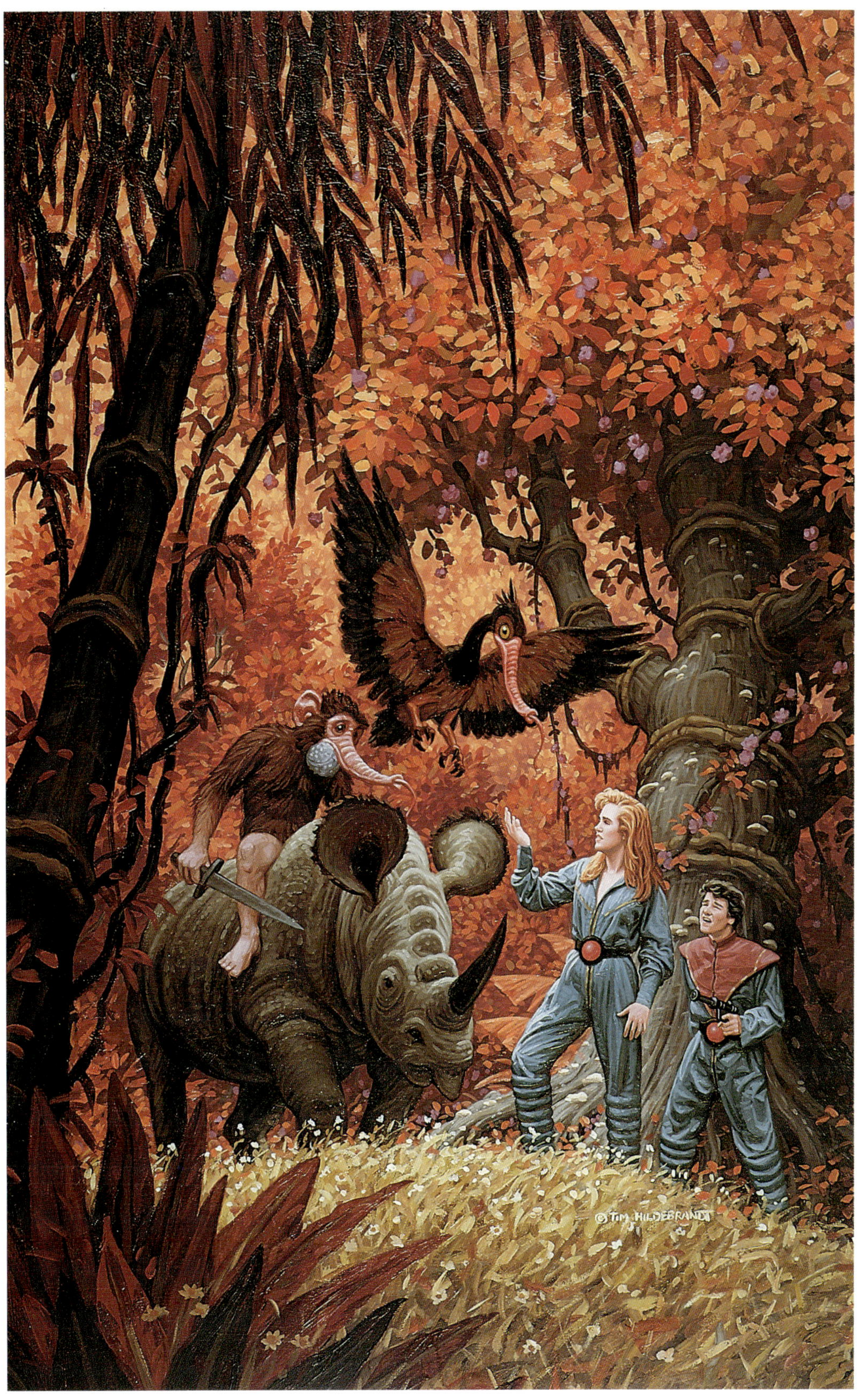

Book cover, New American Library, 1987, acrylic on masonite. Tim: 'This scene is painted with a diffused, overcast sky. Under these conditions all the highlights are cool and all shadows are warm.'

Tim composes the picture, so the problem is to render the sky as realistically as possible. To do this Tim uses our own sky as reference.

Morning and evening skies are identical. If you were to look at a photograph of a sky at sunrise, you would not be able to distinguish it from a sunset. In any sky, the closer to the horizon you get the lighter the values become and the warmer the colours become. This is especially true during sunrise or sunset when the warm colours seem to blaze in the sky. As you look up from the horizon the colours go cooler and darker in value until you finally are looking at a deep, dark blue immediately overhead. This effect is caused by the way our atmosphere affects our visual perception. From any given point to the horizon there is a much greater density of atmosphere and pollution than there is from any given point to directly overhead. The cool, dark values that colour the space beyond our atmosphere are less able to penetrate the increased amount of atmosphere in the distance. At sunrise or sunset the light source is very close to the horizon. It is the effect of this light passing through the many layers of atmosphere that accounts for the spectacular display of colours to be seen in the sky during those times.

Lighting and atmosphere combine to create other effects that must be considered by the artist. The light from the sun gives a scene not just one, but two distinct sources of light: the direct lighting from the sun (or moon) and reflected light bouncing up from the ground. The light is either warmer or cooler, depending on the light source. In addition, the light from the sky itself adds some blue to elements of a scene.

Rendering the sky, as with anything else, often requires some insight as to why things are perceived in the way that they are. This knowledge, combined with the other basic rules of colour and perception, and the careful execution of all of the steps in the previous chapters, constitute a majority of the work involved in painting. The application of paint to the work surface is then academic.

To see how all of these principles come together, then, think back to the example of the morning sky. The first

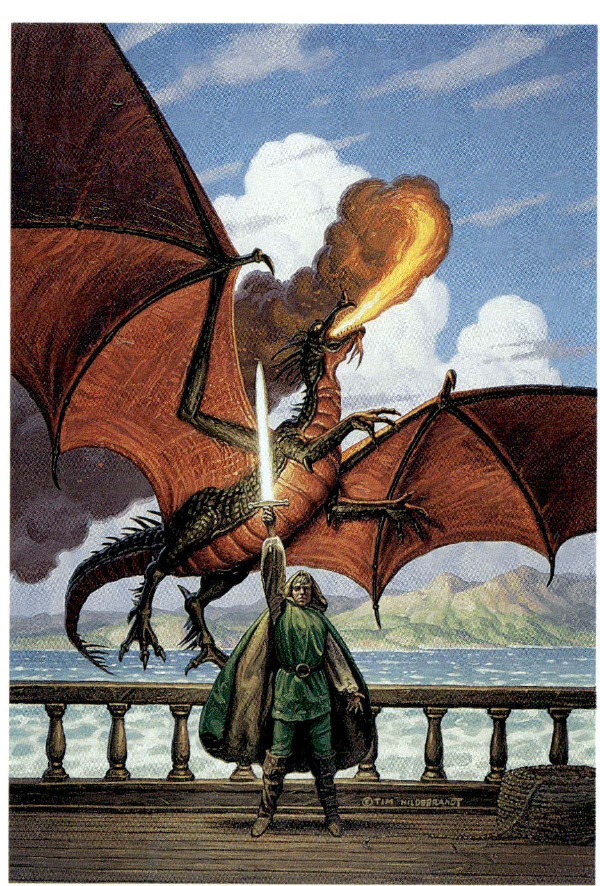

Book cover, Warner Books, 1987, acrylic on masonite.

RIGHT **The King of the Sceptred Aisle**
Book cover, New American Library, 1989, acrylic on masonite. Tim: 'Notice the yellowish light bouncing off the rock. The darkest colour used in the sky is Payne's grey going into cobalt blue with a little purple towards the horizon.'

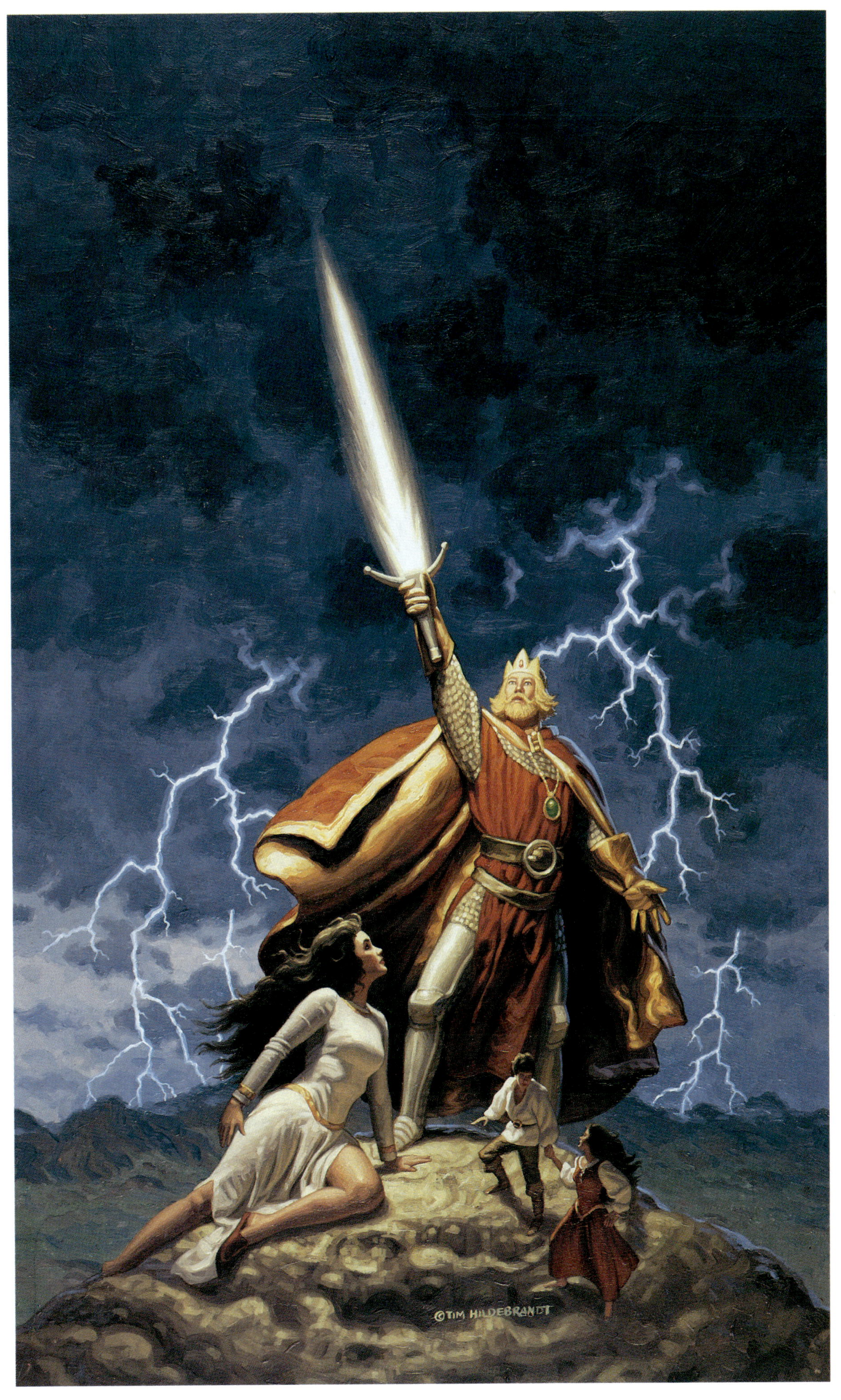
©TIM HILDEBRANDT

order of business would be to establish the palette. Starting at the horizon the first value might be a mixture of cerulean blue, Thalo blue, raw sienna and titanium white. Progressing upward to the next value, you would eliminate the Thalo blue and add more cerulean blue to the first value. These two values are mixed directly next to each other on the palette, blending into each other at the edges to create a smooth transition. In the third value even more cerulean blue is added, and at the fourth value cobalt blue would be introduced. The fifth value would have even more cobalt blue, and even some ultramarine blue. These five values then represent the graduating colours found from the horizon to directly overhead. Once these values are established they are painted on the masonite in exactly the same order, and blended together to form the sky.

When applying these values on the board Tim normally paints in the middle value first, in a broad strip across the middle of the sky area. Working quickly down toward the horizon he applies the next lighter value in another strip next to the first. He then mixes on his palette a tone that is somewhere in between the two values, then blends the two strips together on the board. This is repeated all the way down to the horizon, and all the way up to the darkest value in the sky.

The palette for the sky is then labelled and set aside in air-tight boxes (to keep the paint from drying), and a palette for the next most distant image is established. In this case, these objects could be clouds. Contrary to popular myths, clouds that appear white are not. The atmosphere behind the clouds adds a bluish hue, although in comparison to the sky the clouds should still appear white. In this case, since the light source is warm, the shadows will be cool. Raw sienna is then added to the lighter values to warm up the highlights, and Thalo blue added to the darker to cool down the shadows.

Once the clouds are completed the palette is labelled and stored away in case Tim needs to touch up the clouds. It is difficult to duplicate exactly colours later on, so he is sure to mix more than enough colours for the image or

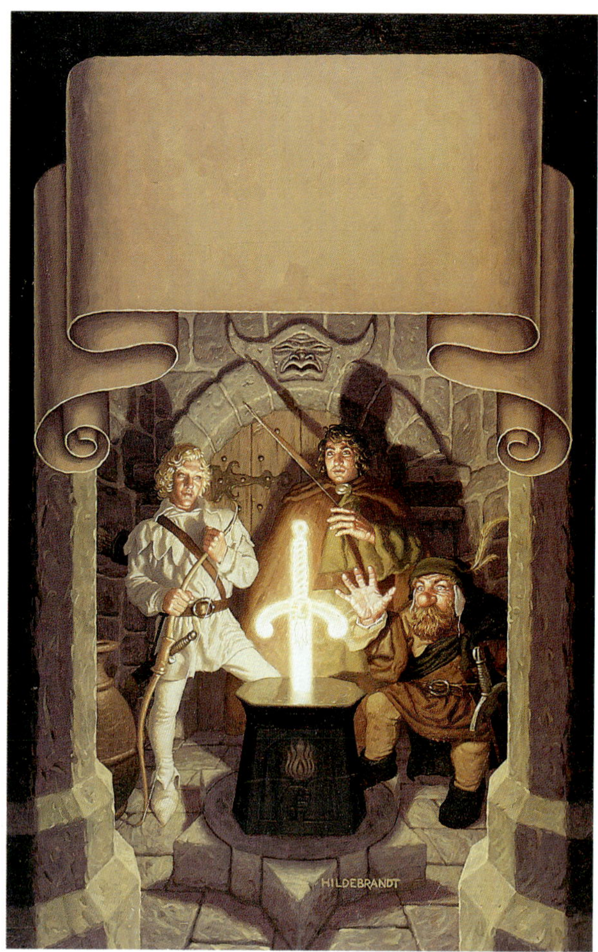

The Sword of Shannara
Book cover, Ballantine Books, 1977, acrylic on masonite. Tim: 'To ensure that something looks like it's glowing it must be the brightest object in the picture.'

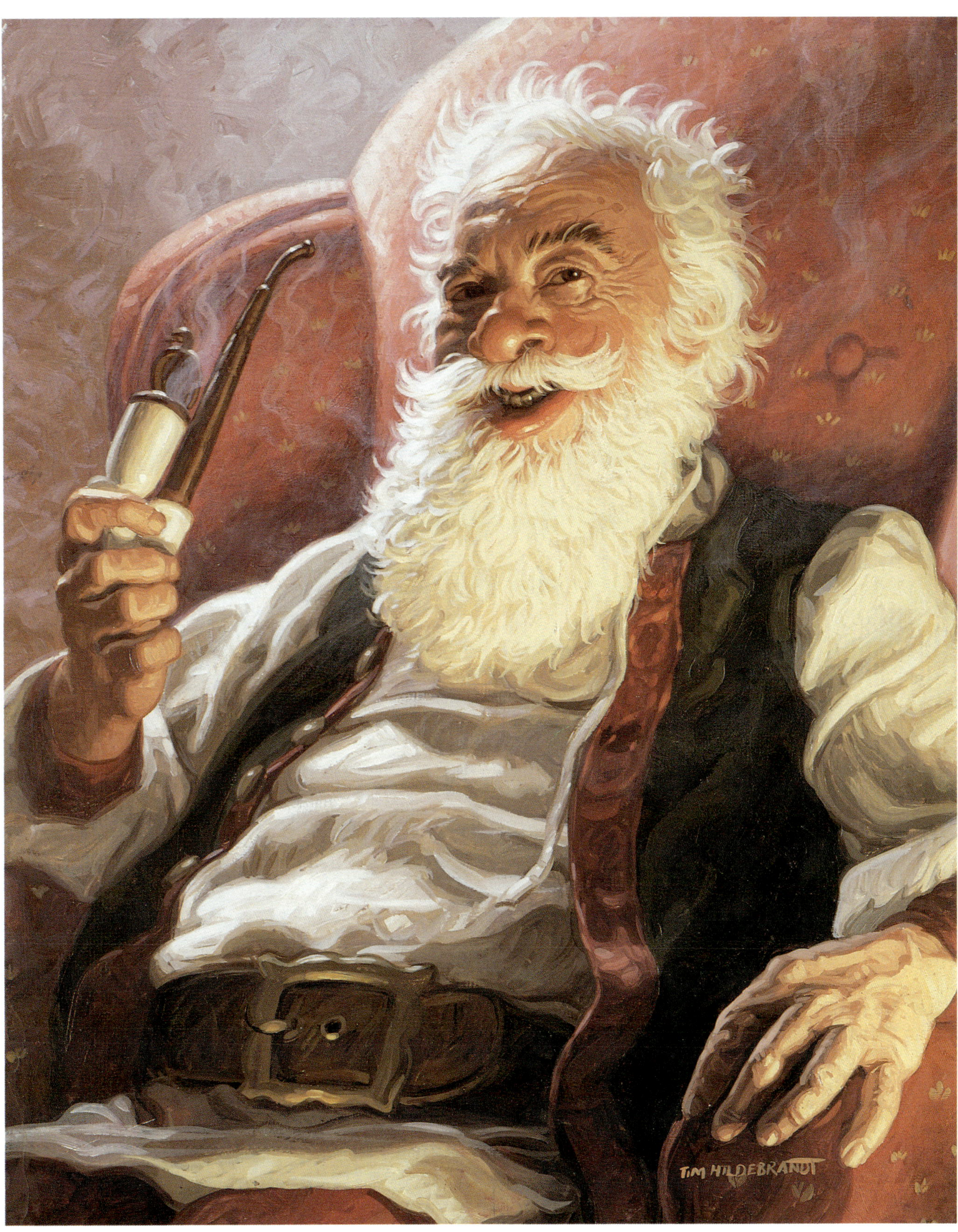

Santa Daydreams
A present from the artist to his wife, 1985. Tim: 'I
used only two values to paint the hair here: raw
sienna and white, and yellow and white.'

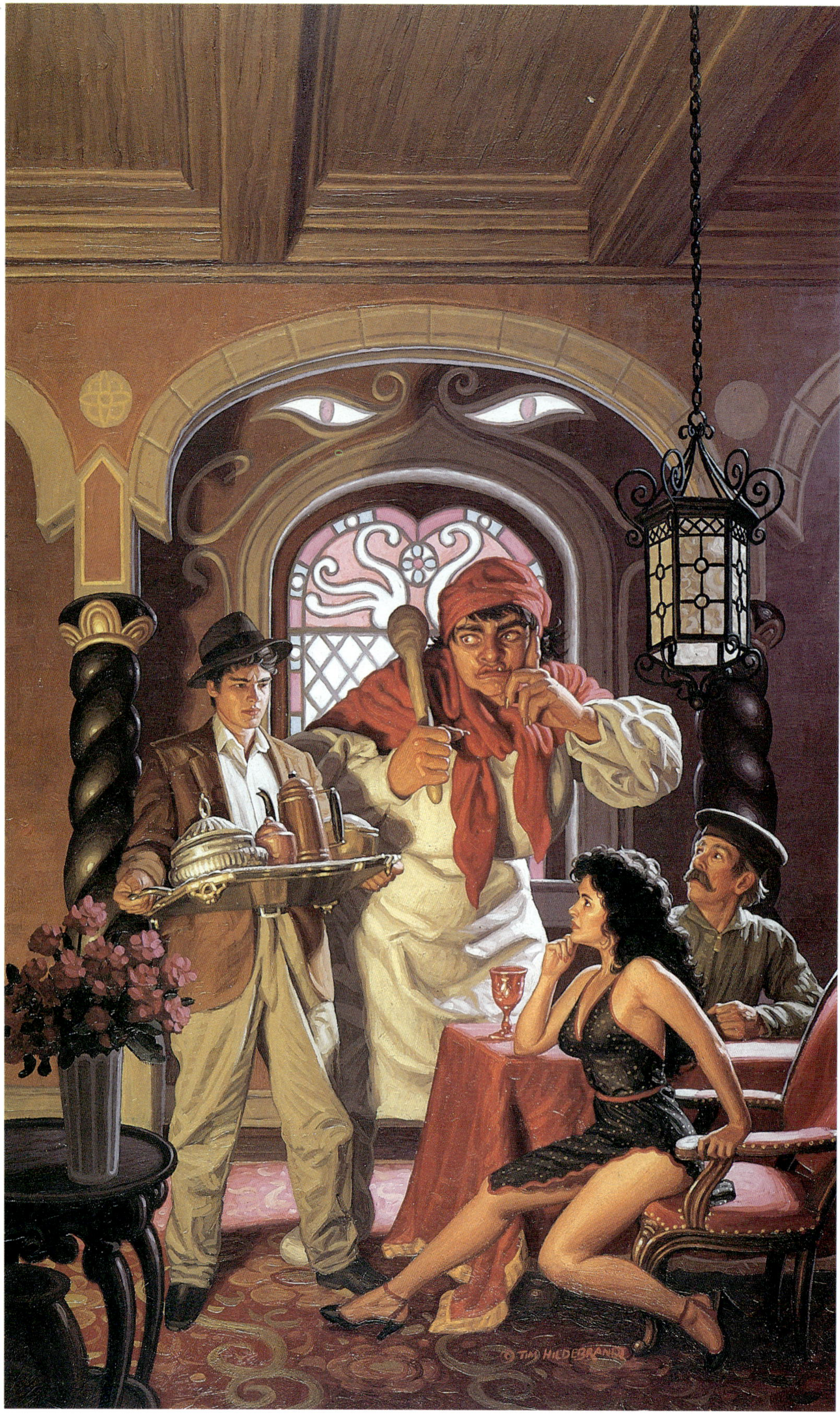

Cover for a Glenn Cooke book, New American
Library, 1989, acrylic on masonite. Tim: 'When I
paint cloth I like to keep it simple – broad brush
strokes quickly applied.'

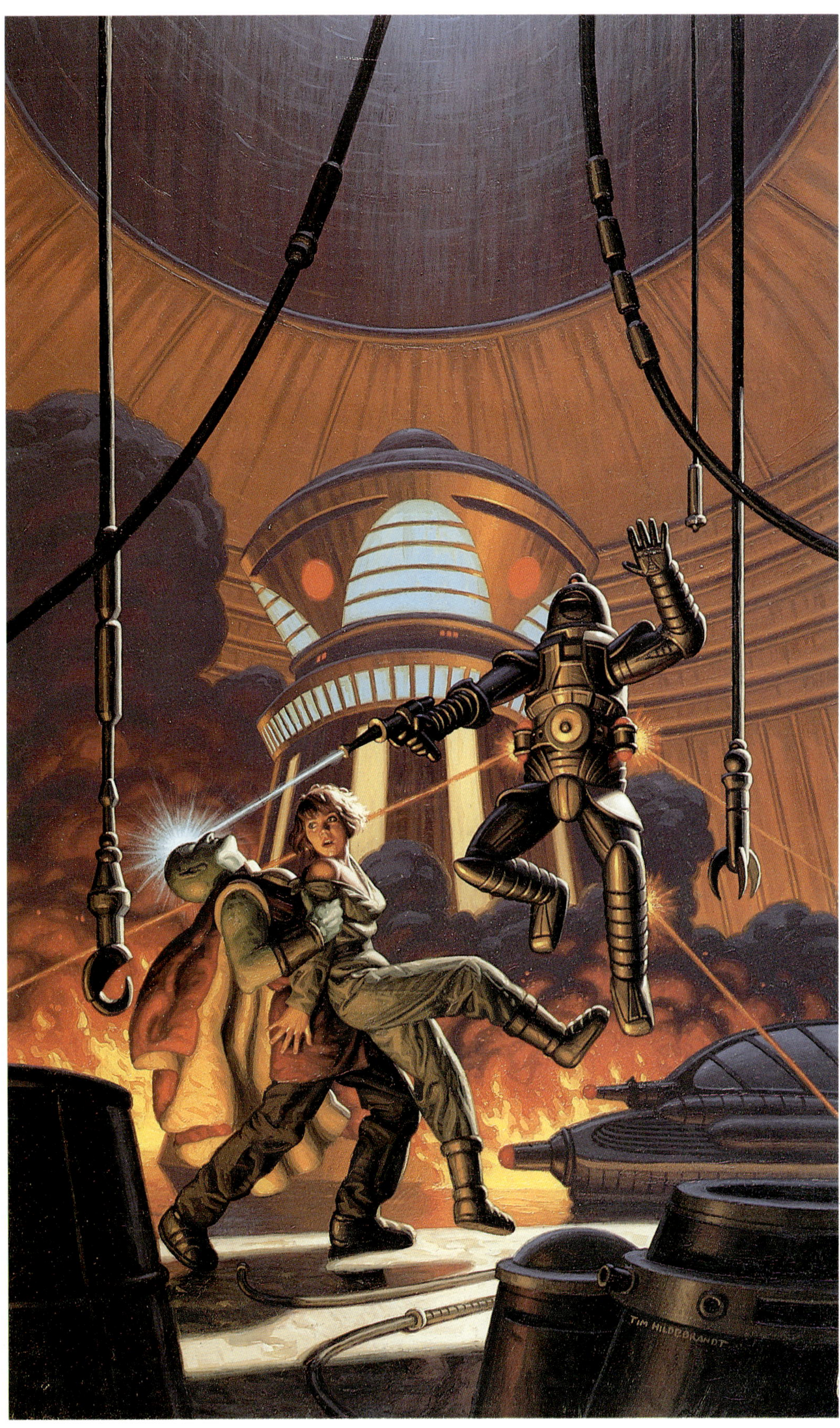

A Knight of Ghosts and Shadows
Book cover, New American Library, 1987, acrylic
on masonite. Tim: 'Metal is painted with hard
edges and plenty of shine.'

object from the beginning. These colours are stored until the painting is finished and the art director has accepted it in its final form.

Every object in the composition is handled in exactly the same way. The colour of the object is determined under the lighting conditions called for in the composition, and it is taken to its highest highlight and its darkest dark. Warm or cool colours are introduced to the dark values, depending once again on the light source. Some objects in a composition present special rendering problems, however. The following will present some possible solutions.

Night skies are never rendered in black due to the presence of moonlight and atmosphere. In addition, black has a tendency to make a painting look flat and lifeless. In a moonlit scene, Tim's palette might begin with a white and yellow mixture that will represent the moon (white is never used straight out of the tube). The second value, representing the glow around the moon, would be a mixture of raw sienna and white. This mixture is slightly darker in value and leaves the moon itself as the brightest object in the sky. The third value would be made by adding raw umber to the second value, and in the fourth cerulean blue is introduced. The fifth value would contain even more cerulean blue and in the sixth value cobalt blue is introduced. These colours radiate from the moon to create the illusion of a dark, moonlit sky, even though black is never used. Edgelights for objects in the scene are rendered in the same colours used in the sky, and warm colours are added to the shadow areas.

If the moon is not present in the scene it could still be handled in much the same way. The colours would not be as bright since there is no direct light source, but would still be lighter in value toward the horizon. Edgelights would again be rendered in sky colours, and shadows would still be warmer.

For a dramatic, stormy sky, the most distant objects would be mostly the clouds themselves. Rendering stormy skies follows the same principles used when rendering any other object, and good reference material is vital here. Tim finds that a good middle value for storm clouds

The Curse of the Werewolf
Book cover, TSR, 1985, acrylic on masonite. Tim: 'Sometimes the sketch is more detailed than the painting. I do this to have a very firm idea of the details before I start the painting.'

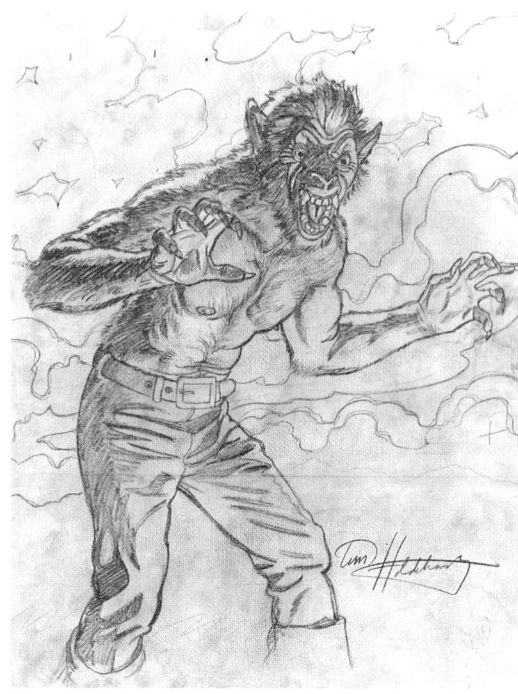

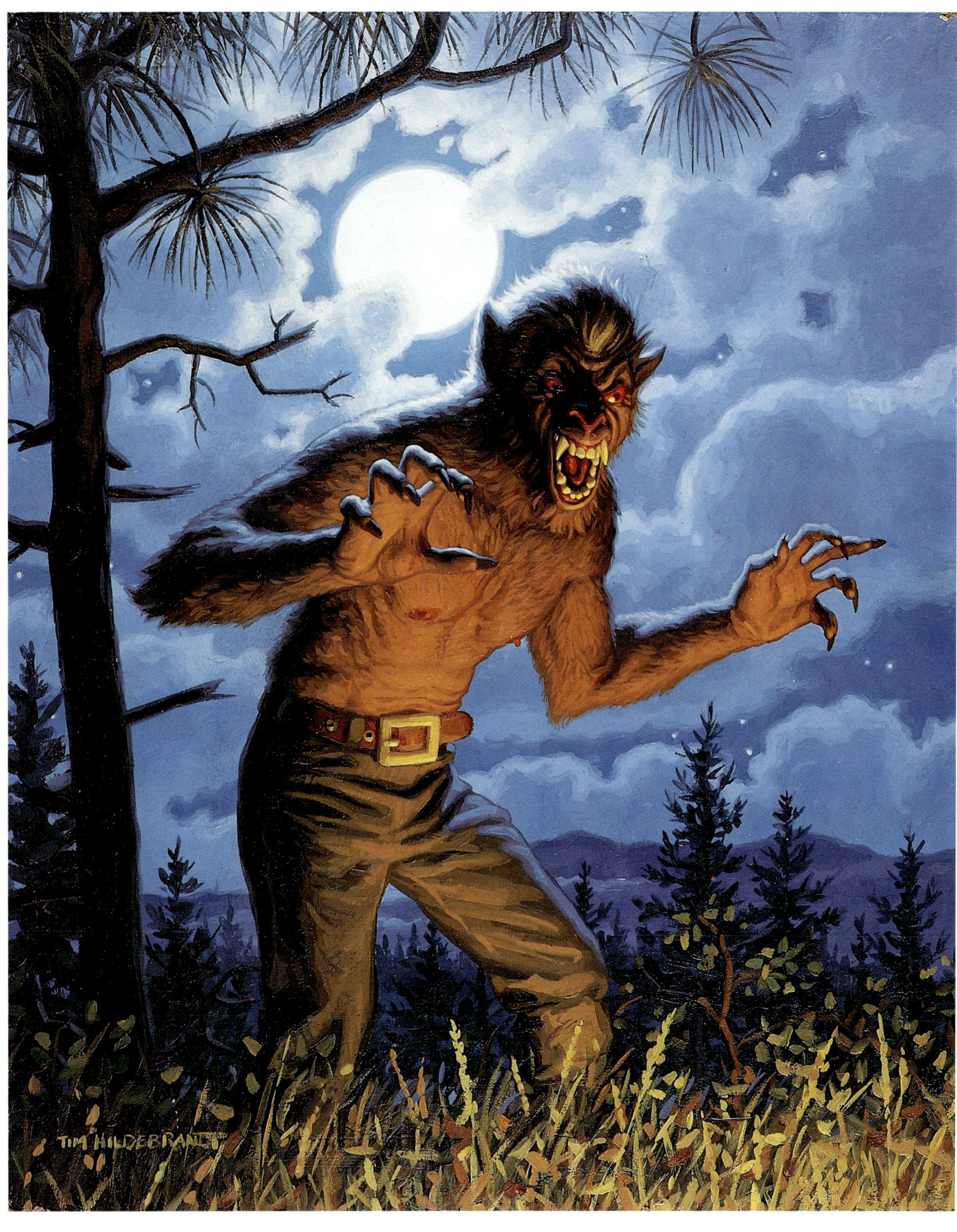
TIM HILDEBRANDT

is a mixture of Payne's grey, white and raw umber. Since the sun is located above the clouds, highlights would be warmer; the colours would include more raw umber, raw sienna and white. Cloud shadows would include ultramarine or cobalt blue. The light source for the rest of the scene is considered cool, however, as the sun is diffused through the clouds. Shadows for the other objects would be warmer, and highlights cooler. Objects in a stormy scene appear more hazed out than in a bright, daylit scene and have fewer contrasting values. This is even more apparent if you choose to include rain in the composition. The rain itself is normally suggested as streaks across the scene, since this is how we *see* rain. Individual drops of rain are never actually seen.

Skies are important compositional elements in outdoor scenes, not only because they are part of the scene but because they determine the intensity, direction and colour of the light that illuminates the entire scene. This is true even when the sky is not present in the scene itself. The effects of the sun or moon on the atmosphere directly influence how objects are perceived. For example, cobalt blue is present in every shadow in every object in the distance since that is the colour of the sky directly overhead.

Indoor scenes are not usually influenced by the colours of the sky, unless there is a large window present in the composition. The most important element in determining colour, however, is still the light source. It could be a candle, a fire, a glowing magical talisman or any number of different sources. In any case, if the light source is present, the brightest highlight of any other object in the scene must be less bright than the source itself. Only if the source of light is not present in the scene can other objects become brighter. It is the relative brightness of an object that determines which object is actually glowing.

Painting an interesting background that represents outer space can be a problem, since true space is pitch black. So Tim will usually introduce some sort of atmosphere. The scene is then rendered according to the light sources called for in the composition.

Underwater scenes are handled in much the same way

And the Sphinx Always Nose
Unused illustration for a book cover, 1985, acrylic on masonite. Tim: 'When painting skin in cool light the shadows or darker areas must be warmer.'

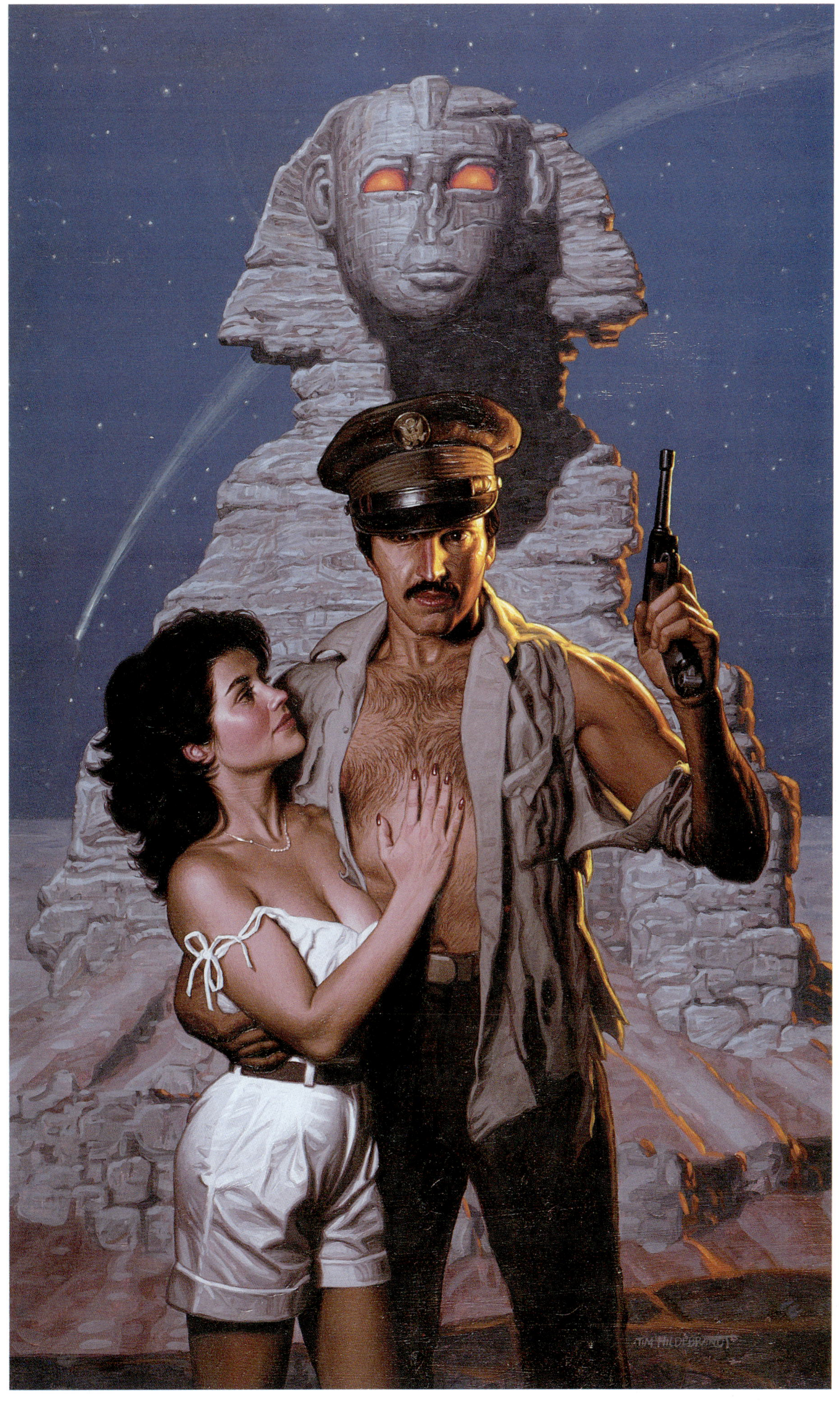

as a scene with a sky for a background, except that the density of water intensifies the effects of atmosphere by about 200 percent. Objects far away seem bluer and more monochromatic and shadows tend to go greener. Usually, a second light source is introduced to keep the picture from becoming too monochromatic.

Rendering objects in a scene requires you to follow the same principles of lighting and colour, whether you are attempting to paint flesh or steel. The only difference is in how you handle texture. For example, hair or feathers can be handled in a very loose manner, suggesting detail rather than revealing it. Steel or glass, however, is more rigid and absolute. The colours must be rendered more evenly, with values that blend gradually from one area to the next. The process for rendering any object is always the same: study your reference material, determine the absolute colour of the object under your specified lighting conditions and take it to its highest highlight and darkest dark. You then add warm or cool colours to the darker values, depending on the light source.

Painting is a process, one that begins with the initial concept and extends all the way through to the completed illustration. The only 'secrets' to creating realism in a painting lie within the artist's understanding of rules that govern colour and perception. The technique is always the same; it is how you apply the technique that determines how successful you will be in creating realism within your own compositions.

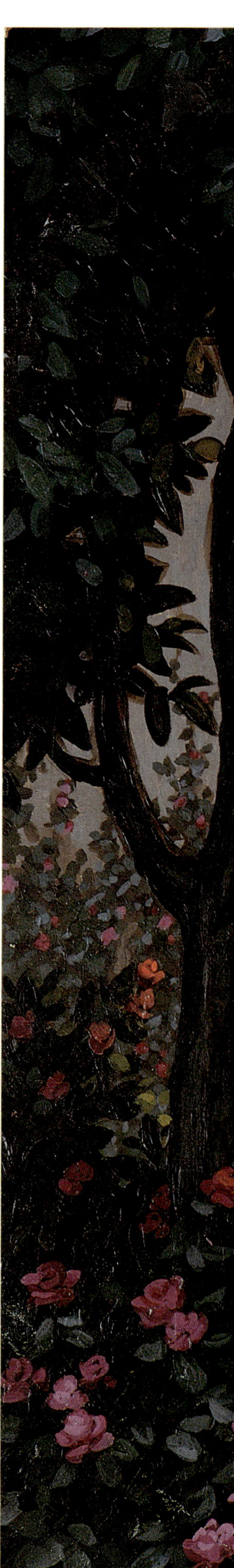

Romeo and Juliet
Unused illustration, 1987, acrylic on masonite.

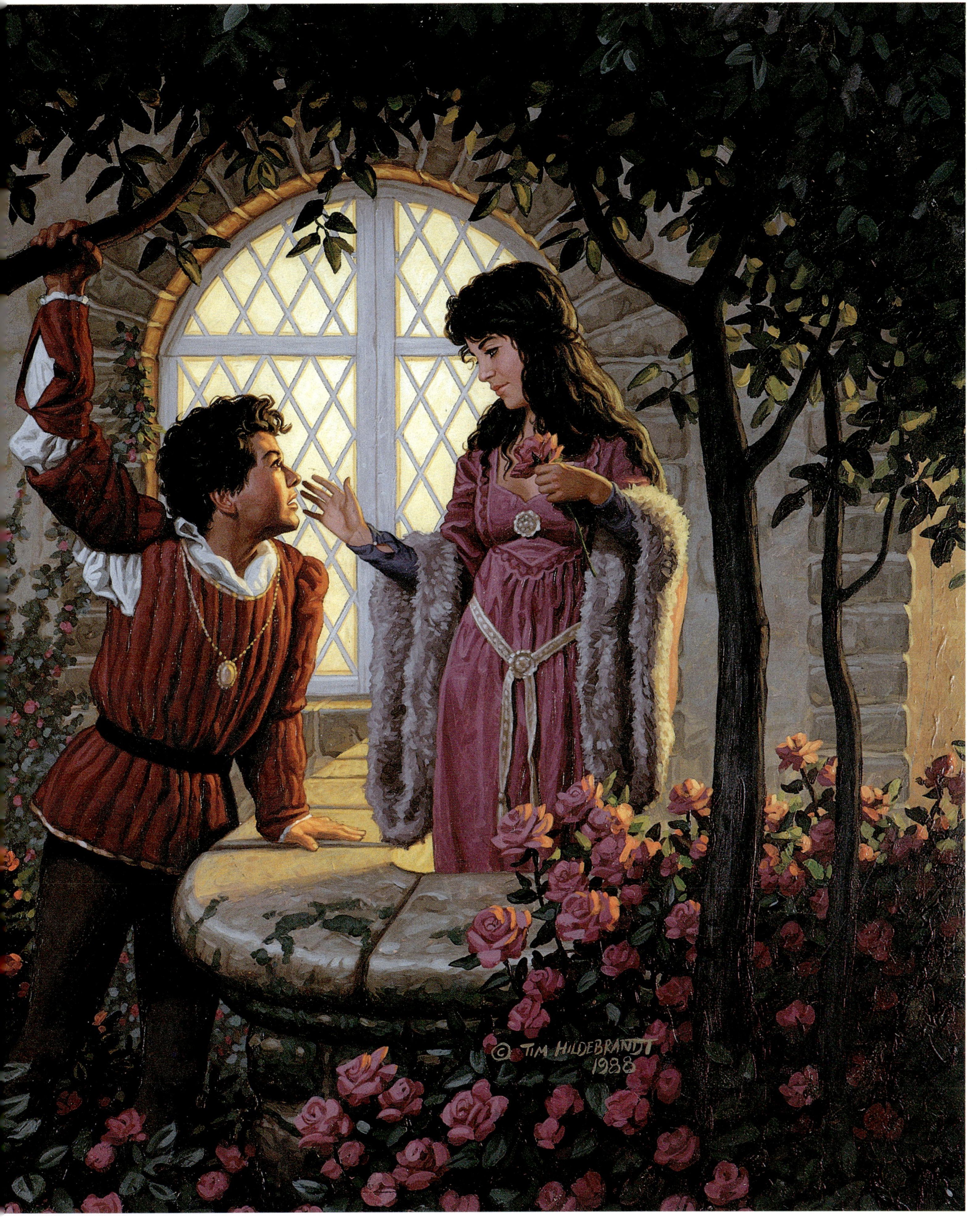
© TIM HILDEBRANDT
1988

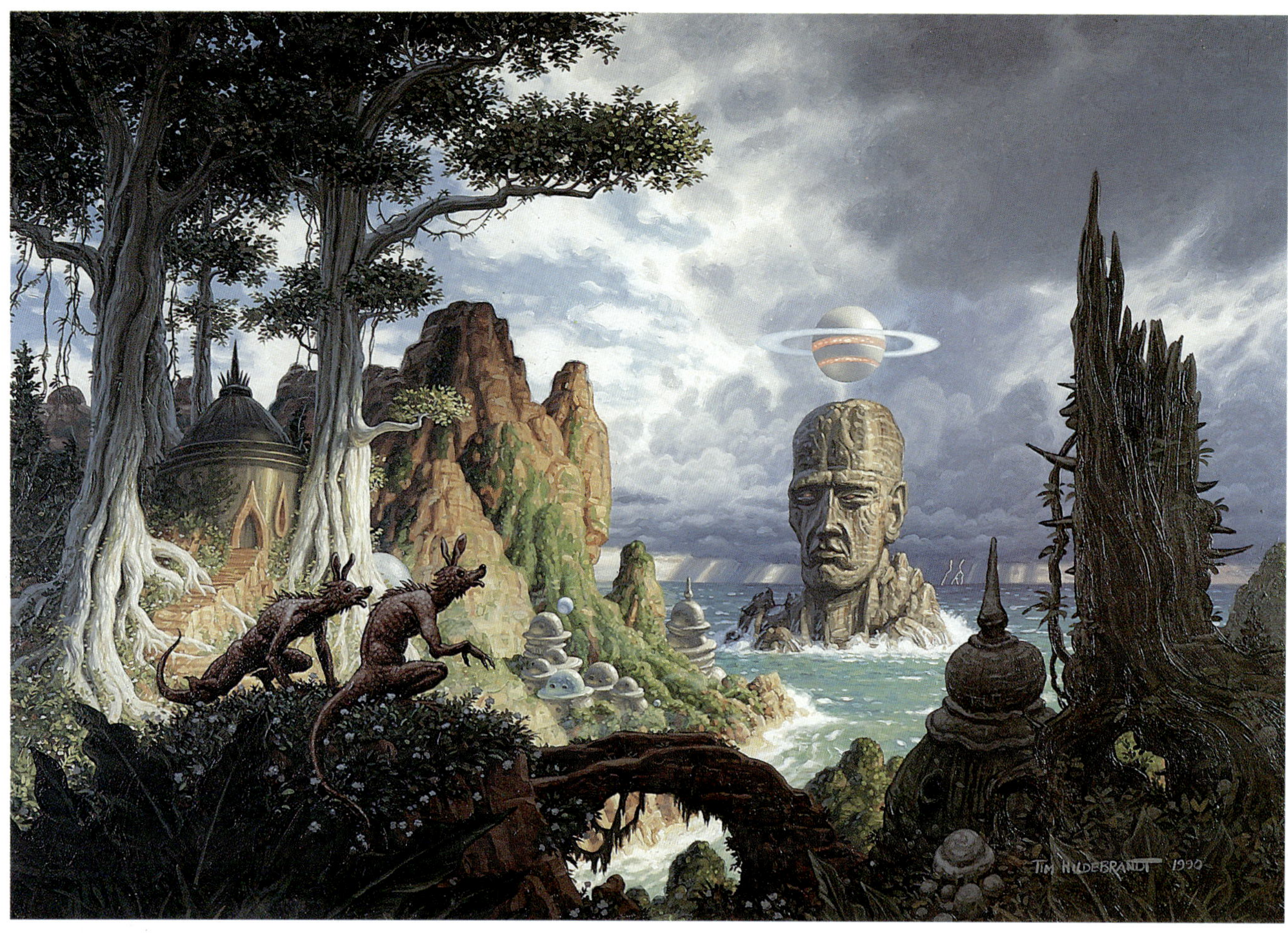

Storm Watch
Private piece, acrylic on masonite. Tim: 'This was
triggered by a photograph of a hurricane
advancing on an island.'

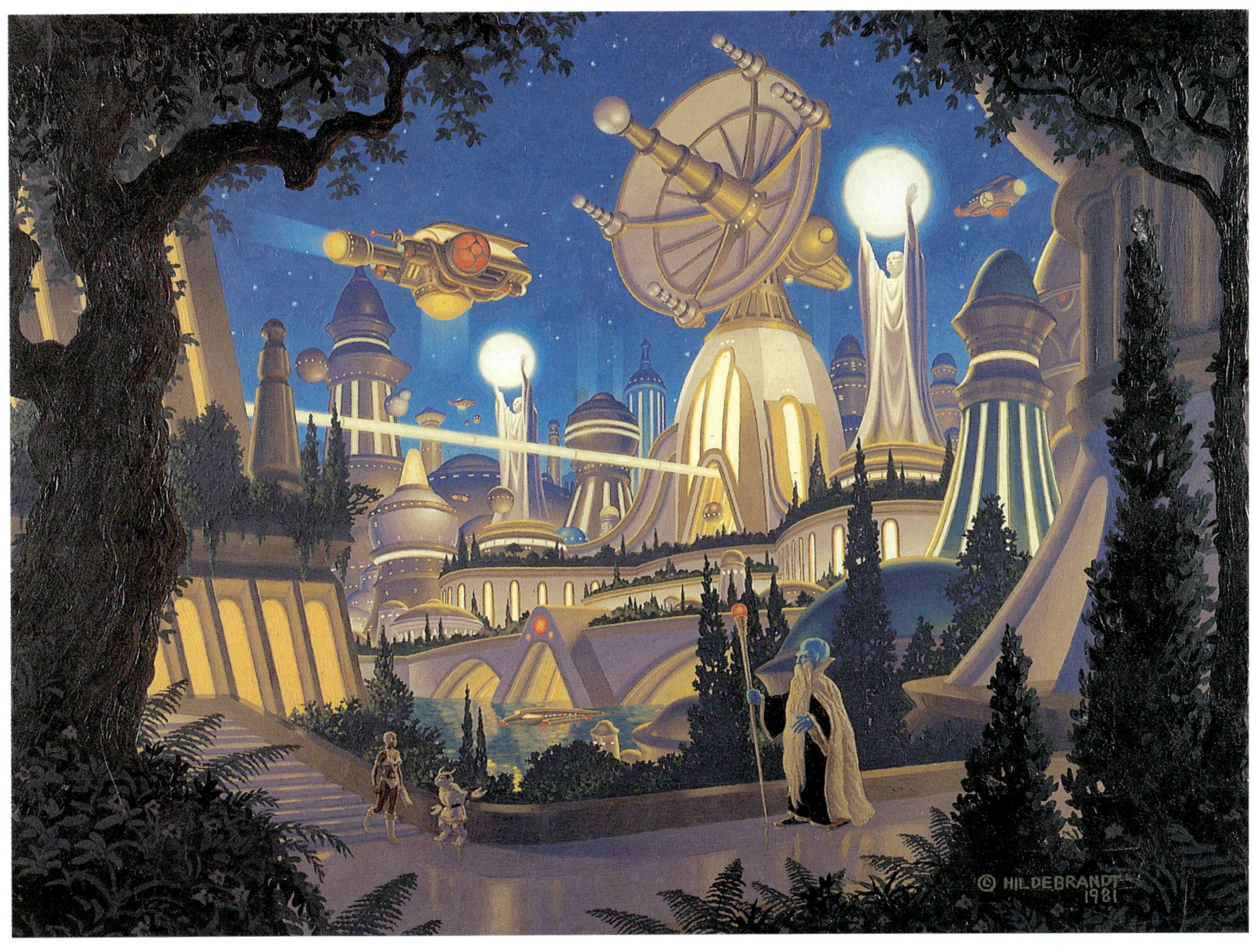

Night Scene in Atlantis
Calendar illustration, Starlog, 1981, acrylic
on masonite.

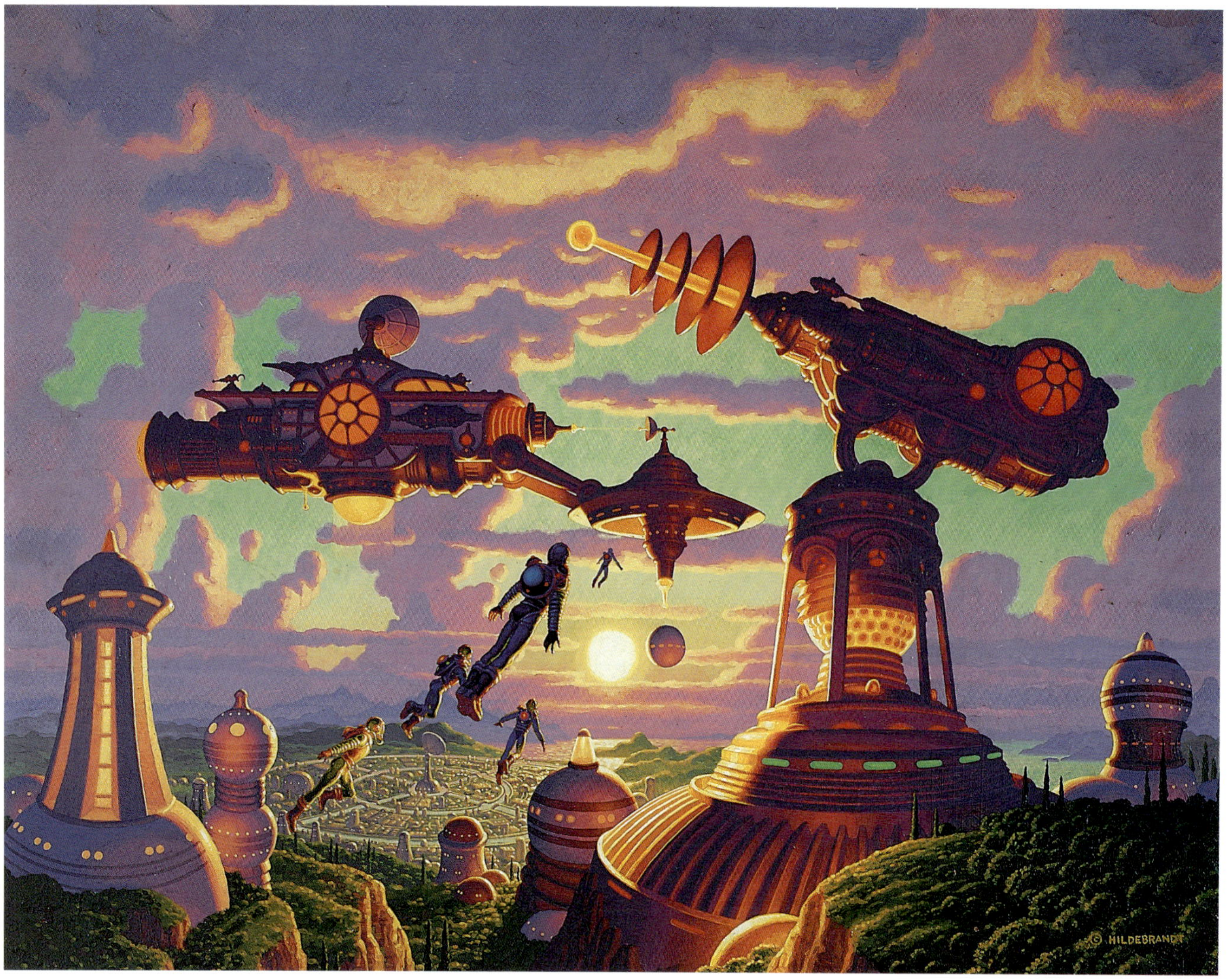

Atlantis: The Lost Continent
Calendar illustration, Starlog, 1981, acrylic on
masonite. Tim: 'Sunrise, sunset, who can really tell
the difference? There isn't any! The effect I was
after here was of the old *Amazing Stories* covers
of the 1930s. Lots of orange and purple.'

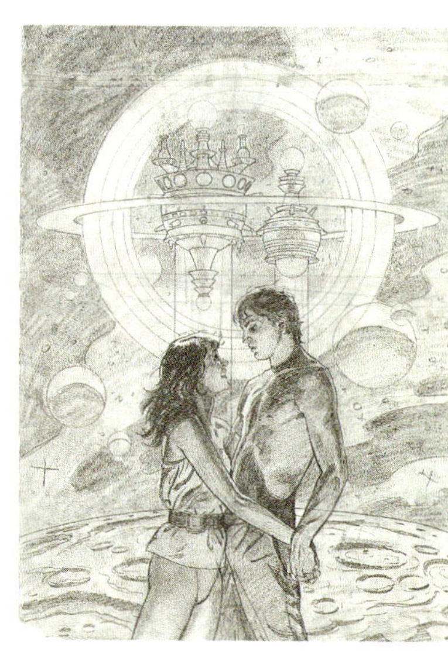

RIGHT **The Byworlder**
Cover illustration for the book by Poul Anderson,
New American Library, 1989, acrylic on masonite.
Tim: 'I read an article about Bob McCall, the artist
who painted the great mural in the Air and Space
Museum in Washington DC. In it he said that when
painting space he didn't use black – too flat – but
burnt umber and ultramarine. I tried it and was
very happy with the results. Thanks Bob!' Of the
unused cover sketch Tim notes: ' I felt that this
was too weak a composition. So did the art
director!'

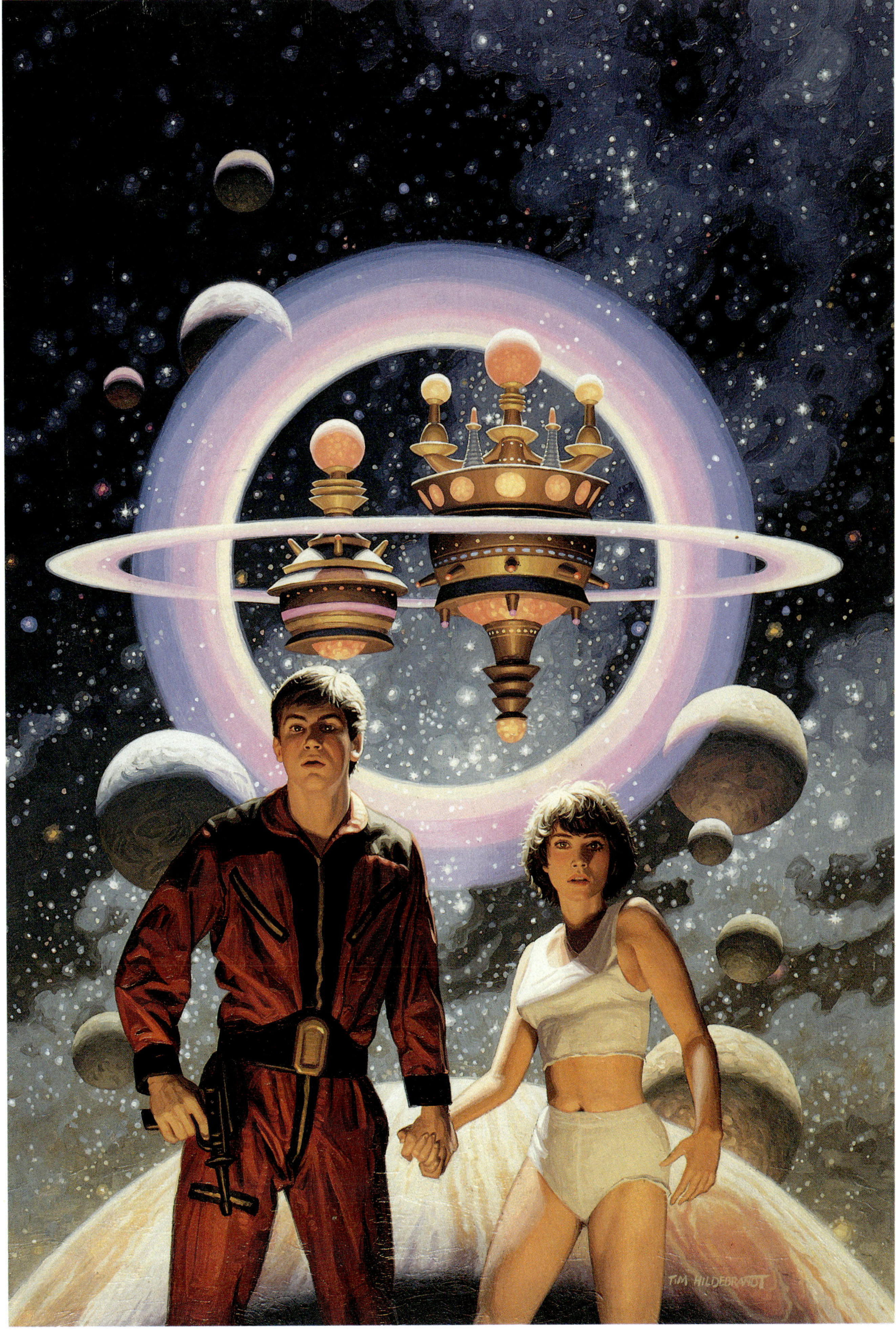
TIM HILDEBRANDT

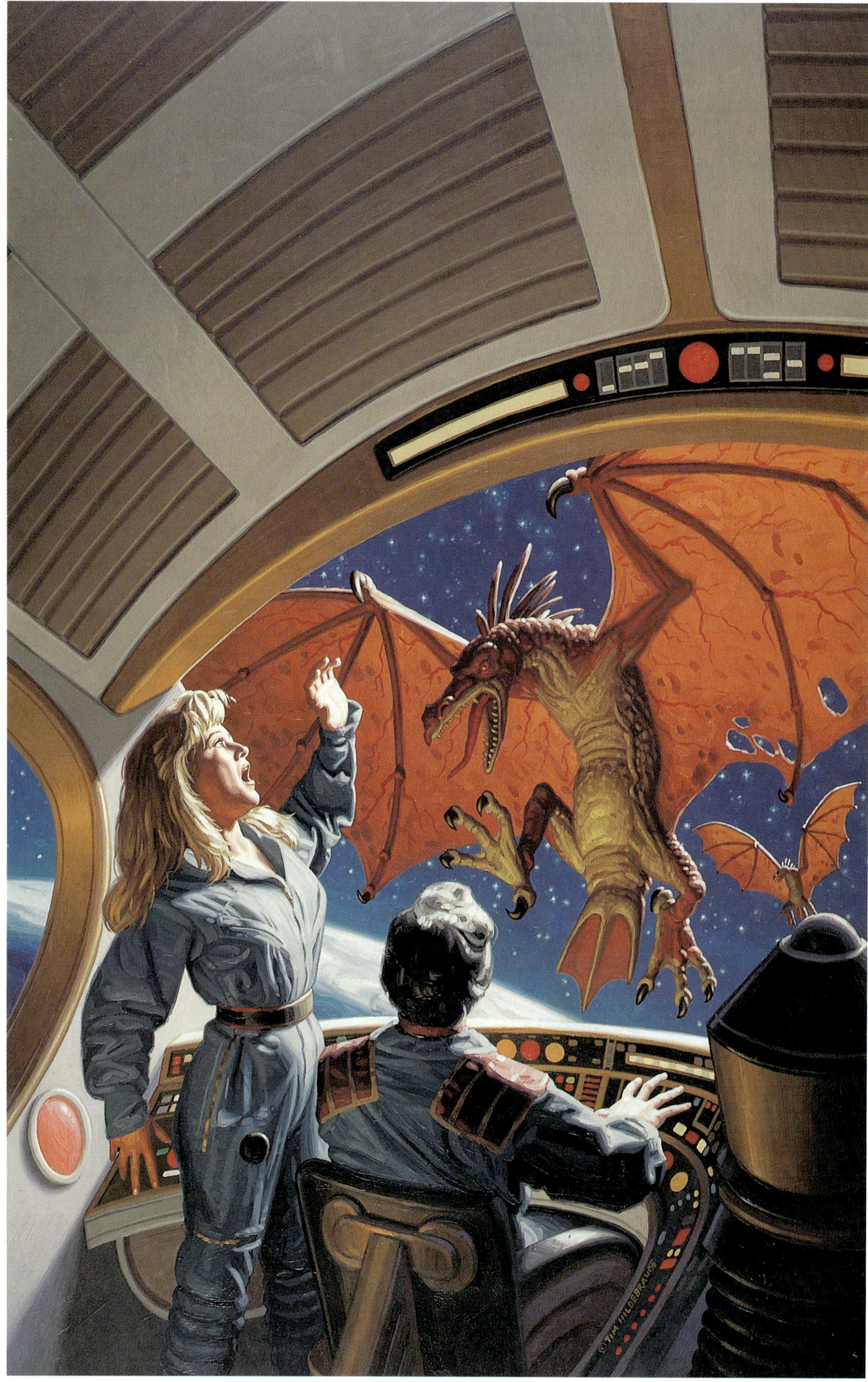

A World of Hells
Book cover, New American Library, 1988, acrylic
on masonite.

RIGHT **Children of Arabel**
This book cover illustration (New American
Library), won the artist the Merit Award from
the Society of Illustrators in 1987, acrylic
on masonite.

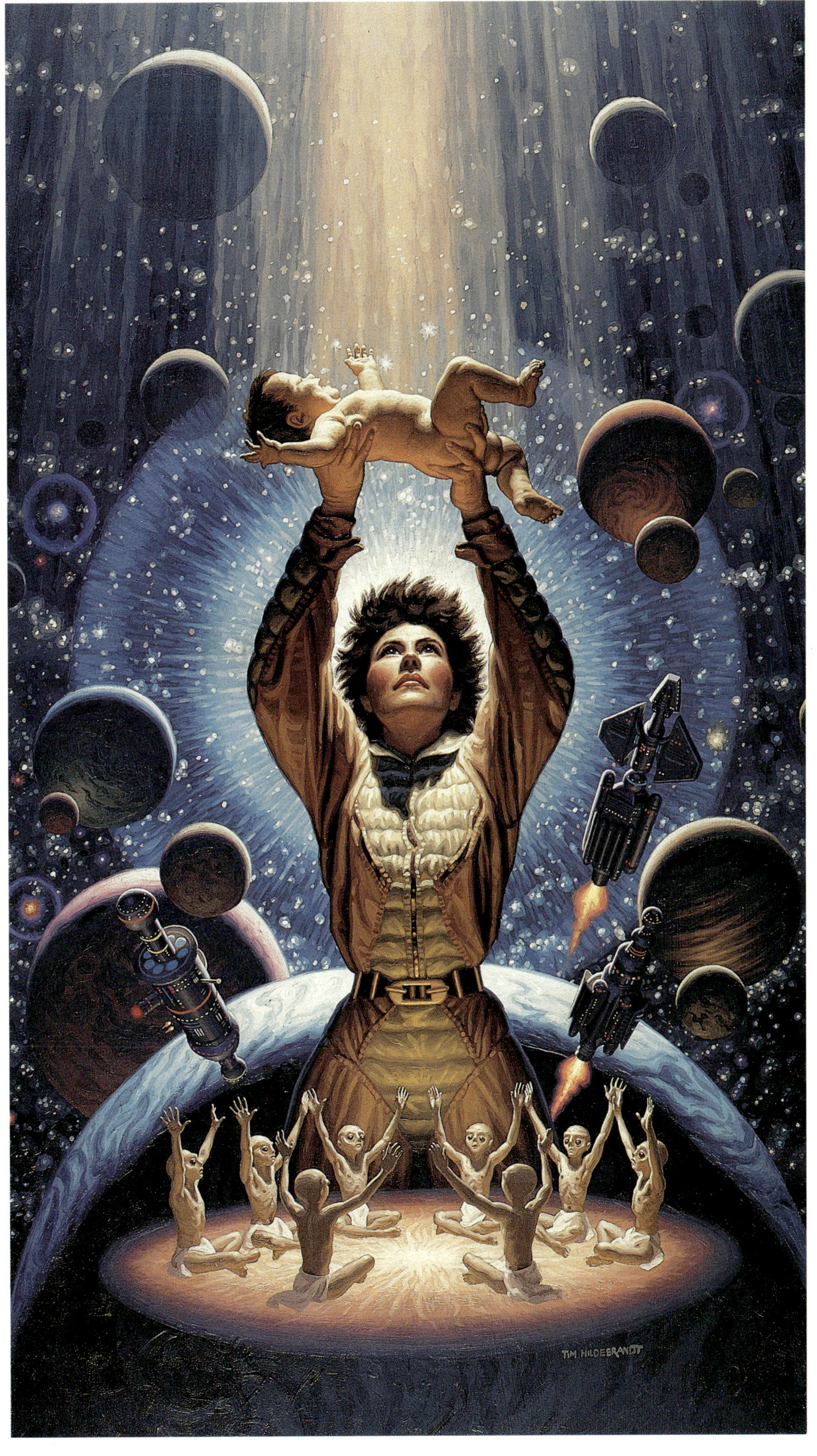

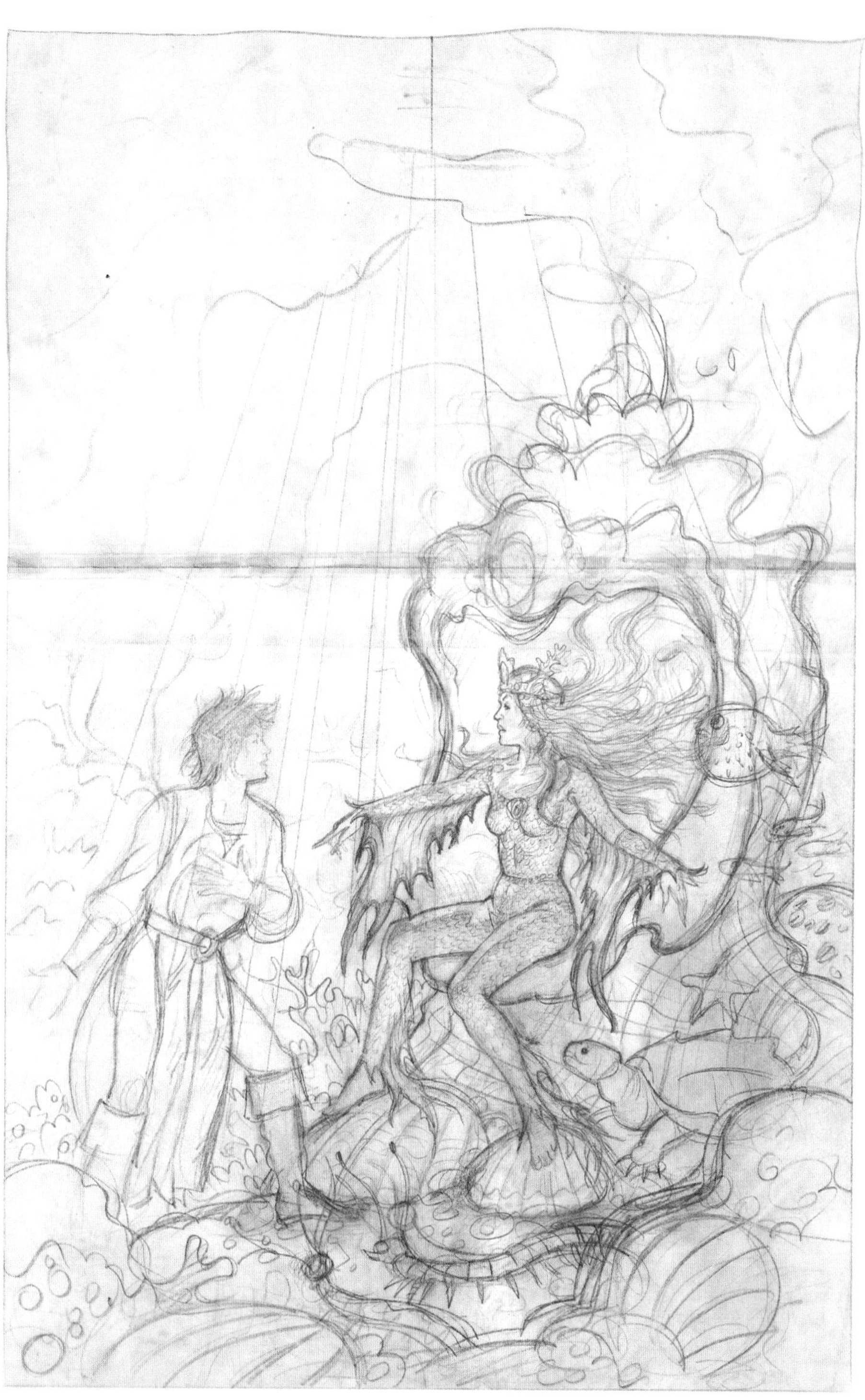

In the Sea Nymph's Lair
Cover illustration for the book by F.J. Hale,
Pageant Books, 1989, acrylic on masonite. Tim:
'Painting an underwater scene is not much
different than one above water. Just make the
background more blue.'

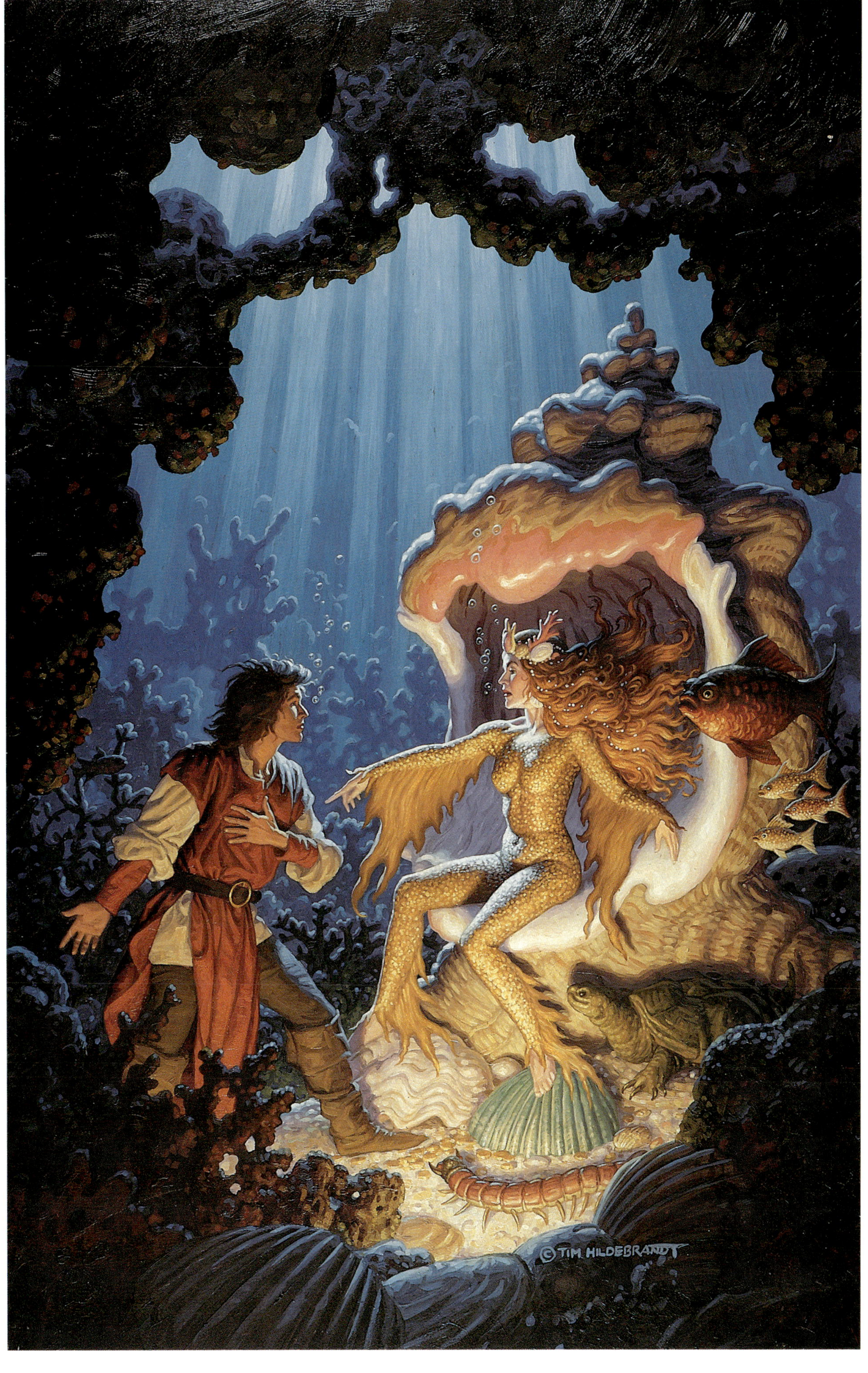
© TIM HILDEBRANDT

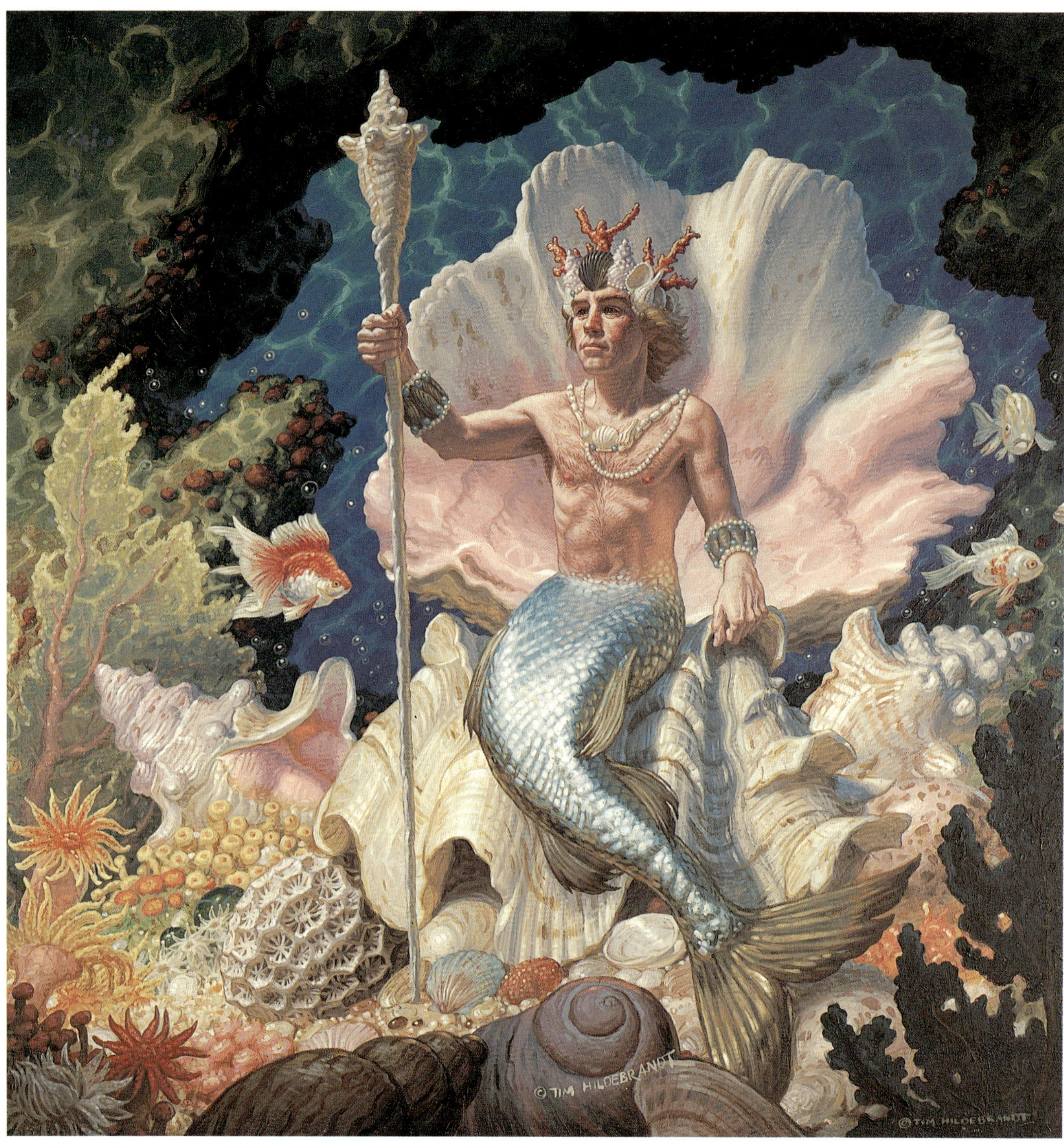

Sea Lord
Illustration from the *Realms of Wonder* calendar,
TSR, 1983, acrylic on masonite. Tim: 'For
reference I used a seashell from my collection
and a fish bought in the supermarket.'

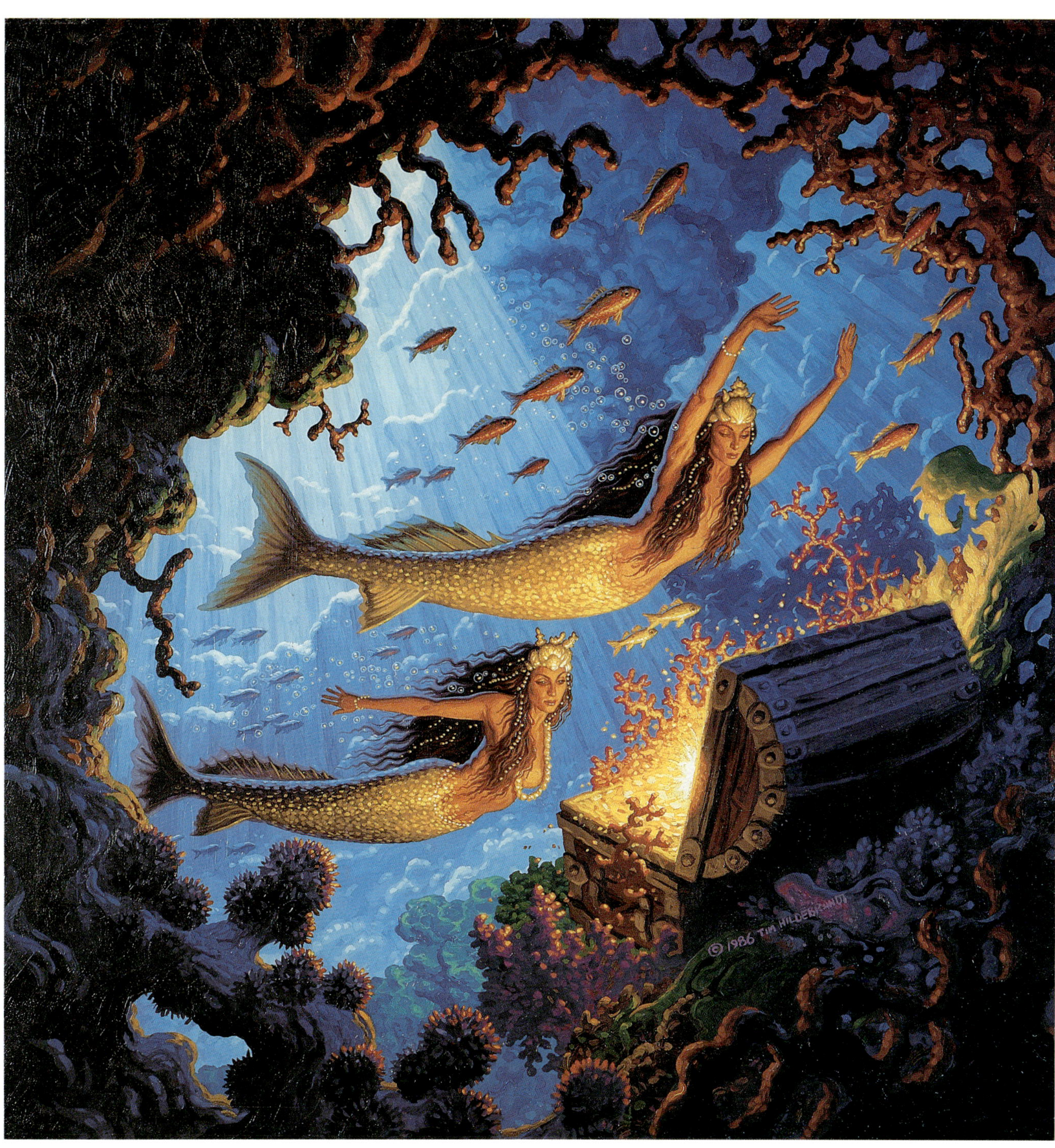

The Mermaid's Grotto
Illustration from the *Realms of Wonder* calendar,
TSR, 1983, acrylic on masonite. Tim: 'The colour
scheme here incorporates the three primary
colours – red, yellow and blue.'

Presentation

Creating art for art's sake is a wonderful thing, in and of itself. However, anyone considering illustration as a profession ultimately must be prepared for dealing with the realities of art as a business, if he or she is to survive. And the first order of business is to establish an effective presentation.

Before launching into a full scale campaign to sell your art it may be helpful if you take some time to evaluate exactly what it is that you hope to accomplish as an illustrator. If you only want to illustrate science fiction or fantasy, that's fine. However, if you have any hopes of actually making a living through your art, it is recommended that you broaden your horizons somewhat.

As a new illustrator, it would benefit you to incorporate as many different styles, techniques, mediums and looks as possible into your portfolio. You never know exactly what that art director has in mind for his next assignment, and by limiting your art to one particular style or genre you are mathematically limiting the number of venues for your work. In the early stages of becoming a professional illustrator your first priority should be simply to survive, and to get your work seen. Specializing in a particular genre almost always follows establishing yourself as an artist first.

A beginner's portfolio could contain a good selection of watercolours, pen and ink drawings, black and white renderings, realistic art, cartoon art and ad layouts. It wouldn't hurt if some of those paintings or drawings had a recognizable 'look' to them. As a young illustrator, many of Tim's paintings imitated the styles of Walt Disney, or Norman Rockwell. He and Greg earned the reputation among art directors of: 'When in doubt, give it to the Hildebrandts'. As a result, he admits that there was no instant development of personal style, but he was able to live comfortably from his work as an artist. Besides, style develops naturally with time, and is subject to change, so it shouldn't be your biggest priority.

There are, of course, some exceptions to this rule of variety. If you know that a publisher is looking for an artist to illustrate their new series of children's books, you

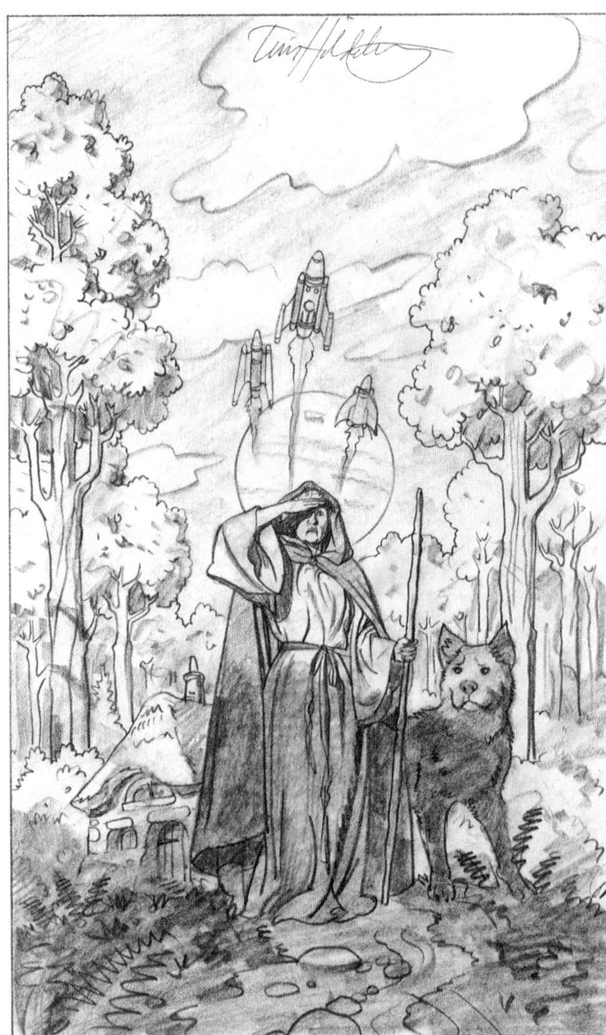

Unused cover sketch for *Vendetta* by M.S. Murdock. Tim: 'Several different pencil sketches of one subject might show an art director your versatility.'

RIGHT **Barbarella**
This illustration for the poster of the reissue of the film *Barbarella* was submitted just too late for it to be considered for use, 1979, acrylic on masonite. Tim: 'It is useful to include in your portfolio a likeness of a famous person.'

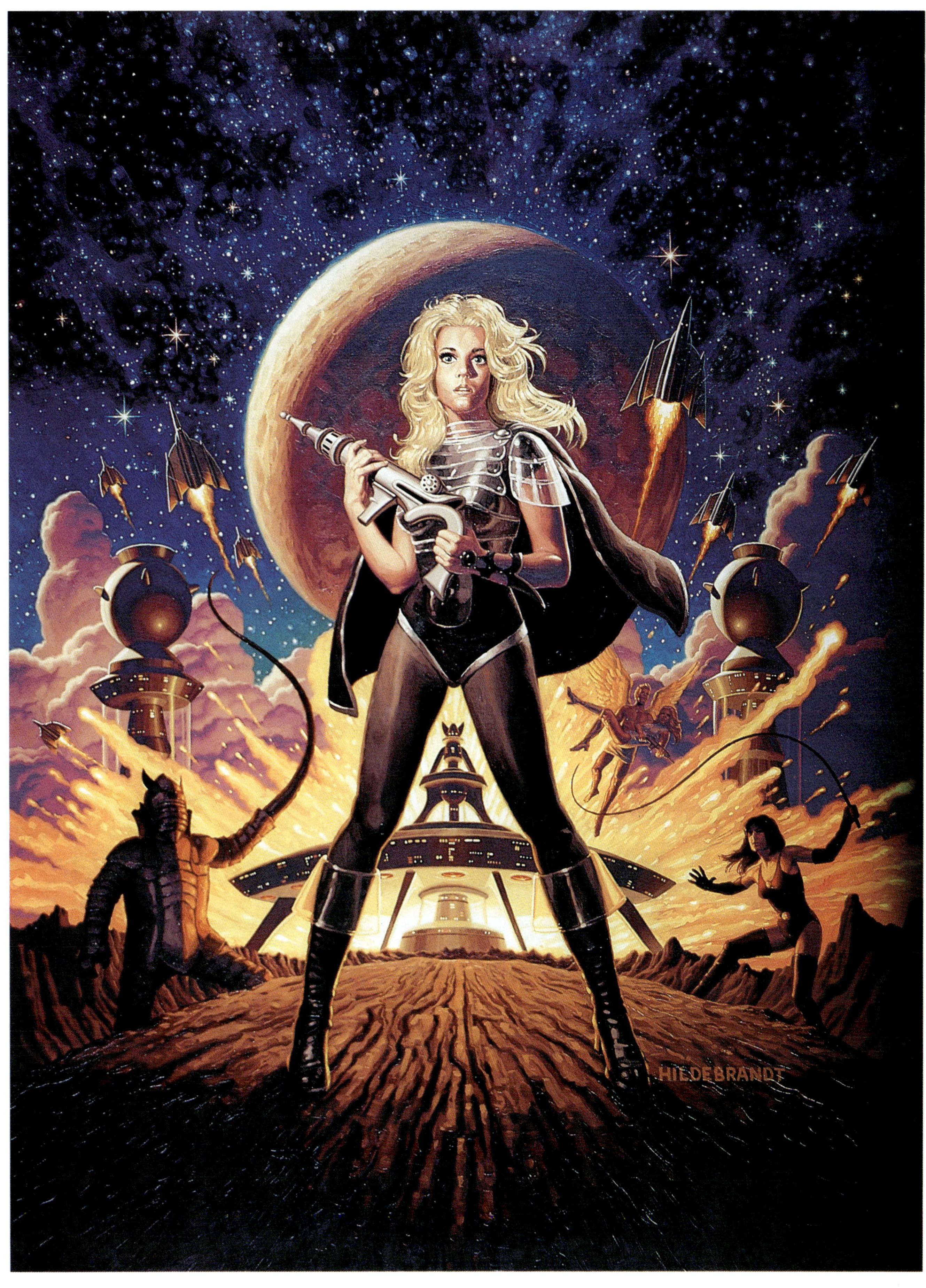

would want to tailor your portfolio to fit that. If you are presenting your artwork for any specific job, you would take that into consideration. Still, you would want to include as many different styles and mediums that could represent that genre.

Once you have your drawings and paintings assembled, you must begin sorting through the artwork, and include only the very best. Beware the inclusion of a 'favorite' painting if it is not your best work; a single bad, or even fair painting or rendering can compromise your entire portfolio. Remember, you are trying to show a variety of styles and genres, so try to represent evenly each style. Never include figure studies by themselves; most art directors are more interested in learning what you can do with those figures in an illustration. Instead, include those figures in an ad layout or a book cover, or some other context that has some value.

Ideally, you want to be perceived as a professional artist, so the next step would be to assemble your artwork into a portfolio case, or some other case that portrays a professional image. These can be found at most art supply stores, and range in both size and price. It isn't necessary to purchase the portfolio with the fanciest design, or most expensive price tag. Find one that is large enough to hold and protect your work, and is sturdy enough to last. Most portfolio cases have a space on the outside for your name, address and telephone number. Use it. That information is perhaps the most critical information an art director will need after evaluating your work.

Once equipped with a high-quality portfolio you are ready to make your presentation. If you are fortunate enough to live in close proximity to a large city, you simply take your portfolio of original art to the various publishing houses and leave it in care of the art director there. With luck, you may receive an immediate appointment to see the art director. In most cases, you won't. As long as you have your name and address on the case, it will be in good hands. You may consider including a simple letter of introduction, explaining who you are and what you do. If you do include a cover letter, be very concise and polite

without too much explanation; they know why you are there, so let your art speak for itself.

You will probably discover that most art directors are not in a rush to evaluate new artists, as they are quite often deluged with other work that they are responsible for. It is not uncommon for art directors to take several months to get back to you. Be patient. It is considered very unprofessional to badger these people with phone calls, asking where your artwork is. Instead, take this time to work on another portfolio, and approach other art directors. Eventually, they will get back to you.

If you don't happen to live close to a city, you can still make it as a professional illustrator. In your case, you would want to send in high-quality transparencies of your work. Most art directors will accept 35mm slides. Address the slides to the art director at the publishing house you are submitting to, and use that art director's name, if you know it. If you don't have a name, simply address the package to the attention of the art director. It will still go to the right place. Remember that, if you want your materials returned, you must include the correct return postage with your submission. Few publishers will return your portfolio without it. Be sure to include a cover letter as before, with your name, address and telephone number where you can be reached. And once again, remember that it can take quite a while for a reply, so be patient. Use the in-between time to contact other art directors, or to improve your work.

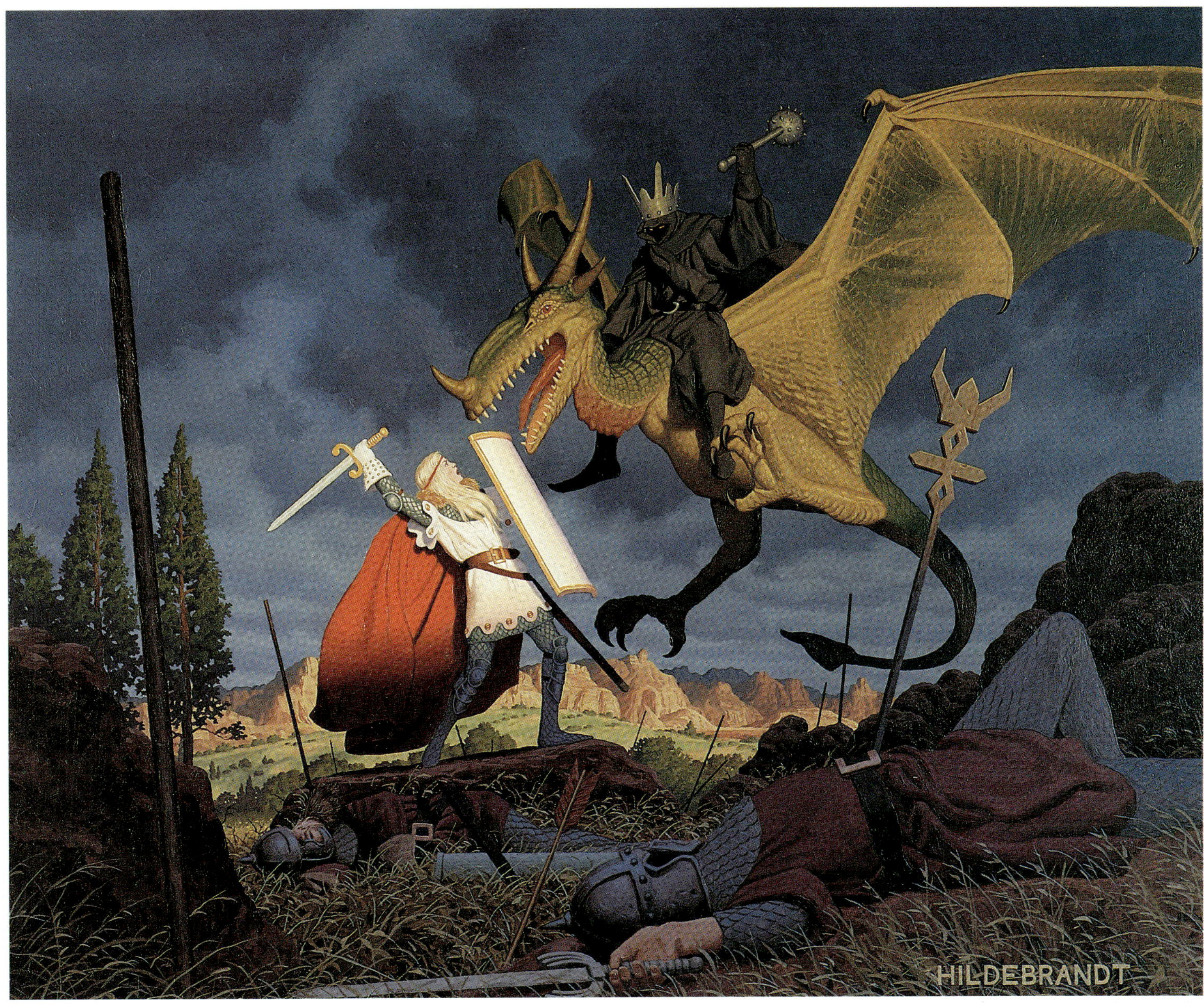

Eowyn and the Nazgul
From the J.R.R. Tolkien calendar, Ballantine
Books, 1976, acrylic on masonite. Tim: 'This
calendar was my first fantasy project.'

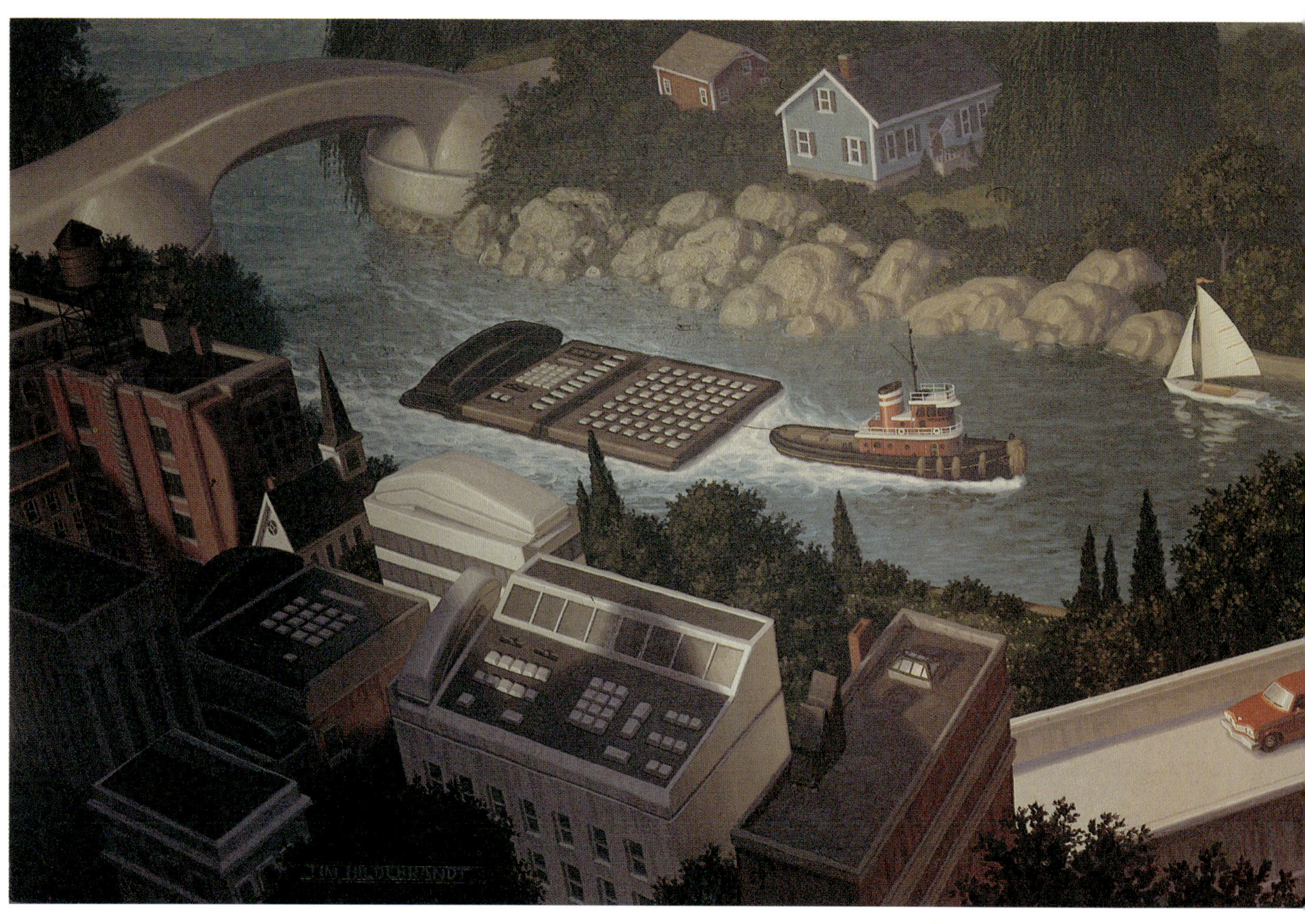

Advertisement illustration for AT&T, 1985,
acrylic on masonite.

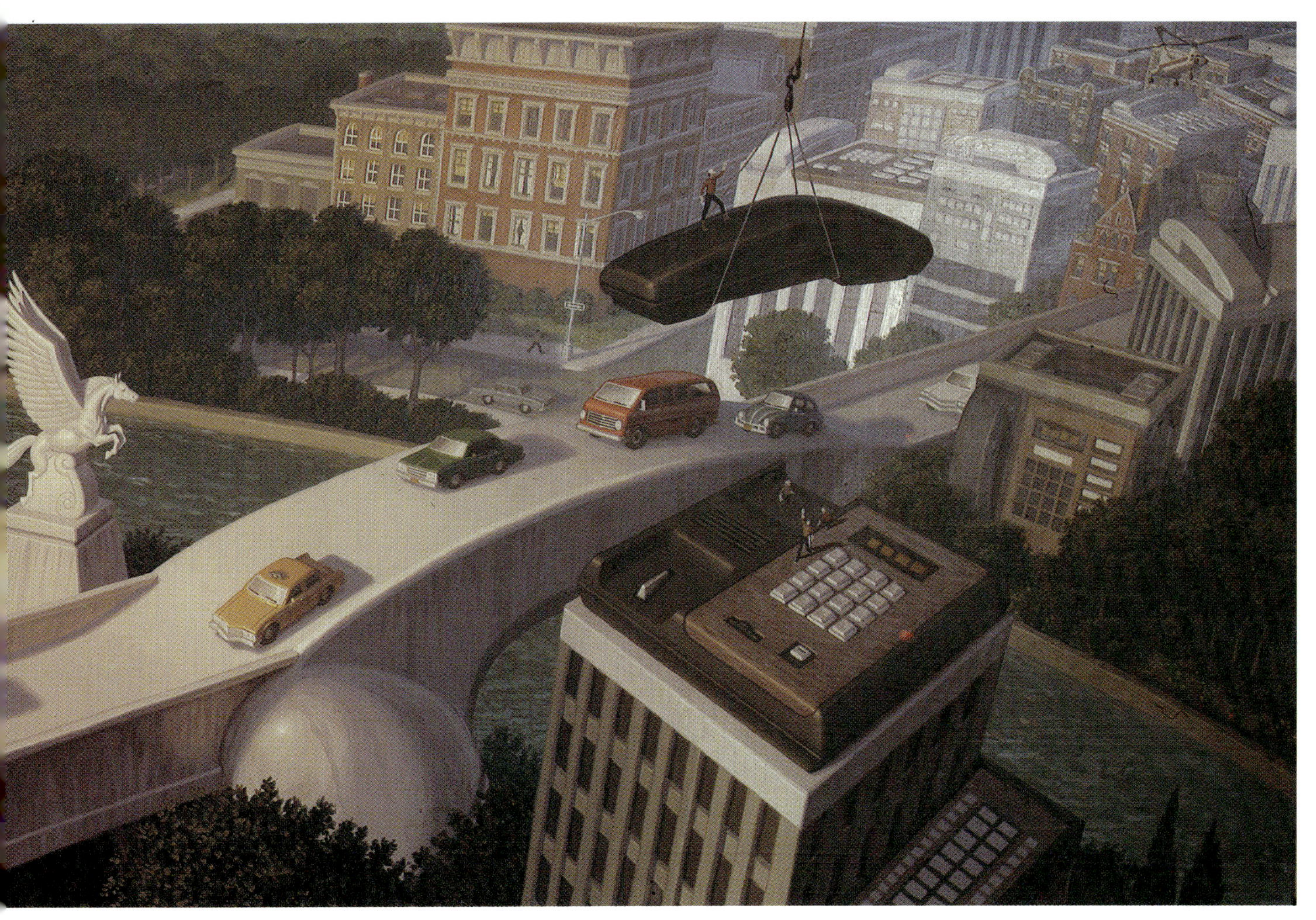

Regardless of where you live, you might at some point consider having an agent or agency represent you. If you live out of town, this could be essential. Working with an agent has its obvious benefits, but it can have some drawbacks as well. Before you decide, you should consider the advantages and disadvantages.

Obviously, the first advantage of having an agent is that they do the legwork for you. In the ideal situation, you would be provided with a continuous flow of work, and all you would have to do is deliver your art. Usually, it doesn't happen that way. Many agents, especially those who are inclined to take on new artists, may represent many other artists at the same time. In his early days, Tim's first agent represented about sixty other artists, and provided Tim with an average of two jobs per year. The rest of his work was sold through his own persistence.

Perhaps the biggest drawback of having an agent represent you is the percentage that they receive for every sale. Most agents receive an average of twenty-five percent on each placement, even if he or she was only involved in the initial contact. For instance, if an agent introduces you to an art director, and as a result that art director buys your work, your agent is entitled to his percentage of every sale to that art director, even if he is not directly involved. On the other hand, a good agent will land you jobs that you might not have been able to get otherwise.

In the end, it doesn't really matter who represents you, as long as that person is directly tied in to the publishing industry. Tim's second representative was Ian Sommers, the art director for Ballantine. He was involved in the sale of *Urshurak*, and was ideal due to his ties in the publishing industry. Following that, he was represented by his wife Rita, which he concluded was the ideal working situation. Today he still maintains an agent, but is only dependent on him to land advertising jobs that often elude unrepresented artists.

If you've decided that agency representation is the right choice for you, the next step is to find one. You can begin by obtaining a copy of the telephone directory. Artists' agents will be happy to describe their agency to

you: take some time to study these prospective agencies carefully. Some questions you want to be sure are answered before you enter into any agreement include: what percentage do they receive for sales? How many other artists do they represent? Are they accepting new clients? What are their submission requirements? Once you have narrowed the list down to your satisfaction you may begin submitting your work. This is essentially the same as submitting to an art director. Try to include a variety of subjects, genres, styles and mediums. Be sure to include information on how you can be contacted. And be patient.

Finding the right agent can be as frustrating for a novice illustrator as making his first sale. It is the same situation that has troubled workers in every profession for years. It's difficult to get the job without the experience, but it's just as difficult to get experience without the job. The key here is perseverance. Take the time between submissions to continually hone your craft. Eventually, the effort will pay off.

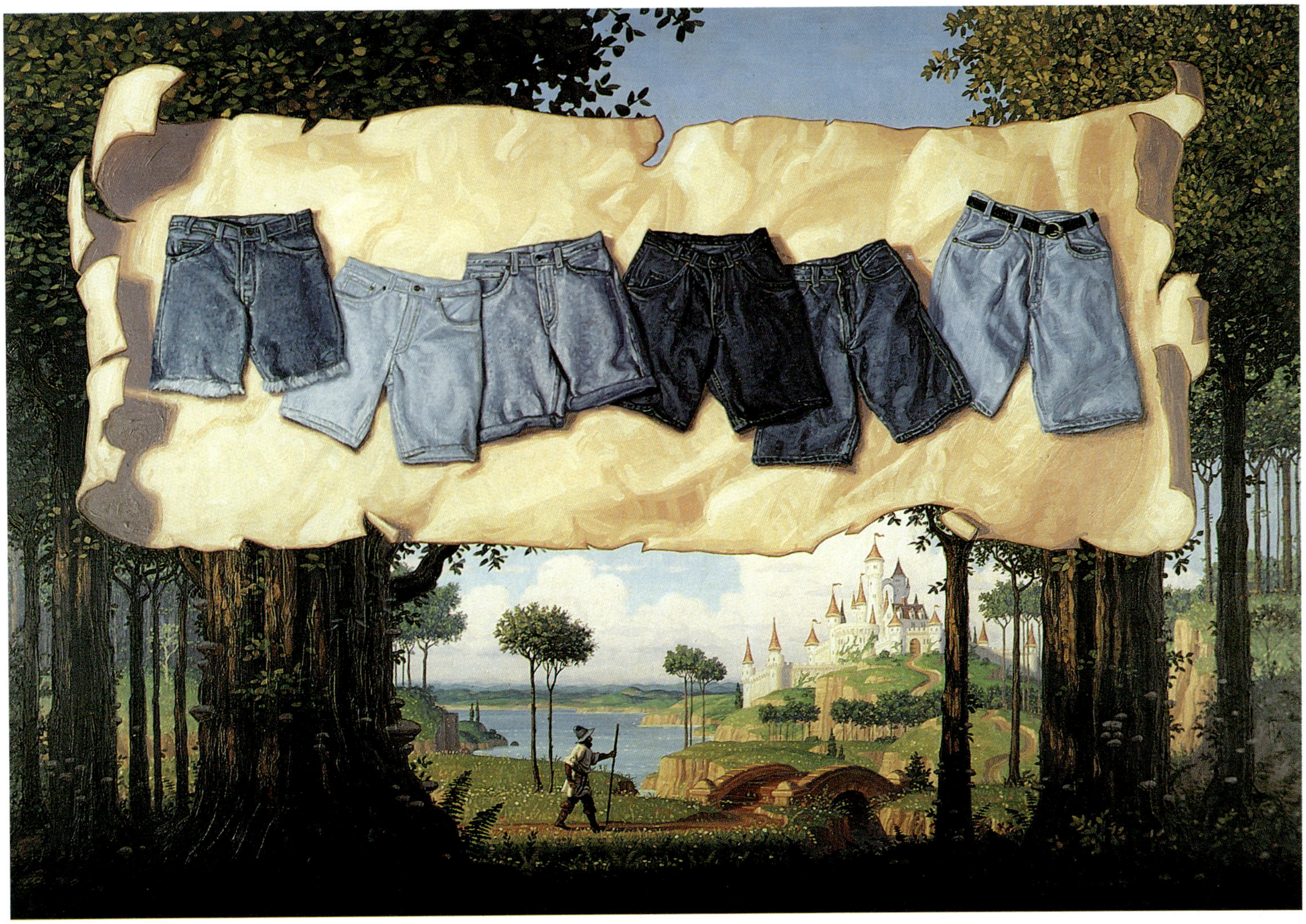

ABOVE Advertisement illustration for Levi Strauss, 1990, acrylic on masonite.

RIGHT Video game cover for Parker Brothers, 1985, acrylic on masonite. Based on the last 'Star Wars' film *Return of the Jedi*.

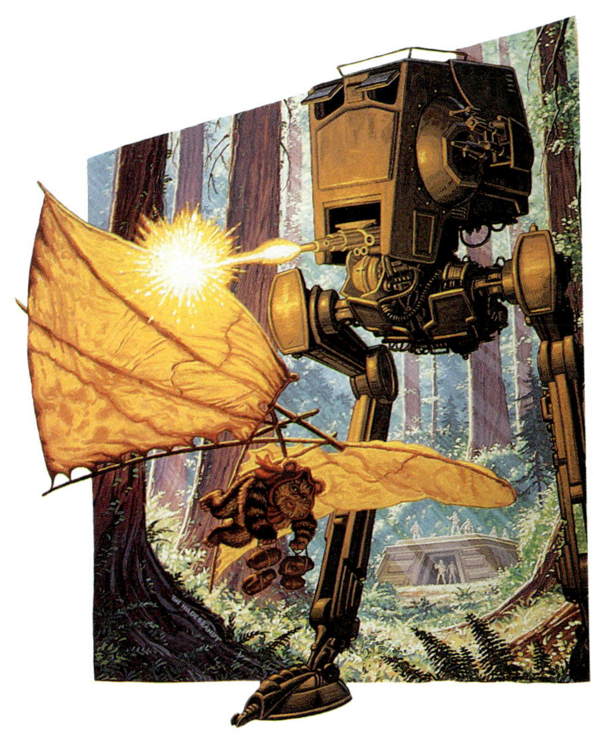

Conclusion

154

There was little hope from the beginning of condensing all of the techniques learned during the thirty years that Tim has been an artist into the few pages here. In retrospect, I don't think that was ever the intent. Tim Hildebrandt is a virtual encyclopedia of artistic knowledge, demonstrating talents that go far beyond those of an ordinary commercial artist. His knowledge of art could easily fill several volumes this size.

Instead, I've tried to include an understanding of the principles that are basic to Tim's technique. These principles are the foundation for virtually all of his work, no matter what the medium. They are the formulae that have enabled him to consistently produce the artwork that makes him the artist that he is.

I have tried, in the space allowed, to describe these specific principles within the different chapters of the book, but perhaps the most fundamental principle can only be seen through a much larger overview: the fact that there is a formula that, once learned, can be used universally by anyone to improve their art.

Not that these are magic formulae, and that by simply following the words I've assembled you will somehow become a great artist. This book is merely a beginning, one that can provide you with a framework from which your own abilities can develop. You still must do the work. It is up to you to learn everything you can about all of the topics presented within this book, and though books can help you, ultimately you learn by doing.

Knowing that art is a learned skill can represent an enormous breakthrough for many people. How often have we told ourselves, or been told by others, that you must have a talent to be successful as an artist? This fallacy has no doubt kept untold numbers of people from reaching their own creative potential. It is probably correct to say that some people develop the necessary skills to create art at a more accelerated rate than others. But, nonetheless, these skills are learned. If there is a gift given by God, it is the gift of determination. It is that burning desire to achieve their goals that compels people to excel, regardless of their chosen profession.

Like all other art forms, fantasy art can be learned. The procedures for choosing a subject, deciding on the most effective composition and rendering the scene is identical to any other genre. What separates the mundane from the fantastic is the imagination of the artist. An artist may see only a woman, or a fish. The fantasy artist, however, might blur the two images, then focus on a mermaid shimmering in the ocean mists. An artist may see a mother and her child, while the fantasy artist might surround them with tiny alien beings against a background of planets and stars.

This deliberate distortion of images that creates fantasy from the ordinary can also be learned. To begin with, simply recognize that fantasy need only be an extension of reality. There are probably hundreds of ordinary items that surround you every day that, with a simple stretch of your imagination, could furnish you with unlimited inspiration for your art. To the fantasy artist, the simple shape of a key might provoke images of huge battleships in space. An oatmeal box readily lends itself to the cylindrical shape of a time-travel machine. A plastic dinosaur, with the addition of a photo of bat's wings, becomes an enormous, fire-breathing dragon. You can train yourself to look at things in a slightly different way, and, once you do, you will suddenly find yourself in the world of fantasy.

Even under the best of circumstances, all of us can get discouraged. What you must realize is that, like everything else, the learning and development of an artistic skill takes time. You must master the basics before you can effectively utilize the more advanced techniques. I can't say that I've ever met anyone who actually enjoyed shading cylinders or spheres, yet without this technique, how could you possibly render a human form? The key is persistence; you can only improve with practise.

Fantasy art can be one of the most challenging, yet rewarding genres to work in. At times it can prove to be quite strenuous, taxing all of your senses to the limit. At the same time, it could prove to be one of the most exhilarating activities you could ever pursue. There is something very remarkable about an artist who can somehow bring to life the most fantastic elements of our imaginations. For that artist, being able to create new worlds, and then populate them in any way he chooses is often reason enough to continue his efforts.

It is true that the most powerful tool an artist can possess is not one that can be bought or sold, nor is it a technique that can be taught or learned. It is undoubtedly that spirit of determination and endurance, and must develop naturally within each artist. Establish that desire first, and perhaps then the techniques presented here will help you along.

Afterword

To me fine art is fashioned of multiples: skilled draftsmanship, mastery of media, facility with the brush and pen, understanding of anatomy, perspective and composition. Place them in the hands of the semi-skilled and they will render on board and canvas the most exquisite corpses. Technically proficient frozen imagos without warmth, without meaning. Without life.

Would-be aesthetic interlocutors will direct you to observe a painting, to study and analyze it. You don't have to look at a Tim Hildebrandt painting: *it* looks at you. I am not being facetious. There is a glow to Tim's work that demands your attention even as it arrests the indifferent eye; chromatic bursts of colour and intensity that slam into the optic nerve and insist you pay attention. You *must* look; the Hildebrandt kaleidoscope gives no quarter. I am put in mind of Maxfield Parrish working with brushes instead of lasers.

To achieve such an effect in two dimensions requires more than mere application of neon shades to canvas. Light in art is a paradoxical manifestation of shadow, of darking and subduing what is in the background to highlight that which is to be crowned prominent. Tim is a master of gradation, a toiler in supple lumens rather than blatant shapes. The result is that his work doesn't attract, it grabs. Big, bold sweeps of, yes, of shadow that roll forward like waves, until the eye is blinded by the comparative brilliance of a lamp, a sidelit face, a mermaid's eyes. It is all a matter of deliberate and skilled contrast. Not, 'I'd like you to look at this' but 'I'm going to *make* you look at this!'

This is the light that illuminates the inspiration, which Tim conjures from his own mind and from the words of those writers fortunate enough to find their creations given shape and form by him. It is one thing to describe a sinister parrot and quite another to paint its portrait, as Tim did on the cover of my novel *The Time of the Transference*. One thing to paint a character, quite another to give shape and form to its spirit, its essence.

One thing to be a painter, and another to be an artist.

Alan Dean Foster, Prescott, Arizona, March 1991

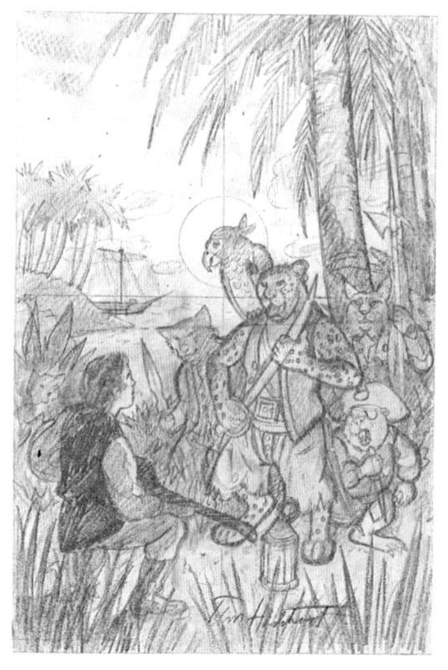

The Time of the Transference
Cover illustration for a book by
Alan Dean Foster, Warner Books,
1986, acrylic on masonite.

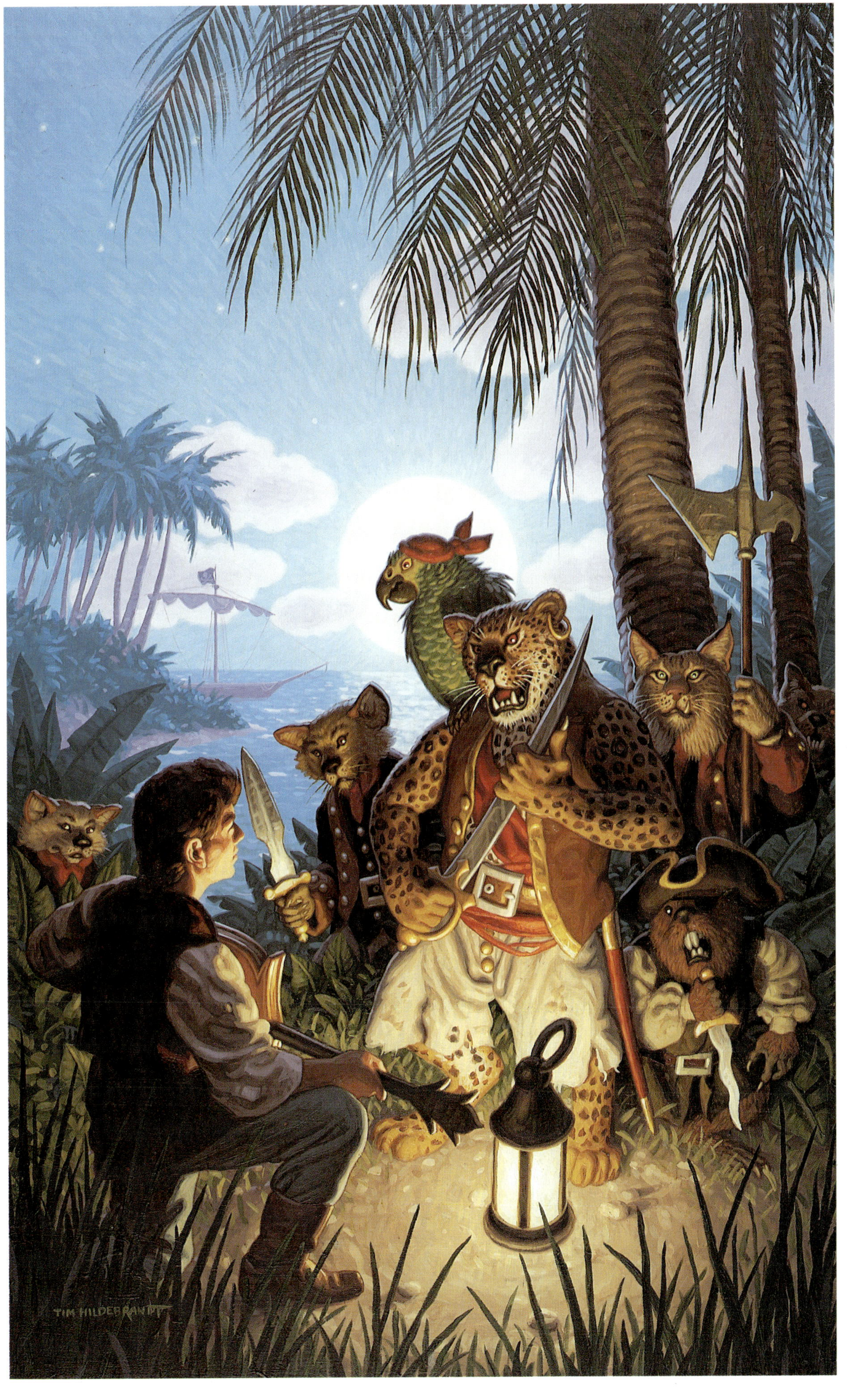

TIM HILDEBRANDT

Index

Entries in bold denote illustrations, those in italics to publications or films.

advertisement illustrations **151—1, 153**
After the Spell Wars: Book One: Ogre Castle 118
agents, representation by 152
Alta 99
Amazing Stories 112
Amazon City of Zandura, The 25
Amazon Fire Crystal, The 17
Amazon Musicians at the Oasis 95
Amazon Tournament 95
Amazons, The 93
And the Sphinx Always Nose 133
art, basic principles of 76, 80, 92, 154
artists, fantasy 154
artists, professional 146, 148, 152, 154
Atlantis (Calendar) 26
Atlantis: The Lost Continent 138
award-winning illustration **141**

Barbarella 147
Billy Goat's Gruff 10
Bitter Gold Hearts 70
Blackfoot Indians Hunting Bear 66
book covers
    After the Spell Wars: Book One: Ogre Castle 118
    Amazing Stories 112
    And the Sphinx Always Nose 133
    Bitter Gold Hearts 70
    Byworlder, The 138—9
    Children of Arabel 141
    Curse of the Werewolf, The 130—1
    Day of Their Return, The 56—7
    Dragon's Carbuncle, The 54—5
    Dread Brass Shadow 48—9
    Dynteryx 58—59
    Fang the Gnome 51, 84
    In the Sea Nymph's Lair 142—3
    King of the Sceptered Aisle, The 125
    Knight of Ghosts and Shadows, A 129
    Lord of Chaos 36—37
    Merovingen Nights: Divine Right 68
    Red Iron Nights 71—5
    Sweet Silver Blues 88
    Sword of Shannara, The 126
    There Will Be Time 42—3
    Those Who Watch 44—5
    Time of Transference, The 156—7
    To Warm the Earth 67
    Tripods, The 52—3, 110

    unnamed **113, 123, 124, 128**
    Vendetta 24, 65, 146
    White Dragon, The 61
    World of Hells, A 140
    Worldstone 50
    Worm Oroborus, The 91
Byworlder, The 138—9

calendars
    Atlantis 26
    Dragonriders of Pern, The (1984) **115, 116**
    Dragonriders of Pern, The (1985) **40—1, 60, 119**
    Dungeons and Dragons 26
    Realms of Wonder (1982) **63, 111**
    Realms of Wonder (1983) **16, 33, 62, 69, 106—7, 114, 144, 145**
    Realms of Wonder (1987) **23**
    sundry other **22, 137, 138**
    Tolkein, J.R.R. (1976) **10**, 24, **46—7, 149**
    Tolkein, J.R.R. (1978) 10, **14—15**, 24, **35**
    Xanth **90, 120—1**
Children of Arabel 141
clouds 106, 112, 126, 130, 132
Coates, Claude 28
colours
    absolute 108, 120, 134
    acrylic 116, 120
    cool 112, 116, 130
    earth tone 116, 120
    lighting, effect of 108, 130
    value 108, 112, 120, 126, 130, 132
    warm 112, 116, 130
composition
    elements, placing of 46, 56, 80
    eyes, cultural use of 44, 46, 50
    final 84, 116
    formal 44, 46
    horizon line 46, 50, 56
    informal 44, 46
    lighting *see* lighting
    perspective 46, 50, 54, 58, 80
    picture plane 44, 46, 56, 80, 92
    rough 56, 84, 92, 94
    thumbnail sketch 54, 56, 84, 92, 94, 100
costumes 34, **38**, 80
covers
    book *see* book covers
    video game *see* video game cover
cross hatching technique 98
Crowning a new Elf Princess 94
Curse of the Werewolf, The 130—1

Day of Their Return, The 56—7
Deadly Spawn, The 26, 27
Dinosaur Rag, The (film) 26
Disney, Walt, influence of 12, 16, 28
distance, effect of 106, 108, **108—9, 110**
dot technique 98
Dragonriders of Pern, The (calendars) **40—1, 60, 115, 116, 119**
dragons 50
Dragon's Carbuncle, The 54—5
Dragon's Keep, The 114
Dread Brass Shadow 48—9
Dungeons and Dragons (calendar) 26
Dwarf Village, The 78—9
dwarves 84
Dynteryx 58—9

Earle, Eyvind 28
Elven Council 106—7
Elven Fortress, The 33
elves 84
Eowyn and the Nazgul 149
erasers, kneaded 94
eyes, cultural use of 44, 46, 50

faeries 50
Fairies, The 92
Fang the Gnome 51, 84
Fantasy Aisle 64
Fantasy Cookbook, The (book) **10, 11, 28—9, 92, 93, 94, 95**
feathers 134
Fever Season (book) **39**
figures
    fantasy 80, 84
    human 80, 84, 106
F'lar and Mnementh 40—1
Forest of the Unicorn 111
Foster, Hal 30

giants 84
glass 134
Gold Dragon, The 115
Great One Sleeps, The 96

hair 134
Henry David's Place 20—1
hobbits 84
Home of Shandar the Sorcerer, The 85
Homeward Bound 76
horizon line **42—3**, 46, 50, 56, **60**
Hugh Oxford's Departure from Vandor 89

In the Sea Nymph's Lair 142—3
indoor scenes 132
**Interior View of Mowdra — Home of Elgan the
    Wizard 82—3**

King of the Sceptered Aisle, The 125
Knight of Ghosts and Shadows, A 129

lighting
    colour, effect on 108, 130
    cool 112, 120
    correct use of 54
    high source **22**
    moon 130
    overcast light **28—9**
    pen and ink design 98
    photography 36, 56
    realism 54
    sources 36, **39**, 54, **56—7**, **58—9**, **65**
    sun 124
    warm 112, 120
    workspace 120
limited edition print **117**
Lord of Chaos 36—7
Lord of the Rings (trilogy) *see* Tolkein, J.R.R.

masonite 116
Meinzinger's Art School 16, 20
Merlin and MaReenie 98
Merlin and the Dragons of Atlantis (book) **96**, **97**, **98**,
    99, **100**, **101**
Merlin and Zaran 100
Merlin and Zaran Duel 101
Mermaid's Grotto, The 145
Merovingen Nights: Divine Right 68
    illustrations from series **108—9**
Messengers of the Dragon Lord 16
Mountain, The 60
Mowdra 122
Mutant Warrior, The 117

Night Scene in Atlantis 137

Old Man Willow 35
Orthanc 46—7
outdoor scenes 132
outer space 132, **138—9**

palettes 116, 120, 126, 130
paper, drawing 92
pen and ink drawings 84, 94, 98, 100

pencil drawings 80, 84, 88, 92, 94, 100
pencils, graded art 88
perspective
    compositional process 46, 50
    picture plane 80
    realism 58
    single point **44—5**, **46—7**, 50, **86—7**
    three point 54
    two point 50, 54, **75**, **85**
photography 30, 32, 34, 36, 38, 80
picture plane 44, 46, 56, 80, 92
Pillars of the Kings 14—15
portfolio, beginner's 146, 148
portfolio pieces **20—1**, **32**
posters
    Barbarella 147
    Deadly Spawn, The 27
    Dynteryx 58—59
    Star Wars 10, 12—13, 24
private pieces **64**, **66**, **136**
Pyle, Howard 28

Quest, The 31

rain 132
Rapunzel 120—1
Realms of Wonder (calendars)
    (1982) **63**, **111**
    (1983 **16**, **33**, **62**, **69**, **106—7**, **114**, **144**, **145**
    (1987) **23**
Rebirth 97
Red Iron Nights 71—5
reference materials 30, **34**, 38, 40
rendering process 134
Return of the Jedi (film) 153
Romeo and Juliet 134—5
rough composition 56, 84, 92, 94

Santa Daydreams 127
Sea Dragon 62
Sea Lord 144
shadows 54, 112, 120
shape *see* picture plane
skies 106, **112**, 120, 124, 126, 130, 132
Snow Giant 69
specialization in art 146
Star Wars 10, 12—13, 24
steel 134
stippling 98
Storm Watch 136
Study in Earth Tones — The Bleeding Earth, A 18—19

sunrise 124, **138**
sunset 124, **138**
surfaces, painting 116
Sweet Silver Blues 88
Sword of Shannara, The 102, 103, 126

Tal-Amon, City of the Azmurians 86—7
Tenggrin, Gustav 28
There Will Be Time 42—3
Those Who Watch 44—5
thumbnail sketches 54, 56, 84, 92, 94, 100
Time of Transference, The 156, **156—7**
To Warm the Earth 67
Tolkein, J.R.R. 10, **14—15**, 24, **35**, **46—7**, 149
transfer of drawings 84, 100, 116
Tripods, The 52—3, **110**

underwater scenes 132, 134, **142—3**
Unicorn Treasury, The (book) **76**, 77, 104, 105
Urshurak (book)
    Amazon City of Zandura, The 25
    Amazon Fire Crystal, The 17
    Dwarf Village, The 78—9
    film project 24
    Home of Shandar the Sorcerer, The 85
    Hugh Oxford's Departure from Vandor 89
    **Interior View of Mowdra — Home of Elgan the
        Wizard 82—3**
    Mowdra 122
    sale of book 152
    Tal-Amon, City of the Azmurians 86—7
    unpublished **80—1**

Valley of the Unicorn 92
Valley of the Unicorns, The 77
Vendetta 24, 65, 146
video game cover **153**

Water Nixie 23
White Dragon, The 61
Wizard Glade, The 22
World of Hells, A 140
Worldstone 50
Worm Oroborus, The 91
Wyeth, N.C. 28, 30

Xanth 90

Zormena's Castle 28—9